FOLK PAINTERS
OF AMERICA

View of Great Barrington, artist unknown, oil on canvas, 1850–1855, Massachusetts. 36″ x 52″. This village in the Berkshires of New England is typical of the communities throughout early America that produced so much great folk art. Photograph courtesy Hirschl & Adler Galleries, New York. (Private collection)

FOLK PAINTERS OF AMERICA

Robert Bishop
Director, Museum of American Folk Art, New York

GREENWICH HOUSE
Distributed by Crown Publishers, Inc.
New York

(Above). *Ship in a Storm* by William H. Coffin, oil on canvas with original painted and grained frame, 1846, probably New England. 21½″ x 30″. The surge and power of a storm at sea is masterfully depicted in this great folk painting. Photograph courtesy Kennedy Galleries, Inc., New York. (Private collection)

(Page 1). *Portrait of a Baby*, artist unknown, oil on canvas, 1830–1840, New England. 34″ x 28″. The folk artist's delight in design and symmetry is evident in this enchanting painting, which also beautifully captures the essence of the child. (Greenfield Village and Henry Ford Museum)

Copyright © 1979 by Robert Bishop
All rights reserved.

This 1983 edition is published by Greenwhich House, a division of Arlington House, Inc., distributed by Crown Publishers, Inc., by arrangement with E. P. Dutton, Inc.

Manufactured in the United States of America

Color inserts printed in Hong Kong

Library of Congress Cataloging in Publication Data

Bishop, Robert Charles.
   Folk painters of America.
   Reprint. Originally published: New York : Dutton, c1979.
   Bibliography: p.
   Includes index.
   1. Painting, American.   2. Primitivism in art—United States.   3. Folk art—United States.   I. Title.
ND205.5.P74B57   1983   759.13   83-8975

ISBN: 0-517-413647

h g f e d c b a

CONTENTS

Color illustrations follow pages 64, 112, 144, 184, 216, 240

ACKNOWLEDGMENTS

I wish to express my sincere gratitude to the many individuals and institutions that have so generously provided pictorial and textual material for this volume. It gives me great pleasure to make a special acknowledgment to Cyril I. Nelson, and to Patricia Coblentz, both of whom helped make this book a reality.

Abby Aldrich Rockefeller Folk Art Center, Williamsburg, Virginia: Mrs. Beatrix T. Rumford, Director; Albany Institute of History and Art, Albany, New York: Roderic H. Blackburn, Assistant Director; America Hurrah Antiques, New York; The American Federation of Arts, New York: Konrad G. Kuchel; Amon Carter Museum of Western Art, Fort Worth, Texas; The Magazine Antiques, New York; The Art Institute of Chicago, Chicago, Illinois: Esther Sparks, Assistant Curator; Austin-Travis County Collection, Austin Public Library, Austin Texas; Cary F. Baker, Jr.; Bancroft Library, University of California, Berkeley, California; Berdan's Antiques, Hallowell, Maine; Bishop Hill, Illinois Division of Land and Historic Sites, Springfield, Illinois; Mr. and Mrs. Jerome W. Blum, Lisbon, Connecticut; Sidney E. Bond; Mr. and Mrs. Edwin C. Braman; Brigham Young University Art Gallery, Provo, Utah; The British Museum, London, England; Chicago Historical Society, Chicago, Illinois: Joseph B. Zywicki; Childs Gallery, Boston, Massachusetts; Church of Jesus Christ of Latter-Day Saints, Salt Lake City, Utah; Patricia L. Coblentz; Columbia County Historical Society, Inc., Kinderhook, New York; Columbus Museum of Arts and Crafts, Inc., Columbus, Georgia; The Connecticut Historical Society, Hartford, Connecticut: Thompson Harlow; Allan Daniel; Daughters of the Republic of Texas Library, San Antonio, Texas: Catherine McDowell; David L. Davies; The Detroit Institute of Arts, Detroit, Michigan: Rosalind Ellis; Richard Dietrich; Dossin Great Lakes Museum, Detroit, Michigan; Joan and Robert Doty; Mr. and Mrs. Richard Dubrow; Earlham College, Richmond, Indiana; Ephrata Cloister, Ephrata, Pennsylvania; Jack T. Ericson; Ralph Fasanella; Howard and Catherine Feldman; Mr. and Mrs. James Fostey; Frankenmuth Historical Association, Frankenmuth, Michigan: Carl R. Hansen; Free Library of Philadelphia, Philadelphia, Pennsylvania: Frank Halpern; Edgar William and Bernice Chrysler Garbisch; Georgia Department of Archives and History, Atlanta, Georgia: Carroll Hart; Georgia Historical Society, Savannah, Georgia: Anthony R. Dees; Greenfield Village and Henry Ford Museum, Dearborn, Michigan: Robert G. Wheeler, Kenneth Wilson, Walter E. Simmons II; William and Florence Griffin; Mr. and Mrs. Charles V. Hagler; Mr. and Mrs. Michael D. Hall; Fred Harvey Foundation Collection, Santa Fe, New Mexico; Mr. and Mrs. William Denning Harvey; Herbert W. Hemphill, Jr.; Hirschl & Adler Galleries, New York: Jane L. Richards; The Historic New Orleans Collection, New Orleans, Louisiana: Linda Faucheux; Index of American Design, Washington, D.C.: Lina A. Steele; IBM Art Collection, New York: Gloria Sullivan; Sidney Janis Gallery, New York; Barbara Johnson; Jay Johnson: America's Folk Heritage Gallery, New York; Mr. and Mrs. Harvey Kahn; Gene and Linda Kangas; Mrs. Jacob M. Kaplan; Mr. and Mrs. James O. Keene; Kennedy Galleries, Inc., New York; Phyllis Kind Gallery, New York; Kinnaman-Ramaekers Gallery, Houston, Texas; Lansing Board of Water and Light, Lansing, Michigan; The Library Company of Philadelphia, Philadelphia, Pennsylvania; Mackinac Island State Park Commission, Mackinac Island, Michigan; Macpheadris-Warner House, Portsmouth, New Hampshire; Maine Antique Digest, Waldoboro, Maine; Susan Taylor Martens; Maryland Historical Society, Baltimore, Maryland: Lois B. McCauley; Massachusetts Historical Society, Boston, Massachusetts; The Metropolitan Museum of Art, New York: Nada Saporiti; Clara Mae Staffel Michel; Mr. and Mrs. Frank J. Miele; The Museum, Michigan State University, East Lansing, Michigan: Kurt Dewhurst and Marsha MacDowell; Mr. and Mrs. R. Lawson Miles, Jr.; Milwaukee County Historical Society, Milwaukee, Wisconsin; The Minneapolis Institute of Arts, Minneapolis, Minnesota: David Revere McFadden; Minnesota Historical Society, St. Paul, Minnesota: Jill M. Christopherson; J. Roderick Moore; Moravian Historical Society, Nazareth, Pennsylvania: E. B. Clewell; The Moravian Archives, Bethlehem, Pennsylvania; Mount Vernon Ladies' Association of the Union, Mount Vernon, Virginia: Christine Meadows; Munson-Williams-Proctor Institute, Utica, New York: Marjorie C. Freytag; Museum of American Folk Art, New York: Kathleen Ouwel; Museum of Early Southern Decorative Arts, Winston-Salem, North Carolina: Rosemary N. Estes; Museum of Fine Arts, Boston, Massachusetts: Laura C. Luckey; Museum of Fine Arts, Springfield, Massachusetts; Museum of International Folk Art, Santa Fe, New Mexico: Christine Mather; The Museum of Modern Art, New York; National Gallery of Art, Washington, D.C.: Elise V. H. Ferber; Elise Macy Nelson; New England Historic Genealogical Society, Boston, Massachusetts: Dr. James Bell; New Mexico Department of Development, Santa Fe, New Mexico; New Mexico State Tourist Bureau, Santa Fe, New Mexico; The New-York Historical Society, New York: Mary Black; The New York Public Library, New York; New York State Historical Association, Cooperstown, New York: Jerry Reese; James Nutt; Ohio Historical Society, Inc., Columbus, Ohio: Douglas White; Old Colony Historical Society, Taunton, Massachusetts: Carolyn B. Owen; Old Dartmouth Historical Society Whaling Museum, New Bedford, Massachusetts; Old Salem, Inc., Winston-Salem, North Carolina: Paula Welshimer; Old Sturbridge Village, Sturbridge, Massachusetts: Barbara D. Caplette; The Peabody Museum of Salem, Salem, Massachusetts: Philip Chadwick, Foster Smith; Pennsylvania Academy of the Fine Arts, Philadelphia, Pennsylvania: Glenn C. Rudderow; Pennsylvania Hospital, Philadelphia, Pennsylvania: Teddy Wilgoss; Philadelphia Museum of Art, Philadelphia, Pennsylvania; Phillips Exeter Academy, Exeter, New Hampshire: Susan MacDougall; Pocumtuck Valley Memorial Association, Deerfield, Massachusetts; Burton and Kathleen Purmell; Dr. and Mrs. Henry Raskin; W. D. Ray; Raynham Hall, Oyster Bay, New York; Rhode Island Historical Society, Providence, Rhode Island; Marguerite Riordan, Stonington, Connecticut; Franklin D. Roosevelt Library and Museum, Hyde Park, New York; Rutgers University Fine Arts Collection, New Brunswick, New Jersey; Helen R. Sailer; St. Lorenz Church, Frankenmuth, Michigan; Salem Academy and College, Winston-Salem, North Carolina: Alicia Stephens; San Antonio Museum Association, San Antonio, Texas: Claudia J. Eckstein; Church of San José de la Laguna Mission, Laguna, New Mexico; George E. Schoellkopf Gallery, New York; Mr. and Mrs. Samuel Schwartz; Ella Sharp Museum, Jackson, Michigan; Shelburne Museum Inc., Shelburne, Vermont: Nancy C. Muller; Sleepy Hollow Restorations, Tarrytown, New York; The Smithsonian Institution, Washington, D.C.; Sotheby & Company, London, England; Sotheby Parke Bernet Inc., New York; Mrs. Bruce L. Stout; Taylor Museum of the Colorado Springs Fine Arts Center, Colorado Springs, Colorado; Telfair Academy of Arts and Sciences, Inc., Savannah, Georgia; Texas State Archives, Houston, Texas; Peter H. Tillou; Virginia Museum of Fine Arts, Richmond, Virginia; Frank W. Kelly; Donald Vogel; Wadsworth Atheneum, Hartford, Connecticut: Peter O. Marlow; Wells Fargo Bank History Room, San Francisco, California: Jo Ann Baldinger; David B. Wiggins; Mr. and Mrs. William E. Wiltshire III; The Henry Francis du Pont Winterthur Museum, Winterthur, Delaware; Thos. K. Woodard: American Antiques & Quilts, New York; Worcester Art Museum, Worcester, Massachusetts; Yale University Art Gallery, New Haven, Connecticut.

PREFACE

To understand the work of the American folk artist it is necessary to suspend the criteria with which academic art is usually considered. The subtleties of elaborate composition, masterly technique, and sophisticated organization are only occasionally the concerns of the folk painter, although they are often unconsciously achieved.

In her introduction to the exhibition catalogue *The Flowering of American Folk Art* (1974) Alice Winchester made the following statement, "One may look for, and find, originality of concept, creativity of design, craftsmanly use of the medium, and flashes of inspiration, even genius. Folk art makes its appeal directly and intimately, even to people quite uninitiated into the mysteries of art." [1]

The first real appreciation of American folk art began during the 1920s. Ever since that time collectors and scholars have attempted to identify and classify the naïve folk paintings that, at different times, have been called by such diverse terms as *amateur, artisan, pioneer, popular, primitive,* and *provincial*. The confusion about this vast body of work, which, for the most part, was executed by self-trained artists in a state of relative artistic innocence, is not surprising, for the paintings fall into several broad categories based upon medium and type.

Oil and tempera paintings on canvas and board, watercolors on paper and cardboard, drawings and sketches, and pastels are the mediums most encountered. Portraits; silhouettes; landscapes; pinprick pictures; calligraphic drawings; theorems on paper, velvet, and silk; wall murals; furniture decoration; coach decoration; shop signs; fireboards; and overmantel paintings are but a few of the types of art that are included in the catchall term *American folk painting*.

There are several characteristics that consistently appear in folk painting regardless of the medium. In the best examples there is a combination of naturalness and simplicity resulting in a directness that has come to be much admired by contemporary art historians, critics, and collectors.

Some scholars have spent much of their lives studying American folk art, and nearly every one has arrived at his own definition. Perhaps the most pertinent was developed in private conversation by Mary Childs Black, former Director of the Abby Aldrich Rockefeller Folk Art Collection at Colonial Williamsburg, first Director of the Museum of Early American Folk Art, New York, and current Curator of Paintings and Sculpture at The New-York Historical Society: "The genesis, rise, and disappearance of folk art is closely connected with the events of the nineteenth century when the disappearance of the old ways left rural folk everywhere with an unused surplus of time and energy. People were free to invent and make simple things for their own pleasure in each household and in each village, until the rise of industrial production toward the end of the nineteenth century. Folk art occupies the brief interval between court taste and commercial taste."

Definitions used by other scholars support Mrs. Black's theories in general, and it is possible to derive from them a consensus of the qualities usually associated with great folk art. Such words as *freshness, directness, simplicity,* and *imaginative* frequently occur in writings on the subject.

Until recent years it was generally thought that the folk artist was essentially anonymous, itinerant, and untrained. Research has somewhat altered these views. Many artists have now been identified. At the same time, it has been established that not all of them were itinerant and, more important, that a good many of them even had the advantages of basic artistic training.

A backward look at the appreciation of American folk art will provide a helpful perspective.

European academic paintings were aggressively sought by a relatively few wealthy Americans during the eighteenth and early nineteenth centuries. Large collections of canvases of "doubtfully attributed, appropriately yellowed 'Old Masters'" [2] provided prestige for American collectors like the New York merchant Luman Reed. He decided to dispose of his holdings in this field in 1834 and in their place hung works of the "native school," which he purchased from the astute dealer Michael Paff. Before Reed's death in 1836 he had acquired outstanding canvases by William Sidney Mount, Asher B. Durand, and George Whiting Flagg. He also commissioned Thomas Cole to paint the extraordinary five-panel cycle *The Course of Empire* in the same year as his death.

Philip Hone, Jonathan Sturges, and Robert Gilmore, collecting contemporaries of Reed, also bought American paintings. None of these distinguished gentlemen is known to have been interested in folk painting.

When The Metropolitan Museum of Art was founded in 1870, certainly no folk art was included in its collection. As a matter of fact, it was not until 1880 that the first director, Italian-born General Louis Palma di Cesnola, announced that the burgeoning institution would attempt to build a collection of academic American paintings.

Early American art historians also tended to ignore the folk artist and his work. Although William Dunlap was vice-president of the National Academy of Design and an artist of note during the 1830s, he is best known for his trailblazing book *History of the Rise and Progress of the Arts of Design in the United States* (1834). He began his preface,

A History of the Arts of Design in the United States, given by a series of biographical notices, which should show not only the progress of improvement in those arts, but their present state, necessarily includes the biography of many living artists.

To publish the biography of the living is objected to by some. They say, if truth is told, the feelings may be wounded; and if mere eulogium is aimed at, truth will be wounded, the public deceived, and that which pretends to be history, will become a tissue of adulatory falsehood. But of public men—and every artist is a public man—the public have a right to demand the truth. The most interesting portion of my work is the biographies of living artists; and it throws a light upon the lives and actions of those who have departed, which could not be obtained in any other way. Every artist wishes, and ought to wish, that public attention should be called to him.[3]

Dunlap failed to include many of the artists represented in this book, for like Reed and his collecting contemporaries, he would not have understood the inversion of perspective and the innocence of vision so evident in their works.

The folk painter fared no better in *Art in America*, written by S. G. W. Benjamin in 1880. Benjamin enjoyed a well-deserved reputation for his critical abilities that had been demonstrated in his earlier books, *Contemporary Art in Europe* and *What Is Art?* In the preface to his work on American painting, he explained: "The aim of this book has been to give a historical outline of the growth of the arts in America. But while this has been the dominating idea in the mind of the writer, criticism has necessarily entered, more or less, into the preparation of the work, since only by weighing the differences or the comparative merits of those artists who seemed best to illustrate the various phases of American art has it been possible to trace its progress from one step to another."[4]

Clarence Cook, the preeminent art critic of the late Victorian period, in the introduction to his authoritative three-volume art history titled *Art and Artists of Our Time* (1888), explained how American art came into being. He believed that since American art traditions were inherited directly from the English, it was not surprising that great artists had not flourished in America. He convincingly pointed out that until the close of the seventeenth century, "no painter of mark had been born in England. . . . But, although so few native names of note are found in the early annals of English art, we must not conclude that there were no English painters until Hogarth, Reynolds and Gainsborough appeared. The Holbeins, Van Dycks, Rubens, Lelys, Knellers, worked for kings and nobles, and the splendor of their pictures has paled the light of a hundred twinkling stars that their light had taught to shine. . . . There were, no doubt, many people in the middle ranks of English society who did desire to have their portraits painted or the portraits of their wives and children, and as the fashion grew, fostered by the pattern set by the upper classes, it may be taken for granted that a native growth of artists would appear to meet the demand. Fashion would also dictate the style of the painting, and those who could not afford to employ a Holbein and a Van Dyck, a Lely or a Kneller, would encourage the artist who could best imitate, or, at the least, suggest, the manner of the master in vogue."[5]

Cook believed that American painting of the Colonial period and the early republic was but a reflection of English artistic endeavors. This premise was taken one step further by Nina Fletcher Little, one of America's most distinguished collectors and authors in this field, who has written, "The American primitive painters of the eighteenth century are a transitional group. They stand midway between the pre-Revolutionary artists of the English school and the indigenous, self-taught, nineteenth-century limners, whose essentially non-realistic approach reached its peak between 1820 and 1850. The nineteenth-century primitives might be considered the first group of truly native artists since they were born during the intensely nationalistic years of the early Republic, and most of them were raised in a rural setting which had little artistic contact with the outside world. They were certainly less affected by foreign traditions than either the colonial artists who had preceded them, or the twentieth-century primitives whose art must necessarily be conditioned by the complexities of a modern environment."[6]

During the 1880s and 1890s appreciation for American art increased and museum collections were being formed at Boston, Philadelphia, Hartford, and Washington. Old Masters continued to be exceedingly popular and modern French painting began to gain recognition around the turn of the century. Still, American folk art remained isolated from the mainstream of art appreciation.

It has been well documented that public interest in American folk art developed prior to the early 1920s. Pioneer modern artists returning home from France after 1910 brought with them an aesthetic refinement that enabled them to appreciate the abstract qualities of folk art. Their revolt against the naturalistic and impressionistic tendencies of the nineteenth century led to a search for their cultural heritage that caused an interest in both primitive and naïve art. They zealously collected American Indian artifacts and purchased from rural families the robust paintings that became the seed from which grew the cult of folk Americana.

By 1920 several modern artists had gathered impressive collections of folk paintings that included such diverse pictures as bright, colorful watercolors, warm-hued theorems on velvet, and stoic effigies from years long past. Interest in American folk art spread like wildfire. "The first public exhibitions of American folk painting were those shown by Mrs. Juliana R. Force at the Whitney Studio Club, and by the Dudensing Gallery, in New York; by Mr. and Mrs. Elie Nadelman in their folk museum at Riverdale-on-Hudson, New York; and by Mrs. Isabel Carleton Wilde in her shop in Cambridge, Massachusetts."[7]

The Whitney Studio Club had grown from the

Studio Club established by Gertrude Vanderbilt Whitney in 1918. This informal center for artists had in turn sprung from the Friends of the Young Artists, which Mrs. Whitney had formed some three years earlier. The exhibition of early American art at the Whitney Studio Club mounted in 1924 was selected and arranged by H. E. Schnakenberg, who borrowed from such important artist/collectors as Charles Sheeler, Yasuo Kuniyoshi, and Charles Demuth.

Perhaps no one was more instrumental in establishing the validity of American folk art than Holger Cahill, who in 1930 staged the first major exhibition of American folk painting at The Newark Museum. In the introduction to the exhibition catalogue, *American Primitives, An Exhibit of the Paintings of Nineteenth Century Folk Artists*, Mr. Cahill accomplished two goals. For the uninitiated he gave his definition of folk art. He also paved the way for a battle that continues even today:

> The word primitive (in the exhibition) is used as a term of convenience, and not to designate any particular school of American art, or any particular period. It is used to describe the work of simple people with no academic training and little book learning in art. The earliest of the paintings shown date from the Eighteenth Century, the latest from the end of the Nineteenth. The work of living men might have been included, for there are many interesting folk artists painting in this country today. Their work finds its way into the big annual no-jury shows, the New York dealers' galleries, and even into the Carnegie International. . . .
>
> . . . Here, as elsewhere, the European influence is at the heart of the native American development. Certain influences, Dutch or English mainly, are definitely recognizable. Most of these artists had seen paintings of one kind or another, or had seen engravings in books. It is evident that they tried to approximate effects achieved by academic artists whose paintings they had seen in the original or in reproduction.[8]

Obviously, Cahill believed that contemporary painters could be validly classified as folk artists. Others, however, continue to maintain that the intrusion of the machine into American society caused the dissolution of the forces that inspired great folk art. In rebuttal, many have taken a firm stand and stoutly defend the validity of the naïve painters of today. This position seems to be attracting museum directors across the country who, in increasing numbers, have begun to exhibit contemporary folk art of all kinds.

Through the years numerous books devoted to the subject of American folk painting have bought new perspectives to the field. The early book *Some American Primitives*, written in 1941 by the enthusiastic New Englander Clara Endicott Sears, is a gathering of anecdotes that might well serve as an antidote for anyone contemplating the collecting of naïve paintings. She smugly chirped, "This book is primarily for collectors, and for those who have a real interest in preserving what is now called the folk-art of America. These are not the grotesque examples that one comes across. I have a great shrinking from anything that departs from the normal." [9] A visit to her collection at the Fruitlands and Wayside Museum, Harvard, Massachusetts, immediately establishes not only her taste but the taste of a whole collecting generation devoted to the "pretty" paintings of bygone years. Several extensive collections of this type have been formed. Current awareness of the experimental art movements of the twentieth century has made these pictures boring to many contemporary folk art collectors. They generally seek tougher art—pictures in which the conventions of academic painting, such as perspective, were not the goal of the folk artist. This does not mean that all naïve painters were incapable of achieving perspective in their paintings. In fact, some, like Edward Hicks, willfully practiced an inversion of perspective in order to give equal importance to many areas in a single canvas.

Jean Lipman, in her book *American Primitive Painting* (1942) and again in *American Folk Painting* (1966), written with Mary Black, and most recently in *The Flowering of American Folk Art, 1776–1876* (1974), spoke out for a new interpretation of the folk artist and his contribution to the mainstream of American art, "I expressed the opinion, 'radical though this may seem,' that a number of gifted folk artists arrived at a power and originality and beauty that were not surpassed by the greatest of the academic painters. I have never changed my mind and am convinced that the entire field of activity of the folk artists was absolutely not, as has often been said, a charming postscript. I believe it was a central contribution to the mainstream of American culture in the formative years of our democracy." [10]

Another early and very important book in the field was written by Carl W. Drepperd (*American Pioneer Arts and Artists*, 1942). He noted that the American people, almost from the beginning, had revered education in its many forms:

> Education in the arts—any one of the classic seven —was an almost desperate desire of our American ancestors. Dancing masters; music masters; Thespians; painting, drawing and writing instructors; teachers of stencil painting, sign painting, decorating and singing, roamed the land with some assurance of patronage wherever they stopped to assemble a class. They visited towns and villages, staying a week, a month or a season, then packed their kits and pushed on to the next place. Big towns and cities gave continuous encouragement (as they were at some pains to call patronage in those democratic days) to all teachers of art.

The future of painting in America appeared assured to the keenly observing eye of Paul Svinin of the Russian Diplomatic Corps on duty here in 1811, 1812 and 1813. A cultured gentleman and himself an artist of considerable talent, M. Svinin makes this comment in his memoirs: "Drawing has already been made a part of the school curriculum"; and, since "education here is for all classes," Svinin looked for painting as a "universal accomplishment." "Already mothers are exhibiting the works of their daughters to each other." In Newport, Svinin notes "a young girl who, although her teacher was barely able to instruct her in the first principles of drawing, *copies* paintings in oil and *paints portraits* with a feeling and facility only to be met with in the works of the best masters." [11]

To illustrate the major contributions of the folk artist has become the goal of many collectors and scholars. Most of the major collections that are available in museums today have grown out of private collections. Probably the finest was formed by Mrs. John D. Rockefeller, Jr., and originally was given to The Museum of Modern Art and to The Metropolitan Museum of Art. In 1957 her entire collection was reassembled, and the Abby Aldrich Rockefeller Folk Art Collection, housed in its own building at Colonial Williamsburg, became a reality. Through the years numerous acquisitions have made this the single richest gathering of folk art.

During the 1920s Mrs. J. Watson Webb established an impressive group of paintings and related material, which she later installed at the Shelburne Museum, Shelburne, Vermont. This collection too has been expanded extensively. Henry Francis du Pont and Henry Ford also were avid collectors of folk art during the 1920s. The Du Pont collection became part of the Winterthur Museum at Winterthur, Delaware, and Henry

Ford's collection is housed at Greenfield Village and the Henry Ford Museum, Dearborn, Michigan. During the 1940s, 1950s, and 1960s the distinguished collectors Colonel Edward W. and Bernice Chrysler Garbisch assembled an unmatched collection, which in recent years they have divided between several museums, including The National Gallery of Art, The Metropolitan Museum, The Philadelphia Museum, and The Chrysler Museum at Norfolk, Virginia.

By 1962 The Museum of Early American Folk Art was established in New York City, and a loan exhibition presented at the Time and Life Exhibition Center brought to international attention the richness of America's folk heritage. The museum, renamed The Museum of American Folk Art, continues to be, through its exhibitions, a pivotal force in the field.

Perhaps no single exhibition to date has made Americans more aware of folk art than "The Flowering of American Folk Art," a major loan exhibition mounted at the Whitney Museum of American Art in New York by Jean Lipman and Alice Winchester in 1974. Miss Winchester, in the introduction to the exhibition catalogue, explained one of the more recent concerns about the study of folk art: "The emphasis here is upon the art in folk art, not the folk. That is another way of saying that the approach is esthetic rather than historical." [12]

In this book I have attempted to rethink and reevaluate the entire folk expression and to illustrate a point of view that is perhaps broader than that stated by Mrs. Lipman. Not only the supreme masterpiece but the simple genre picture and the crudely painted portrait have been included in an effort to indicate more fully the incredibly broad range of the folk artist's concern.

1 (left). Overmantel from the Gardiner-Gilman House, Exeter, New Hampshire, artist unknown, oil on panel, *c.* 1775, 28″ x 47¾″. This handsome panel, showing an imaginary rather than an actual scene, is a splendid example of overmantel painting. (Amon Carter Museum of Western Art)

INTRODUCTION

One of the reasons that American folk painting has attracted such popular interest is that much of it depicts the common man—the backbone of the American experience—and the farms, towns, and cities of this nation prior to the changes in lifestyle that came about as a direct result of the Industrial Revolution.

The great body of work left behind by the folk painter can be divided into two broad categories: pictures that recorded people, places, and time, and paintings that decorated essentially utilitarian objects, such as signs, fireboards, mantels, room ends, floors and floor carpets, windowshades, walls, ceilings, and furniture.

Portraits, landscapes, and seascapes—the art that was framed, hung, treasured, and preserved—were a touch of the old world in the new. These more formal pictures, in their way, provided a sense of security in what was oftentimes a hostile land. Even the modest farmer somehow could find a way to embellish his life with art.

The primary purpose of utilitarian folk painting was to enliven and embellish both country and town dwellings.

Religion inspired the folk painter, especially in the Southwest, where brightly painted crucifixions; reverent, idealized depictions of the Holy Mother; and a vast array of church martyrs and saints provided a close link with the Catholic church for the Spanish colonials and native Indians. Colorful, trumpeting angels and other religious symbols also abound in the Fraktur drawings and watercolors of the culturally isolated German communities scattered throughout Pennsylvania.

As the movement toward political and economic freedom accelerated in the mid-eighteenth century, a new thread was woven into the tapestry of American folk painting. History pictures and blatantly nationalistic themes began to permeate American folk expression.

With freedom won and independence established, the folk painter of the early nineteenth century became preoccupied with American heroes. Men like George Washington caused the folk artist's bosom to swell with pride. Likenesses of this revered leader peppered the land, appearing on tavern signs and windowshades, as furniture decoration, and, of course, in more conventional portraits. This hero worship caused Paul Svinin to observe, "It is noteworthy that every American considers it his sacred duty to have a likeness of Washington in his home, just as we have images of God's saints." [13]

Also in the early nineteenth century, genre pictures became more numerous. People with a sense of belief in America rushed to record the land they loved in its every aspect. The rustic farm and its people and animals, the thriving town with its new industries, and the bustling city with its busy harbor were all captured in paint at one time or another by the naïve artist.

During the early 1800s a new spirit was evident in American folk painting. A consciousness of the Romantic movement and its effect upon English and European art had reached the American shores. At the same time education became a preoccupation. Young girls of good families were sent to seminary schools in which the gracious arts, including painting, were part of the curriculum. A seemingly endless stream of theorem pictures, mourning pictures, tinsel pictures, reverse paintings on glass, and marble dust, or sandpaper, pictures resulted. Young women also learned to decorate furniture. Brush in hand, they approached the handcrafted, specially constructed chair or table with a meticulous concern that would put to shame the modern-day housewife's attempt to decorate mass-produced, unpainted pine pieces.

As the nineteenth century drew to a close, new waves of immigrants came to America. Many brought with them inherited cultural traditions that reinfused European ideas into the American way of life. Ultimately many of these immigrants or their descendants spread across the entire nation and enthusiastically recorded their country in paint.

For those who insist that folk painting died at the close of the nineteenth century, many of the illustrations in this book will be a real eye-opener. To be sure, the contemporary naïve painter is oftentimes a bit more self-conscious, but folk painting of today—the art of the people—is no less valid a statement than that made in the nineteenth century.

Many idealists prefer to believe that the early folk painter sprang from no place, was influenced by nothing, and was simply a creative entity isolated from outside experience. This idealistic notion has time and again been successfully refuted. The seemingly spontaneous creativity often had its origins in early prints, art manuals, and, later on, photographs. Even the idea that the folk painter was without painterly training can be dispelled, for early newspapers abound with advertisements announcing the arrival of an artist in a town and the establishment of a painting school for the local citizens, as when William Birchall Tetley advertised in the November 14, 1774, edition of *The New-York Gazette and the Weekly Mercury*: "Dancing, Taught at Home and Abroad by Wm. Birchall Tetley. Late apprentice to Monsieur Gherarde, of London; He teaches on the usual terms the minuet, cottilions, Allemande, English Country dances; single double, and treble hornpipes, &c. &c. as they are now danced at London and Paris, which last place he has lately visited. Those Gentlemen and Ladies who please to favour him with their commands, at the corner of Beaver-street, shall be duly attended. An Evening School at home, three times a week.

"Continues painting Portraits in oyl or miniature, as usual, Teaches Ladies and Gentlemen drawing and painting in crayons or water colours."

Men like the Scotsman John Smibert, a famous

painter in his own right, greatly influenced American art and more specifically the American folk painter. In 1728 Smibert accompanied George Berkeley to America, where they hoped "to lay the foundation of a College for all sorts of literature on Bermuda." [14] After residing briefly in Newport, Rhode Island, in 1729 Smibert finally settled in Boston, where he was "lookt on at the top of his profession." [15]

In addition to Smibert's efforts to make cosmopolitan New Englanders aware of art, he sold supplies as well. An advertisement in the October 10/17, 1734, *Boston News-Letter* and the October 14/21, 1734, *Boston Gazette* records, "JOHN SMIBERT, painter, sells all Sorts of Colours, dry or ground, with Oils and Brushes, Frames of several Sorts, the best Metzotinto, Italian, French, Dutch and English Prints, in Frames and Glasses, or without, by Wholesale or Retail, at Reasonable Rates; at his House in Queen-Street, between the Town-House and the Orange Tree, Boston."

Smibert is credited with organizing the first art exhibition ever held in America. His collection of copies of Old Masters was shown in conjunction with his recently executed portraits of New England's gentry. The Smibert studio became an informal academy where young artists were allowed to copy the Old Masters and learn the basic principles of traditional European painting. Smibert advertised again in the *Boston News-Letter* of May 15/22, 1735: "JOHN SMIBERT.—To be Sold, at Mr. Smibert's, in Queen Street, on Monday, the 26th Instant, A Collection of valuable PRINTS, engrav'd by the best Hands, after the finest Pictures in Italy, France, Holland, and England, done by Raphael, Michael Angelo, Poussin, Rubens, and other the greatest Masters, containing a great Variety of Subjects, as History, etc, most of the Prints very rare, and not to be met with, except in private Collections: being what Mr. Smibert collected in the above-mentioned Countries, for his own private Use & Improvement: The Price of each Picture, to be mark'd upon it. N.B. The Sale will last from Monday morning till the Saturday Evening following, and no longer: Those Prints, that shall remain then unsold, will be sent to England."

Smibert's variety of artistic activities was no different from those engaged in by numerous European artists journeying to America's cosmopolitan areas. Throughout the entire eighteenth century, ambitious, adventuresome men sailed for America hoping to make their artistic fortune.

The print was a very important source of instruction for the naïve painter. Spanish religious engravings and English portrait engraving were among the first prints in America. English portrait prints, commonly referred to as *heads*, with their frequently elaborate architectural backgrounds, served as models for the American folk painter. Direct borrowings from imported prints are especially evident in the wonderful naïve paintings of the early Hudson River Valley, which represent the first major school of indigenous American art. The print also influenced portraiture in New England and the South as well, and the source for many background settings in early paintings will be clearly established in this work.

Almost from the beginning of the Colonial period books were possessions much prized by the settlers. In fact, numerous religious and political leaders, as well as wealthy merchants, attempted to build libraries. Many of them were eminently successful, and by the close of the seventeenth century Cotton Mather, the Boston divine; Samuel Sewall, the noted diarist and merchant; and William Byrd II, the Virginia planter, owned large personal libraries numbering between three and four thousand titles. The first Colonial press began operations at Cambridge, Massachusetts, in 1639, and the second was set up by the Library Company of Philadelphia, Pennsylvania, in 1692.

It is possible to find the genesis of the self-made man in this love for the printed word. For him, education was crucial and the "do-it-yourself" or "how-to" type of book enabled the man desiring an education to attain it without attending formal schools.

Books greatly affected American art as well. *The Graphice, or The Most Ancient and Excellent Art of Limning*, written by Henry Peachem and published at London in 1612, is especially important, for it is probably the earliest instructor in portrait painting.

Not only art books but artworks and even frames (called *lists*) were imported into nearly every major city. Very often English books on painting, drawing, and sketching were reprinted by American entrepreneurs. George Washington possessed a copy of the 1794 edition of *Artist's Assistant,* which was originally published in London in 1750.

Many painters, frequently known as *limners*, might have gained their first elementary training from early books; however, art instruction books were not confined to portraiture.

The Artist's Assistant in Drawing, Perspective, Etching, Engraving, Mezzotinto Scraping, Painting on Glass, in Crayons, in Water Colours, and on Silks and Satins, the Art of Japanning, etc. was the sixth edition of a work originally produced by Carrington Bowles, an English publisher and print seller, who released the book in London about 1750.

The School of Wisdom or Repository of the Most Valuable Curiosities of Art was published at New Brunswick, New Jersey, in 1787. This was a pocket instructor in which amateur artists were introduced to the mysteries of drawing, water and oil colors, etching, engraving, gilding, staining glass, marble, wood, bone, horn, ivory, paper, parchment, etc.

In 1810 *Hints to Young Practitioners in the Study of Landscape Painting*, written by J. W. Alston and published at London, was shipped to America, where it sold for ten shillings and sixpence.

In 1824 *Progressive Lessons,* by the popular writer Thomas Clay of London, was offered to amateur painters by numerous American booksellers.

Perhaps no book was as popular with the amateur

American artist as the publication *A Key to the Art of Drawing the Human Figure*, which was written by John Rubens Smith and published by Samuel Stewart of Philadelphia in 1831. Smith—an art instructor in Boston from 1811 to 1816, in New York City from 1816 to 1826, and in Philadelphia from 1826 to 1837—chose a huge 17½-inch by 11½-inch format for his book, which contained a wealth of significant material and earned for him a reputation that brought many of the best-known Federal painters to his studio for instruction. Among his pupils were Thomas Sully and Emmanuel Leutze.

After the 1830s art manuals and art instruction books became increasingly popular, and as the various branches of artistic endeavors proliferated, numerous publications dealing with a specific type of painting reached the booksellers. Books on theorem painting, painting for young ladies, ornamental painting, graphic art, flower painting, and drawing for children flooded the marketplace.

Art instruction was introduced into the public schools in New England by *An Introduction to Linear Drawing Adapted to Use of Public Schools in the United States*, written by William B. Fowle and published in Boston in 1825. It was so successful that subsequent editions were issued in 1828 and 1830.

By the end of the nineteenth century elementary art classes had become fairly standard for students in the public school systems of major cities. Even at this late date Fowle's publication could have reached the hands of country artists and greatly influenced their artistic endeavors.

The publication *The Knickerbocker* in 1839 enthusiastically heralded a new age: "We have seen the views taken in Paris by the 'Daguerreotype' and have no hesitation in avowing that they are the most remarkable objects of curiosity and admiration, in the arts, that we ever beheld. Their exquisite perfection almost transcends the bounds of sober belief. . . . There is not an object even the most minute, embraced in that wide scope, which was not original; and it is impossible that one should have been omitted. Think of that!" [16]

Think of that indeed! Few American artists, even those who earned their living by painting portraits, realized that this new process would ultimately drive many of them from their profession.

In 1838 Samuel F. B. Morse (1791–1872) traveled abroad hoping to secure patents for his electromagnetic telegraph in England, Russia, and France. He visited Louis-Jacques-Mande Daguerre (1787–1851), inventor of the daguerreotype, in Paris and viewed some of his photographs.

In September 1839 practical photography was born. Daguerre's method of producing daguerreotypes had been described in most of the major cities, and the account was adequate enough for America's amateurs to begin. Morse, in addition to being an inventor, was a portrait painter of distinction. He considered the daguerreotype from an artist's point of view, for he recorded, "The impressions of interior views are Rembrandt perfected." [17]

Morse commissioned a Mr. Prosch, an instrument maker, to construct a Daguerrean camera for him. He was not without competitors, and the *New York Morning Herald* for September 30, 1839, carried the following news story: "THE NEW ART—We saw the other day, in Chilton's, in Broadway, a very curious specimen of the new mode recently invented by Daguerre in Paris, of taking on copper the exact resemblances of scenes and living objects, through the medium of the sun's rays reflected in a *camera obscura*. The scene embraces a part of St. Paul's church, and the surrounding shrubbery and houses, with a corner of the Astor House, and, for aught we know, Stetson looking out of a window, telling a joke about Davie Crockett. All this is represented on a small piece of copper equal in size to a miniature painting."

This daguerreotype had been made by D. W. Seager, and the enthusiastic reporter, like Morse before him, saw in the daguerreotype a competitor for the portrait artist, for he concluded, "The specimen at Chilton's is a most remarkable gem in its way. . . . Ladies, if they are pretty, with small feet and delicate hands, fond of science, ought to call and see it."

Portrait galleries quickly sprang into existence everywhere. As early as 1840 the products of the Daguerrean camera must have begun to create economic hardships for the folk painter. Both the camera operator and the painter in many instances were itinerant. Both would go to a town, rent rooms, and execute portraits for the local citizens. An advertisement from the June 30, 1840, *National Intelligencer* stated that a Mr. Stevenson "would inform the citizens of Washington and the District that he has taken rooms at Mrs. Cummings' on Penn. Ave. a few doors from the Capitol where he is prepared to take miniature likenesses by the Daguerreotype every fair day from 10 A.M till 4 P.M."

In time, daguerreotypes came to be tinted by hand, making them even more like miniature paintings. With the advent of the daguerreotype the history of miniature paintings abruptly ends.

While the photograph forced the miniature painter and the silhouette artist to seek other ways of earning a living, it also all but drove the naïve portrait painter from the rural scene. As new photographic techniques were introduced and the cost of photographic portraiture became less expensive, demand for the folk painter's work declined sharply. Practically no one wanted an artistic approximation when a "true as life" photograph could be had at a fraction of the cost.

Religion, however, continued to nourish the folk painter, and during the twentieth century a fervent belief in God has produced compelling soul-searching pictures, such as *Crucifixion*, painted by Peter Charlie (fig.206), and *Modern Inventions* by Sister Gertrude Morgan (plate 54).

The naïve painter also continues to be occupied with the land that surrounds him.

Most of the important naïve painters of today base their art upon a backward look. Their compelling scenes of rural America record a fast-vanishing way of life. Memory pictures like those by Grandma Moses, Mattie

Lou O'Kelley, Tella Kitchen, and Emily Lunde document for future generations simple lifestyles and happy childhood experiences.

With the study of psychoanalysis and the preoccupation with the theories and teachings of Freud, new interest has arisen in art created by schizophrenics, such as Martin Ramirez.

There are the artists who paint for joy. Men like Philo Willey, better known as The Chief, transfer to canvas in acid tones and bright-hued raw colors their love of life.

Sometimes it seems as though the whole world is painting. Though a flood of pictures is being created by a virtual army of contemporary naïve painters, only a handful possess the talent to create pictures that will stand the harsh test of time.

I have attempted to include in this book many of the contemporary naïve painters who I think will survive that test and who are every day expanding the concept of American folk painting.

2 (below). *Old State House* by James B. Marston, oil on canvas, 1801, Boston, Massachusetts, 37¼" x 51". At the opening of the nineteenth century, many Bostonians were as conscious of London fashions as anyone living in the English city. Notice the Classical design of the building in the right foreground. (Massachusetts Historical Society)

3 (opposite page). *The Reverend Jedediah Morse Family* by Samuel Finley Breese Morse (1791–1872), watercolor on paper, 1810, Massachusetts, 19" x 23". This painting is said to be the first picture executed by Morse, who later became a well-known artist. He is best known for his invention of the telegraph. It was not unusual that in 1810 a conservative New England family like the Morses still lived with Chippendale furniture, which had long gone out of style. (The Smithsonian Institution)

NEW ENGLAND

4 (above). *Portrait of David, Joanna, and Abigail Mason*, artist unknown, oil on canvas, 1670, Massachusetts, 39½″ x 42^{11}/$_{16}$″. The young people depicted in this painting were the children of Arthur Mason and Joanna Parker. The picture is inscribed "Anno Dom 1670." At the time this group portrait was executed, David was eight years old, Joanna six, and Abigail four. This painting and that of Mrs. Freake and Baby Mary, page 19, reflect inherited medieval traditions. In these pictures, nearly every subject is shown with a decorative accessory such as a fan, gloves, or a flower. The artists have attempted a realistic representation of the subjects, and the Mason children appear to be youthful rather than miniature adults. (Private collection)

NEW ENGLAND

Almost from the day of its first settlement, the economy of New England was derived from the sea. Prosperity grew from shipbuilding, fishing, and trading since the colonists found much of the soil unsuitable for farming and the growing season precariously short.

By 1675 over 225 vessels with a 50-ton capacity traveled to the West Indies, Europe, and as far afield as Syria and Madagascar. At Boston, the hub of New England life, aggressive and astute merchants became rich and powerful.

Prominent citizens of this cosmopolitan area sought ways to demonstrate visibly their worldly success. What could be better than recording oneself for posterity! Portraiture flourished!

This art form was acceptable to zealous religious leaders provided it did not draw the artist or his patron from proper attention to devotional duties. Tolerance of portraiture was consistent with popular English attitudes of the same period.

Recognition of the Bay State as the center of artistic activity in New England came early. The Reverend William Bentley, in a letter to John Adams dated October 10, 1809, remarked, "The portraits of the Seventeenth Century are of high value if they regard Massachusetts." [18]

The early colonists in the New World did not attempt to ignore their heritage. In architecture, art, and the decorative arts, craftsmen modeled the things they fashioned in the New World on those they had left behind in the Old World. Early painting in New England was little more than a provincial development of English painting of the sixteenth and seventeenth centuries. Many of the most important artists of the period worked in England before and sometimes after settling in America.

During the early seventeenth century most of England remained medieval and unaware of the artistic developments of the Renaissance. Medieval attitudes were transported to America by New England settlers, and as a settlement like Boston grew, it looked much the same as an English town of the Middle Ages.

During the seventeenth century New England life remained relatively difficult. Death, which generally occurred early, was a primary artistic stimulant. American sculpture was born and nourished in the graveyard. As the eminent scholar Harriette M. Forbes indicated, "In the carvings of the gravestones, often very beautiful, always thoughtful, we meet the most characteristic expression of the Puritan as artist." [19]

A dark strain of passion and mystical symbolism was everywhere evident in popular attitudes toward death. Several customs surrounding burials furthered the careers of nearly every limner. Important citizens left this world amid elaborate ceremonies in which painted hatchments bearing the coat of arms of the deceased were displayed. On February 14, 1698, Samuel Sewall noted in his diary that the funeral equipment for Colonel Samuel Shrimpton included a painted "Mourning Coach . . . and Horses in Mourning: Scutcheon on their sides and Deaths heads on their foreheads." [20]

Many of America's most important Colonial artists began their careers as sign painters. Practitioners of this craft occasionally developed their talents to the point where they could earn a profitable living just from limning.

The term *limner* probably developed from *illuminer*, a medieval manuscript decorator. As early as 1949 Alice Ford attempted to characterize the American limner of the previous two centuries. She noted that though his work was "nearer in time to the Renaissance, [he] is much closer to the Middle Ages in his approach to picture-making. Unable to achieve true perspective and foreshortening, the limner shows deficiencies relating his portraits to the simple, sincere work of the early primitive painters rather than to the masters of the Renaissance with their passionate creative search for the ultimate in beauty. When the varied obstacles with which he had to cope in Colonial days, and even later, are considered, this fact should not seem surprising. He had no possibility of studying masterpieces in the great painting collections of Europe whenever he might feel the need of such technical inspiration; added to this the materials with which he worked were limited and rudimentary." [21]

An exhibition of seventeenth-century American painting in New England mounted in 1934 at the Worcester Art Museum, Worcester, Massachusetts, revealed two distinct approaches to portraiture.

An early group of pictures, dating about 1670, all reflected an inherited medieval tradition. In these canvases children were shown full-length, generally standing on black-and-white tile floors. Nearly every subject held an object, either a glove, a fan, a bird, a flower, or a piece of fruit. Men were usually depicted in half- or three-quarter length, and if the subject was a clergyman, he held a Bible, and if a layman, a glove. Women were also shown in three-quarter length, and they too held a decorative object in their hands. Backgrounds were plain and dark, and on more than one occasion a stiffly painted, draped curtain helped fill the background space. In these paintings meticulous attention was paid to costume, which was, on occasion, rather sumptuous. Such elegant dress was, of course, in direct defiance of sumptuary laws, and as early as 1637 Governor Winthrop received a letter from England criticizing the colonists' pride and their "going as farr as they may" in their writing home for lace, "though of the smaller sort," [22] to trim their costumes.

The features of the sitters were sensitively drawn. The children's faces were unquestionably those of children and not of miniature men and women.

In the catalogue for the Worcester exhibition Louisa Dresser says of one of the artists who created these pictures, "His conception was decidedly two dimensional but he knew instinctively how to place a figure on the canvas and how to make telling use of brilliant, decorative, local color. He had no idea of having his figures exist in space . . . bright color, so widely used in the seventeenth century, is in contrast to the paler pastel shades of the eighteenth."[23]

It is generally believed that these pictures represent a sign painter's approach to art and have little in common with the main developments of seventeenth-century European painting.

The portraits of the Mason children, David, Joanna, and Abigail (fig. 4), and of Mrs. Elizabeth (Clarke) Freake and Baby Mary (fig. 6) are of this type. David, Joanna, and Abigail Mason were the children of Arthur Mason, who died in 1708 and Joanna Parker Mason (1635–1708). David Mason was born in Boston in 1661 and died in 1724; his sister Joanna was born in Boston in 1664; and Abigail was baptized in Boston in 1666. David is fashionably dressed for the period and wears a dark brown suit with slashed sleeves and a short skirt and white undergarments. The square white collar is edged with lace. His stockings are gray and he wears brown square-toed shoes. He holds a pair of gray gloves in his right hand. Joanna and Abigail wear white caps, grayish brown dresses that have slashed sleeves tied with red ribbons, puffed white undersleeves, and white pinafores. Both of the girls wear necklaces of double strands of red beads.

Elizabeth Clarke was born in Dorchester, Massachusetts, in 1642 and married John Freake on May 28, 1661. Their daughter Mary was born in 1674. Mrs. Freake was painted wearing a white muslin cap, a gray green dress, a white apron, and a red underskirt, which is trimmed with embroidery. Her white collar is decorated with a border of tightly worked lace and red and black bows. A pearl necklace, a bracelet of black beads, and a gold thumb ring add an air of elegance to the portrait. Baby Mary wears a lace-trimmed bonnet, a long yellow dress, a white pinafore, and a lace-trimmed collar.

A second group of pictures included in the Worcester exhibition dates from slightly later and represents a decided break with the medieval point of view that is more concerned with "the hem of a garment hanging in nervous folds over the knees of a seated figure . . . than the form of the legs underneath."[24] These pictures are part of a tradition that was derived from Italian painters of the Renaissance and transmitted to Sir Peter Lely (d. 1680) and his followers in England during the seventeenth century by Peter Paul Rubens (1577–1640) and Anthony van Dyck (1599–1641). In quality they are three-dimensional. These later pictures demonstrate the artists' keen interest in form and mass. The painters attempted to establish the existence of figures in space through the use of light and shade. The outlines of figures are no longer quite as sharp and distinct. Colors are infinitely more somber and they are no longer used in a decorative manner. They become an integral part of the composition. Keen interest in facial expression is

5 (above). *Robert Gibbs*, artist unknown, oil on canvas, dated 1670, New England, 40″ x 33″. Robert Gibbs stands on a geometric-patterned floor that might have been a painted canvas floor cloth, a painted floor, or simply an artistic convention. Many American portraitists utilized this convention as well as that of columns and draperies in the backgrounds of their pictures. (Museum of Fine Arts, Boston; M. and M. Karolik Fund)

6 (opposite, above). *Mrs. Elizabeth (Clarke) Freake and Baby Mary*, artist unknown, oil on canvas, c. 1674, Massachusetts, 42½″ x 36¾″. This painting is inscribed "Aetatis Suae 6 moth." Mrs. Freake (1642–1713) was the daughter of Thomas Clarke. She married John Freake of Boston in 1661 and Elisha Hutchinson in 1677. Mary Freake (1674–1752) married Judge Josiah Wolcott of Salem in 1694. This portrait of mother and child is one of the most celebrated of all seventeenth-century American paintings. (Worcester Art Museum)

7 (opposite, below). *Self-Portrait of Captain Thomas Smith*, oil on canvas, before 1700, Massachusetts, 24½″ x 23¾″. Captain Smith is thought to have immigrated to New England from Bermuda around 1650. Attempts to identify the naval engagement depicted in the background have not been successful. One ship carries the red ensign of England, which is cantoned with the cross of St. George on a white field. This device became popular in the early 1650s. The portrait of Captain Smith reveals much about the man; it is a powerful characterization and contrasts dramatically with the portraits of Robert Gibbs and Mrs. Freake and Baby Mary, which lack individual personality. (Worcester Art Museum)

everywhere evident in the second group of portraits. The heads now dominate the canvases, and costumes become subordinate to the keen characterizations of the sitters.

Typical of this group is the painting of Captain Thomas Smith (fig. 7), believed to be a self-portrait. Captain Smith is thought to have come to New England from Bermuda about 1650. His sturdy features are well defined and the characterization is particularly strong when compared to those of Mrs. Freake and the Mason children. A real man stares out from the canvas. Of special interest is the vignette of a seascape with a naval battle in progress visible through an open window in the background. A tassel hangs over the subject's left shoulder, and his hand rests on a skull, which in turn sits atop a piece of paper that is inscribed, "Why should I the world be minding/therein a World of Evils Finding./Then Farc(e) well World: Farwell thy Jarres/thy Joies thy Toies they Wiles thy Warrs/Truth Sounds Retreat; I am not sorye,/The Eternall Drawes to him my heart/By Faith (which can thy Force Subvert)/To Crowne (after Grace) with Glory." [25]

As during the Renaissance, the individual personality of the sitter played an all-important part in the art of the late seventeenth century. Early eighteenth-century limners like John Smibert (1688–1751) and Joseph Blackburn, emigrating from England, continued to strengthen this tradition. They brought with them a training that few previous New England artists possessed.

Smibert, during his youth, had been apprenticed to a house painter and for some time had worked for coach painters. He spent three years in Italy copying the Old Masters and, upon his return to London, enjoyed success as a portrait painter. Notebooks kept by the English engraver George Vertue, now in the British Museum, describe Smibert as "a good ingenious man [who] paints and draws handsomely" and whose studio was considered "the rendezvous of the most celebrated artists." [26] Smibert's art gallery was not without appreciative visitors and inspired a poem, *To Mr. Smibert, on the Sight of his Pictures,* which appeared in the London *Daily Courant* on April 14, 1730. It was generally believed that his paintings were so well executed that they illustrated the difference between the artistic talents of the Old Masters: "*Vandike* and *Rubens* show their Rival Forms." [27]

Joseph Blackburn transmitted to New England the artistic precepts taught by the Englishman Sir Godfrey Kneller (1649–1723). Blackburn worked in America from 1754 to 1763. His paintings display a fondness for the play of light and dark on gorgeous fabrics. Blackburn's preoccupation with shining folds and occasionally gleaming jewels is especially evident in his delicate rococo portraits of women. He appears to have possessed little interest in true characterizations. As a painter of textiles, he left an indelible mark upon New England portraiture, for he influenced many aspiring folk painters, including the youthful John Singleton Copley, who cast aside his early primitive style and became one of America's most accomplished masters.

During the first half of the eighteenth century several

8 (left). *Self-Portrait of Robert Feke,* oil on canvas, *c.* 1750, Newport, Rhode Island, 42″ x 32″. Feke died before he could complete this self-portrait and the accompanying portrait of his wife. Later owners employed James S. Lincoln to "finish them" around 1878. Feke is considered one of the best of the Colonial limners. Family tradition indicates that he was a mariner and made several trips to the Continent. Feke had established himself as an artist by 1741 in Boston, and in 1745 he moved to Newport, where he resided until 1750. This limner's painting career took him to Philadelphia in 1746 and Boston in 1748. In 1750 he is said to have traveled to Bermuda and Barbados, where he died. Few of Feke's contemporaries traveled as far afield in their search for commissions. (The Rhode Island Historical Society Library)

9 (below). *The Winslow Family* by Joseph Blackburn, oil on canvas, 1757, Boston, Massachusetts, 54½″ x 79½″. By the mid-eighteenth century, numerous European artists such as Joseph Blackburn brought to America a fragmentary knowledge of the English rococo. Blackburn arrived from Bermuda about 1754 and was active in Boston between 1755 and 1760. Between 1760 and 1763 he commuted between Boston and New England's other major cities. The Winslow family portrait quite possibly was known to John Singleton Copley. (Museum of Fine Arts, Boston; Abraham Shuman Fund)

10 (above). *The Gore Children* by John Singleton Copley, oil on canvas, *c.* 1753, Boston, Massachusetts, 41″ x 56½″. It seems apparent that Copley was thoroughly familiar with Blackburn's complex family portraits, such as *The Winslow Family*, page 20. In the early work of several of America's young artists, there are many pictures that might be considered in the folk tradition. With training and experience, the highly gifted Copley progressed from the rather stiff handling of pigment and elementary composition evident in this painting to become America's foremost Colonial artist. (The Henry Francis du Pont Winterthur Museum)

11 (left). *James Badger* by Joseph Badger, oil on canvas, dated July 8, 1760, Massachusetts, 42½″ x 33⅛″. Badger is known for his somber likenesses, which often lack technical ability and are often dull in color. This portrait is especially attractive and is notable for its stiff provincial charm. Quite possibly Badger lavished special attention on the execution of this painting, for it is a portrait of his grandson. (The Metropolitan Museum of Art; Rogers Fund, 1929)

New England-born artists rose to prominence. Robert Feke (c. 1705–1750)—who lived in Newport and is known to have worked at Boston in 1741, at Newport in 1745, at Philadelphia in 1746, at Boston in 1748, and again at Philadelphia in 1750—is almost universally considered the region's outstanding artist prior to Copley. Feke derived his inspiration from Smibert; however, he was an infinitely more competent technician. Feke, like nearly all eighteenth-century artists, both trained and self-taught, relied heavily upon the use of prints and engravings. He must have been intimately familiar with Lord Shaftsbury's essay on art, *The Judgment of Hercules,* for he copied in oil the engravings after Paulo Dematthaeis that were included in it. It can be assumed that he studied other writings on art and used engravings after European painters as a source of inspiration.

Feke was visited by the itinerant diarist Dr. Alexander Hamilton of Annapolis, who journeyed to Newport in 1744 and recorded that "Feykes, a painter [has] exactly the phizz of a painter, having a long pale face, sharp nose, large eyes with which he looked upon you stedfastly, long curled black hair, a delicate white hand, and long fingers" (fig. 8). Hamilton believed Feke to be "the most extraordinary genius" he ever knew, doing pictures "tollerably (*sic*) well by the force of genius, having never had any teaching." [28]

Joseph Badger (1708–1763), Feke's contemporary, was a man of modest means who lived nearly all his life in Boston. Perhaps his longest trip from the bustling port was in 1737 to Dedham, Massachusetts, where he is known to have painted a house. Badger painted signs and hatchments as well. He began to execute portraits about 1740 and frequently borrowed background compositions from mezzotints based on English portraits. By the late 1750s Badger had developed his own distinct style. In his 1760 portrait of his grandson James Badger (1757–1817; fig. 11), he relied less upon European ideas of composition than in most of his earlier portraits.

John Singleton Copley (1738–1815), stepson of the artist Peter Pelham, possibly received instruction from Badger. He must also have been familiar with Blackburn's paintings, since the older man was working in Boston until the time Copley was twenty-six. By 1755 Copley had established himself as a professional painter. His brilliant power of characterization was most certainly his own, even in his very early portraits, which are naïve in

12 (left); 13 (opposite). Two life-size murals from the Macpheadris-Warner House built at Portsmouth, New Hampshire, around 1716 by Captain Archibald Macpheadris, a Scots fur trader. The murals show two of five Iroquois sachems who were taken to England by Captain Peter Schuyler in 1710 and presented at the court of Queen Anne. These murals are based on prints that were created soon after the Indians had arrived in London, where they caused great excitement. (Macpheadris-Warner House)

execution. In his painting of the Gore children (fig. 10), executed in 1753, when he was fifteen, there is only a vague hint of the great artistic achievements that the artist would attain in his later years. None of the painters discussed so far possessed the ability to transfer to canvas the New England matrons and their affluent husbands from the mercantile aristocracy as convincingly as Copley. His penetrating portraits remain the masterpieces of American Colonial art. They are not only great works of art, but during the entire nineteenth century they influenced self-taught painters, like William Matthew Prior, who probably saw Copley's pictures in both public and private collections in Boston.

Winthrop Chandler (1747–1790) is without doubt one of the most important New England artists of the second half of the eighteenth century. Though well known for his stylish portraits of New England's prominent citizens, this house and general fancy painter is perhaps most recognized for his decorative overmantel landscapes, such as the complex rural scene depicted in the overmantel from the Elisha Hurlbut house in Scotland, Connecticut (fig. 19). Overmantels and fireboards are considered by many to be the progenitors of landscape painting in New England. Several of Chandler's remarkable overmantels are still located in homes originally owned by his relatives or friends in both Connecticut and Massachusetts.

Ralph Earl (1751–1801) opened a studio in 1775 at New Haven, where his attempts at painting likenesses in the manner of Copley were surprisingly successful. Like Copley's, Earl's early portraits are naïve in execution and illustrate one stage in the process of his development. The Angus Nickelson family (fig. 25) is crude when compared with his later works. During the summer of 1775 Earl traveled to Lexington and Concord, Massachusetts, to make sketches of several local scenes that he later used for his now famous battle paintings. In his book *History of the Rise and Progress of the Arts of Design*, William Dunlap referred to these as "the first historical pictures, perhaps, ever attempted in America, which were engraved by his companion, in arms, Mr. Amos Doolittle." [29] In the spring of 1778 Earl sailed for England, where he attempted to master European techniques. His return to America in 1785 was noted in the *Independent Journal: or, the General Advertiser*, on November 2: "RALPH EARL.—Last Sunday arrived in town from England, by way of Boston, Mr. Ralph Earl, a native of Massachusetts; he has passed a number of years in London under those distinguished and most celebrated Masters in Painting, Sir Joshua Reynolds, Mr. West, and Mr. Copley. The gentleman now proposes to enter upon his profession in this city, where a specimen of his abilities may be seen on calling at Mr. Rivington's No. 1 Queen Street." [30] For the next decade and a half he painted portraits and an occasional landscape in New England and in New York City.

By the mid-eighteenth century Boston had well established her preeminence as the center of New England cultural activity. The English-oriented society frequently patronized such artists as Joseph Blackburn, Robert Feke,

14 (below); 14a (above). Paneling and overmantel from an upstairs room of a house built by Joseph Pitkin at East Hartford, Connecticut, in 1723, artist unknown, late eighteenth or early nineteenth century, 15″ x 37½″. The wooden paneling above fireplaces in Colonial homes was sometimes decorated with oil paintings, which eventually came to be called *overmantels*. The overmantel painting, like the wall murals from the Macpheadris-Warner House, is probably based upon a print. The raised panels, which surround the fireplace and the overmantel, are painted in "marble" and are an effort to create the same rich decorative interior that was used in the House of Burgesses at Williamsburg, Virginia, in 1705, when the "wanscote and other Wooden work" was marbleized. (Wadsworth Atheneum; gift of Mrs. William B. Goodwin)

15 (opposite). *Moses Marcy*, artist unknown, oil on wood paneling, mid-eighteenth century, Moses Marcy House, Southbridge, Massachusetts, 41½″ x 27⅞″. Decorative mantels and overmantels were often used in homes like the gambrel-roofed dwelling included in the portrait of Moses Marcy. This splendidly dressed New England gentleman is shown with a clay pipe, a punchbowl, and a glass of punch. On the table rests a book, which quite possibly is an account book used to record the prosperous merchant's financial activities. (Old Sturbridge Village)

16 (above). *Seat of Colonel George Boyd,* artist unknown, oil on canvas, 1774, New Hampshire, 17″ x 32″. The house illustrated in this painting was built at Portsmouth by Colonel Nathaniel Meserve in 1740. Behind the house was his shipyard, where in 1749 the fifty-gun man-of-war *America* was built for the Royal Navy. To the left of the house is a mill. In 1768 the house became the property of Colonel George Boyd, who extended the garden to the dimensions shown in the painting. After the Revolution, Colonel Boyd returned to America from England and brought with him a new coach, a coachman, and a gardener. Paintings such as this are important not only as works of art but as social documents as well. This picture amply illustrates New England architecture of the period and reveals much about the social conditions existing at the time of its execution. Photograph courtesy Museum of Fine Arts, Boston. (Phillips Exeter Academy)

17 (right). *Newburyport Harbor* by Thomas A. Hamilton, oil on canvas, *c.* 1870, Massachusetts, 19¾″ x 32″. Throughout much of the eighteenth century, Newburyport was a major shipping port, which served as a center of commerce for the surrounding communities. Of special interest in this painting are the many shop signs indicating an extensive number of commercial establishments, including one shop that specialized in "room paper" or wallpaper. (New York State Historical Association)

18 (opposite, above). Overmantel from Burk Tavern, attributed to Jared Jessup, oil on board, *c.* 1812, painted at Burk Tavern, Bernardston, Massachusetts, 46½″ x 76½″. The Burk Tavern was kept by Major John Burk as early as 1763. The painting depicts a view of Boston harbor and is believed to have been painted by Jessup, a guest of the tavern, who was afterward arrested as a British spy. From 1809 to 1813, the artist traveled northward along the Connecticut Valley, and in the *History of Bernardston* the following information is given: "A man came from parts unknown, doing the work in payment for board. He was here as far as can be learned for some months. One day men arrived from the east part of the State of New York, some say from Albany, departing with this man as their prisoner, and it was always supposed that he was arrested as a spy, the War of 1812 being then in progress." The ships in the painting fly American flags. (Memorial Hall Museum, Pocumtuck Valley Memorial Association)

19 (below). Overmantel from the Elisha Hurlbut House by Winthrop Chandler, oil on board, painted before 1790, Scotland, Connecticut, 41⅞" x 59½". This lively view is one of several overmantels by Winthrop Chandler, a house and general fancy painter who is considered to be one of the most important folk artists of the Revolutionary period. Chandler is also well known for his striking portraits of family members, neighbors, and friends who lived in and about his hometown, Woodstock, Connecticut. From 1785 until his death in 1790, Chandler lived in Worcester, Massachusetts, where in 1788 he gilded the courthouse weathervane, "laying on of 8 books of gold leaf at 2 shillings per book."[1] (Private collection)

20 (below). *Phebe King Turner* (1740–1818) by Rufus Hathaway, oil on canvas, 1796, New England, 34½″ x 33″. The subject in this picture was the wife of the Reverend Caleb Turner. Hathaway frequently used an ornamental fan as a prop in his portraits. The drapery is another convention that Hathaway relied upon. It made the painting of the background substantially easier. Hathaway is believed to have been born in Freetown, Massachusetts, and in the early 1790s traveled on horseback as an itinerant painter. By 1795 he had settled at Duxbury, Massachusetts, and he married Judith Winsor in December of that year. His father-in-law was a prominent merchant, who convinced the young artist to enter the medical profession. Hathaway practiced medicine for some twenty-seven years in the town of Duxbury and in 1822 was elected an Honorary Fellow of the Massachusetts Medical Society. (Old Colony Historical Society)

21 (above). *Portrait of an Unidentified Woman* sitting in a Chippendale side chair by J. Brown, oil on canvas, *c.* 1800, Massachusetts, 29¼″ x 23″. Little is known about the artist, J. Brown. Paintings that can safely be attributed to him have been found in Massachusetts, Connecticut, and New York. It is quite possible that Ammi Phillips was familiar with his work and patterned his early efforts on lessons learned from studying Brown's portraits. (Mr. and Mrs. William E. Wiltshire III)

22 (opposite). *Deacon Eliphaz Thayer and His Wife*, attributed to John Brewster, Jr. (1766–1854), oil on canvas, *c.* 1800, New England, 30″ x 40″. John Brewster, Jr., was born a deaf-mute. At an early age, he was taught to write and soon displayed an aptitude for portraiture. He studied with the Reverend Joseph Steward and during the late 1700s executed several handsome portraits in Connecticut. Upon the marriage of his brother Royal Brewster, he moved with him to Buxton, Maine, where he made his permanent home. His physical handicap did not deter him, for he traveled extensively and advertised his abilities as a portraitist and miniature artist in local newspapers throughout New York, Connecticut, and the northern New England states. When the Connecticut Asylum for the Deaf and Dumb was established at Hartford in 1817, Brewster moved to that city and enrolled in the opening class. He remained there for several years while studying lip reading and speech. Deacon Thayer sits in a handsome Windsor armchair, and his wife, Deliverance, sits in what appears to be a loopback Windsor. (New York State Historical Association)

John Greenwood, John Smibert, and, toward the end of the century, John Singleton Copley and Ralph Earl. Away from the cosmopolitan city, numerous other painters enjoyed a similar patronage from rural dwellers. Men like John Durand, Joseph Steward, and William and Richard Jennys probably had received some professional instruction, for their technical competence as artists exceeded that of self-taught men like Rufus Hathaway, Richard Brunton, and Winthrop Chandler.

Most of the portraits executed during the last quarter of the eighteenth century were of three-quarter figures on large canvases. Occasionally classical details, such as columns, draperies, and window views, were included. New Englanders appear to have possessed a definite preference for the portrait.

Because of religious restrictions on frivolous decoration, the landscape remained relatively unpopular in New England throughout much of the seventeenth century and the first half of the eighteenth century.

John Foster, probably best known for his woodcut portrait of the Reverend Richard Mather, believed to have been made about 1670, was born at Dorchester, Massachusetts, in 1648. After graduating from Harvard in 1677, he taught school in his native village, which he had left by 1675 to become a printer at Boston. Foster is also credited with printing the first map ever engraved and published in the Colonies. Between June of 1675 and the fall of 1676, an epidemic of Indian raids occurred. The Reverend William Hubbard, a teacher at the First Church of Ipswich, Massachusetts, wrote an account of the struggle, which ultimately became known as King Philip's War. Foster printed an edition of this effort in the spring of 1677 at Boston and included the map.

Foster was a true Renaissance man. He not only printed books and woodcuts but appears to have been one of the first native-born portrait and landscape painters. His *View of Boston and Charleston from East Boston* was engraved in Amsterdam. The original, now lost, might well have been America's first indigenous landscape.

By the mid-eighteenth century religious strictures began to soften and popular attitudes toward landscape painting changed. Patrons, in their zeal to decorate elegant houses, realized the potential decorative value of the landscape, and their general acceptance of the art form caused it to become a status symbol. If one could

24 (above). *The Reverend Thomas Robbins* by Reuben Moulthrop, signed on the back before relining: "R. Moulthrop Pinxit. Sept. 1801.," oil on canvas, New England, 30″ x 29½″. The Reverend Thomas Robbins was well known by his contemporaries for his zealous ministerial work. Today he is best known for the impressive library that in time became the property of The Connecticut Historical Society. Robbins was elected recording secretary in 1825, when the society was founded, and was its first librarian. This painting by Moulthrop is considered one of his best. The sitter noted in his diary on September 5, 1801: "Agreed with Mr. Moulthrop to take my portrait." On September 8th he added: "Sat for Mr. Moulthrop to take my likeness."[2] (The Connecticut Historical Society)

not afford a realistic, carefully painted "landskip" by a famous artist, more crudely painted decorative examples by the lesser trained and the folk artist were perfectly acceptable. The day of the landscape had arrived, and for the New England folk artist interest in recording the native scene has never waned.

New England's first artists who attempted to paint the sea tended to focus their attention upon the harbor and the land masses, avoiding the unknown, threatening aspects of the open water. This is evident in the portrait of *Moses Marcy* (fig. 15) executed by an unknown artist circa 1760. Time and again the artists' preoccupation with the harbor is evident throughout all of the Colonies during the seventeenth and much of the eighteenth centuries. Very few marine views of this early period are known. However, the custom of including an emblematic seascape visible through an open window in the background of portraits was established early. In the self-portrait of Captain Thomas Smith (c. 1690; fig. 7), it is obvious from the naval battle depicted in the background that the seaman, although the conqueror of

hostile waters himself, was ever conscious of the possibility of death associated with his profession.

In time the painter of American seascapes broadened his horizons. He no longer concerned himself exclusively with the shore. By the mid-eighteenth century paintings of large bodies of water dotted with sprightly sailing ships were created. As the Romantic style developed during the nineteenth century, the American artist turned his back on the shore and recorded the turbulent open sea. Woodcuts, engravings, and mezzotints provided the marine artist with sources of design that he boldly copied and on occasion adapted, at the same time developing his own artistic ability. From this point onward, the innovative American painter looked upon the recording of the sea as a great adventure. Throughout the next hundred years the awe of the sea felt by earlier painters gradually dissipated, until ultimately the naïve painter came to celebrate the natural wildness and fury of the untamable waters.

Formal portraiture flourished in the new American republic and no artist was more successful than Gilbert

25 (above). *The Angus Nickelson Family* by Ralph Earl (the Elder), oil on canvas, *c.* 1800, New England, 42½″ x 58″. Family pieces such as the multiple portraits of the Angus Nickelson family are relatively rare in American painting. The Nickelsons were obviously well-to-do and fully aware of the latest European fashions. (Museum of Fine Arts, Springfield, Massachusetts; gift of Robert Lewis Mason, great-great-grandson of Angus Nickelson)

Stuart (1755–1828), favorite painter of the republican court. Stuart's paintings influenced nearly every American portrait painter of the nineteenth century. He encouraged young artists to observe him at work. Many journeyed long distances to visit his studio and to discuss his methods of painting. Others, including John Trumbull, Thomas Sully, and William Matthew Prior, improved their technique by copying his masterpieces.

While Americans such as Benjamin West, John Singleton Copley, and Mather Brown dominated the English artistic scene during the last years of the Colonial period and in the early Federalist years, naïve masters continued to paint throughout New England in relative obscurity.

Reuben Moulthrop (1763–1814) was born at East Haven, Connecticut. His first artistic endeavors included modeling portraits in wax. In time he became proprietor of a waxworks museum and a traveling waxworks exhibition. Moulthrop's paintings were always experimental and his work was strikingly uneven. One week he might paint an absolute masterpiece, the next week a very poor likeness. In his portrait of the Reverend Thomas Robbins

(1777–1856; fig. 24), the artist rose to the occasion. The Reverend Robbins was a distinguished Connecticut gentleman, well known as an inspiring clergyman, a book collector, and a librarian, who, when Moulthrop executed his portrait in 1801, had already earned his master's degree from Williams College.

The New England folk painter used his brush in many ways. Thorough study is merited by the career of John S. Blunt (1798–1835), detailed in the catalogue *The Borden Limner and His Contemporaries*, which accompanied a special exhibition of paintings by this artist at the University of Michigan Museum of Art in 1976–1977.

John Blunt advertised on December 31, 1822, in the *New Hampshire Gazette* that he did "profiles, profile miniature pictures, landscapes and ornamental paintings." He announced a new venture in the *Portsmouth Journal* on April 2, 1825: "Drawing and Painting School. The subscriber proposes to open a school for the instruction of young ladies and gentlemen in the arts of drawing and painting. The following branches will be taught: oil

26 (above). Tavern sign from Saybrook, Connecticut, painted wood, 1796, 52½" x 27¼". Few eighteenth-century signs remain, as it was a common practice to repaint an old inn sign when it became worn by the elements or when an establishment changed owners. Few painted signs can safely be attributed to an artist, for they were rarely signed. Many signs were created by artists who practiced other branches of the trade. Abner Reed of East Windsor, Connecticut, is most famous as an engraver; however, he is known to have executed signs on wood, canvas, tin, and glass. In 1808 he advertised: "a number of Tavern Signs; ready painted of various devices, the name only wanting to complete them for hanging."[3] (The Connecticut Historical Society)

painting on canvas and glass, water colors, and with crayons. The school will commence about the first of May provided a sufficient number of scholars can be obtained to warrant the undertaking. Terms made known on application to John S. Blunt. Painting in its various branches attended to as usual."

In August 1826 Blunt moved to a new location and in October announced a special "Exhibition of paintings for three weeks only, open evenings and brilliantly illuminated. The people are respectfully informed that a number of paintings will be exhibited at No. 4 State Street among which are six views of Niagara Falls, a view of the Notch of the White Mountains, a view of Lake Winnipiseogee, a likeness of Sir William Pepperell, to-gether with a great variety of other paintings. Admittance to the public 12½ cents, children half price, season tickets 25¢. Tickets for sale at Mr. B. Hutchinson's store. N.B. The entrance to Mr. Blunt's painting room will be for the present through Mr. Hutchinson's store."[31]

Blunt was a collateral descendant of William Pepperell, who had died in 1759. Quite possibly the painting of him was based upon an engraving or other early source. Blunt is known to have owned several prints, for the inventory of his estate recorded seven framed prints valued at $5.25.

John S. Blunt advertised again in the 1827 Portsmouth Directory, where he was listed at the corner of Court and State Streets. In this advertisement he announced that he would execute "THE FOLLOWING BRANCHES, VIZ. Portrait and Miniature Painting, Military Standard do. Sign Painting, Plain and Ornamented, Landscape and Marine Painting, Masonic and Fancy do. Ships Ornaments Gilded and Painted, Oil and Burnish Gilding, Bronzing, &c &c."[32]

Blunt obviously had been frequently patronized by the Masons, for in his ledger he recorded many entries for 1825 and 1826 similar to the following:

May 26, 1826:	DeWitt Clinton Encampment to painting 10 Aprons and Sashes	$12.50
July 3, "	Washington Chapter to painting banner	11.00
" " "	St. John's Lodge to All seeing Eye and Painting do.	2.25 [33]

A typical page from John Blunt's account book indicates the great variety of painterly tasks performed by New England folk artists during the first quarter of the nineteenth century.

On August 8 he painted for Robert Foster, Jr., Co. a pair of signs for $3.50. Robert Foster is identified in the 1821 Portsmouth Directory as a printer and bookseller maintaining an establishment on Daniel Street. Also on August 8 he lettered a coffin plate for Samuel M. Docham, for which he charged 25 cents. The same day he charged Ann Folsom $4.20 for mending three chairs and painting a set of eight.

On August 24 he repainted letters for the Robert

Foster, Jr., Co., charging them 20 cents and on the same day charged the Town of Portsmouth $3.34 for painting a guideboard and board. On August 29 Blunt painted for John Trundy parts of a small carriage, charging him 12 cents, and on September 3 he earned $1.75 by painting a sign for Nathaniel O. Ham. John Trundy was listed in the 1827 *Portsmouth Directory* as a compass maker who maintained a shop on Penhollow Street and resided on South Street. Nathaniel Ham in the same directory was listed as a watchmaker with a shop on Congress Street and a residence on Vaughan Street.

Folk artists were indeed jacks-of-all-trades and were forced to supplement their incomes in many ways. On September 4 Blunt charged Langley Boardman $1.75 for staining a bedstead rose. On September 16 he painted a small coffin plate, earning $1.00. The entry for September 21 deserves note, for it expands the spectrum of John Blunt's artistic endeavors. On that date he charged $1.00 for painting five dozen tin boxes for Joshua Hubbard. Hubbard was a druggist, who in the 1827 *Portsmouth Directory* was located at 2 Market Street. The boxes probably were apothecary containers. Throughout New England painted and decorated tin was an acceptable alternative to imported French tole. Nearly every home had at least one document box that was made decorative by the addition of painted flowers or stylized designs. Blunt probably decorated this type of tin as well.

In 1831 John Blunt and his wife moved to Boston, where he opened a studio on Cornhill and acquired a house on Castle Street. In 1829 he had exhibited at the Boston Athenaeum the view of Lake Winnipiseogee mentioned in his Portsmouth announcement of October 1826.

On September 12, 1835, the Portsmouth *Journal* carried in the "Death" column the notice, "At sea, on board ship Ohio, on his passage from New-Orleans for Boston, Mr. John S. Blunt, aged 37, painter, of Boston, formerly of this town."

Blunt has long been known for his seascapes, winter scenes, ship portraits, and genre pictures. A large body of portraits has now been attributed to this unusually gifted folk painter as well. One of the handsomest is the portrait of Eliza Anthony Brownell (plate 17).

The work of William Matthew Prior corresponds to Reuben Moulthrop's in that his paintings, too, were especially uneven. It has been surmised that Moulthrop simply did not care to strive for a steady progression toward a distinguishable style. Prior's unevenness resulted from economic factors. If a client wanted an inexpensive portrait, he would readily paint one. If a patron was affluent and wished a more realistic likeness, Prior was capable of this, too. It simply cost more!

Prior and his painting in-laws, the Hamblens, are worthy of careful detailing, for their experiences and growth as artists were probably fairly typical.

William Matthew Prior, like most folk painters, relied upon his own ingenuity and ability to develop a viable technique for portraiture. Although many academic American painters of the same period studied in Europe, European study remained outside Prior's realm.

27 (above); 27a (below). Tavern sign inscribed "Worrick's Hotel," paint on a wooden panel, second half of the nineteenth century, W. 38". Modes of transportation were especially popular with tavern-sign painters. This example depicts a steam-operated locomotive on one side and a sidewheeler on the reverse, indicating that the hotel probably served both land and sea. It is conceivable that this sign was used in Massachusetts, for the ship is named the *Mayflower*. (Greenfield Village and Henry Ford Museum)

34

30 (left). *Memorial to George Washington* by Mehitabel Wingate after an engraving by E. G. Gridley, watercolor on paper, *c.* 1810, New England, 15⅝" x 17⅛". The tablet on the memorial carries the legend, "Sacred to the Memory of the truly Illustrious GEORGE WASHINGTON. He was possessed of every qualification to render him worthy the Title of a GREAT and GOOD MAN." (Greenfield Village and Henry Ford Museum)

31 (below). *Memorial to George Washington* by A. D. Reid, watercolor on paper, 1834, New England, 21½" x 16¾". It is interesting to compare the design of this watercolor with the William Matthew Prior view of Washington's tomb, page 34. In this version, the Potomac separates the tomb from Mount Vernon. (Mr. and Mrs. Edwin Braman)

28 (opposite, above). *George and Martha Washington*, attributed to William Matthew Prior, reverse painting on glass, *c.* 1850, Boston, Massachusetts, 24½" x 18½". During the last half of the eighteenth century and throughout much of the nineteenth, reverse paintings on glass were especially popular. Prior is well known for his single portraits of George and Martha Washington. This is the only known example where the two portraits are included on a single large sheet of glass. (Private collection)

29 (opposite, below). *Mount Vernon and George Washington's Tomb* by William Matthew Prior, oil on canvas, *c.* 1855, Boston, Massachusetts, 19⁵/₁₆" x 25". Several versions of this scene are known and are unquestionably based upon prints. Nearly every American printmaker offered his view of the final resting place of "The Father of Our Country." This painting is stamped on the back of the canvas: "PAINTING GARRET/No. 36 Trenton St./East Boston/W.M. PRIOR." (Greenfield Village and Henry Ford Museum)

32 (above). *Historical Monument of the American Republic* by Erastus Salisbury Field, oil on canvas, *c.* 1876, New England, 111″ x 157″. This fantastic picture was painted to commemorate the hundredth anniversary of American independence. James Ackerman, a sign and ornamental painter, ran a display advertisement in the *New York City Directory* for 1849. This advertisement probably gave Field the idea for the *Monument.* Numerous printed sources provided elements for this painting: *The Tower of Babel,* which appeared in a New Hampshire Bible; *The Garden of Eden,* the Bible illustration after John Martin; and Thomas Cole's *The Course of Empire* and *The Architect's Dream,* variations on compositions by John Martin; and John Trumbull's *Signing of the Declaration of Independence* and *The Surrender of Lord Cornwallis at Yorktown* were the source of two of the subjects reproduced on the walls of the *Monument* in painted imitation of bas relief. Field was immensely pleased with his painting and in 1876 had printed at Amherst a ten-page key that was to serve as a guide for each level of each tower. In the same year, an engraving of the *Monument* was made by E. Bierstadt, and in a letter to a Mr. Hubbard, the painter discussed darkening the shading and the lines of the painting so that a second edition of the print would be stronger. Through the years, Field continued to be concerned about the *Monument,* and about 1888 he added two more towers. Field's religious conviction caused him to support abolition and Lincoln's efforts to preserve the union. The new towers painted in 1888 strongly state his views on slavery. (Museum of Fine Arts, Springfield, Massachusetts; the Morgan Wesson Memorial Collection)

33 (right). *Portrait of an Unidentified Child,* attributed to Erastus Salisbury Field, daguerreotype, second half of the nineteenth century, New England, 4½″ x 3½″. This daguerreotype has been tinted with watercolor and stylistically displays many of the characteristics of Erastus Salisbury Field's portraits of children executed in oil on canvas. (Marguerite Riordan)

34 (above). *Master Burnham*, attributed to R. W. and S. A. Shute, watercolor and pencil on paper, *c.* 1833, Massachusetts, 27⅜″ x 19″. The son of Josiah and Abigail Burnham of Grafton, Massachusetts, this sober youngster's portrait is a major work by the Shutes. Photograph courtesy Sotheby Parke Bernet Inc. (Private collection)

35 (left). *Portrait of a Young Girl*, attributed to Ruth Henshaw Bascom, pastel or crayon on paper, *c.* 1840, Fitzwilliam, New Hampshire, 16″ x 12″. This winsome young lady is said to be a member of the Payly family of Fitzwilliam. (Old Sturbridge Village)

36 (below, left). *Lady with a Nosegay* by A. Ellis, oil on panel, *c.* 1830, New Hampshire, 22½″ x 26½″. This highly decorative portrait is a boldly styled painting by an untutored naïve artist. The vibrant colors and abstract modeling are common characteristics in works by the artist. (New York State Historical Association)

37 (above). *Mary Ann Wheeler* by Isaac Sheffield, oil on panel, 1835, Stonington, Connecticut, 30″ x 24″. (Mr. and Mrs. William E. Wiltshire III)

38 (opposite, above left). *Charles Mortimer French* by Asahel Powers, oil on panel, *c.* 1832, Vermont, 36″ x 21¾″. This painting is signed on the reverse: "Charles Mortimer French/taken at 6 years old/Asahel Powers./Painter." (New York State Historical Association)

39 (opposite, above right). *Young Boy* by William Bartoll (1817–1859), oil on canvas, 1840–1850, Marblehead, Massachusetts, 36⅛″ x 30¼″. The young boy holds an alphabet book in his left hand, and his right hand rests upon the head of his favorite dog. (Greenfield Village and Henry Ford Museum)

40 (opposite, below). *Double Portrait of Members of the Stiles Family*, oil on canvas, second quarter of the nineteenth century, Malden, Massachusetts, 32¼″ x 47″. The woman in this painting wears colored glasses. (Mr. and Mrs. Edwin Braman)

Prior, the second son of Sarah and Matthew Prior, was born at Bath, Maine, on May 16, 1806. Several searches by such distinguished art historians as Nina Fletcher Little have uncovered little evidence of formal training.

Prior was a thoroughgoing Yankee. Though he possessed a more than competent technical skill, he was willing to adapt his style to suit the pocketbook of any potential sitter. At one point in his career, he advertised, "Persons wishing for a flat picture can have a likeness without shade or shadow at one quarter price." [34] On the reverse of the frame on one of Prior's flat portraits is the printed label, "PORTRAITS/PAINTED IN THIS STYLE!/Done in about an hour's sitting./Price $2.92, including Frame, Glass, &c./Please call at Trenton Street/East Boston/WM. M. PRIOR." [35]

On June 5, 1827, Prior advertised in the *Maine Inquirer,* "Ornamental painting, old tea trays, waiters re-japanned and ornamented in a very tasty style. Bronzing, oil guilding and varnishing by Wm. M. Prior, Bath. No. 1 Middle Street." [36]

The earliest known portrait signed and dated by Prior was executed at Portland, Maine, on August 14, 1824, indicating that already, at the age of eighteen, he was traveling in search of commissions.

Prior first advertised as a painter of portraits in the *Maine Inquirer* on February 28, 1828: "Portrait painter, Wm. M. Prior, offers his services to the public. Those who wish for a likeness at a reasonable price are invited to call soon. Side views and profiles of children at reduced prices."

At various times throughout his career Prior indicated the versatility of his talent. He not only advertised for fancy sign and ornamental painting but also offered to execute commissions for military and standard paintings. Prior's large portraits ranged from $10 to $25 apiece. Obviously he was held in high esteem as an artist, for many of his contemporary competitors were actually executing large family portraits for as little at $10.

William Matthew Prior married Rosamond Clark Hamblen in 1828 at Bath. Like many painters with aspirations, he named at least one of his children after a famous artist. Gilbert Stuart Prior was born at Bath in 1831.

An advertisement in the April 5, 1831, issue of the *Maine Inquirer* indicates another aspect of Prior's work: "Fancy pieces painted, either designed or copied to suit the customer, enameling on glass tablets for looking glasses and time pieces."

Sometime between 1831 and 1834 Prior moved his family to Portland, Maine, where they resided on Green Street with his brother-in-law, Nathaniel Hamblen, a painter. By 1837 he had established his own residence, and his relatives, Joseph G. and Sturtevant J. Hamblen, also painters, resided with him. Soon after the death in 1839 of Eli Hamblen, a third brother, the Hamblen–Prior clan moved to Boston, where they resided at Nathaniel Hamblen's house on Chambers Street. Of the three Hamblens, only Sturtevant J. Hamblen was a portrait painter. It is believed that the other brothers earned their living by house, sign, and fancy painting.

The two families continued to live together and in 1842 moved to Marion Street, East Boston. Between 1842 and 1844 Prior appears to have been on one of his many painting trips, which ranged sometimes through the New Bedford–Fall River–Sturbridge, Massachusetts, area. Prior frequently took at least one or two of his children on his trips, and Grace Adams Lyman, in an interview with William Matthew Prior, Jr., recorded, "This son recollects traveling with his father through New Bedford, Fall River, and all along the coast, and spending four or five months in Baltimore. Often several members of the family accompanied him on these journeys." [37]

Prior's intense belief in the teachings of William Miller, a leader of the Advent Movement during the early 1840s, caused him to publish in later years two books: *The King's Vesture, Evidence from Scripture and History Comparatively Applied to William Miller, the Chronologist of 1843,* released in 1862, and *The Empyrean Canopy,* released in 1868. In the latter book he related information about painting a chronological chart under the direction of Miller and of being so influenced by the man's magnetic personality that he was moved to paint his portrait.

In true Yankee fashion, Prior turned his deep religious conviction to financial advantage. Because of his spiritualistic powers, "he painted portraits of children who had died in infancy, declaring that they had come to him from the spirit world. The practice of phrenology was another avocation. Varied as were Prior's accomplishments, however, it is for his copies on glass of portraits of the Washingtons that he will be longest remembered." [38]

Many beginning artists were without adequate supplies and adapted what was easily available to suit their needs. A few of the paintings signed by Prior that have come to light were executed on cotton bed-ticking. It seems probable that Prior not only prepared his own canvases and ground his own paint but also made his own frames.

In 1846 William Matthew Prior built a house at 36 Trenton Street, East Boston, and the third story became his "Painting Garret." He hung one of his large paintings over the door as a combination sign and advertisement and continued to work at this location until his death in 1873. Many of the portraits and ornamental landscapes executed from this studio bear a stamp on the reverse side that includes Prior's name, the name of his studio, and the location.

The popularity of daguerreotypes caused Prior's portrait commissions to decrease significantly. In his later years he turned to copying portraits of famous people. Many of these paintings were executed by reverse painting on glass.

Prior quite possibly had met Gilbert Stuart personally. He obviously admired him and in 1850 persuaded the Boston Athenaeum to allow him to copy a portrait of George Washington by the American master. Prior's paintings of famous personages must certainly have been successful, for numerous examples remain, including likenesses of Martha Washington, Abraham Lincoln, Ulysses

41 (left). *Parke Family Tree* by William Richardson, ink and watercolor on paper, *c.* 1838, Massachusetts, 19¾" x 13¾". In this family record, two upside-down hearts unite the family names of Ayeres and Parke. One side of the tree depicts an architectural scene; the other a nautical scene. Beside one apple appears the following inscription: "Sarah Parke departed this life Oct. 6, 1836—Aged 2 years, 18 days—So faids the lovely blooming flour." (IBM Art Collection)

42 (below). *Memorial Picture*, artist unknown, ink and watercolor on paper, *c.* 1830, New England, 28" x 32". Sylvia W. Proctor died at age twenty-one. This memorial picture includes a severed willow tree representing the cutting off of life. The figure of the mourning woman resembles a watercolor silhouette. (Private collection)

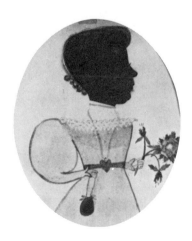

S. Grant, Theodore Parker, and Napoleon. These fragile pictures were originally framed in narrow gilt moldings and sold for $3 to $4 each.

Prior also specialized in landscapes in the latter part of his career. His winter scenes are numerous. One view, titled *Moonlight,* which he painted time and again, and two fantastic landscapes, one dated 1855, indicate his attempt to interest the public in Romantic imaginary pictures that contained castles, humble cottages, and gently flowing streams.

Prior freely borrowed from prints. He painted many views of Mount Vernon and Washington's tomb seen at various seasons. These were based upon engravings and lithographs.

Nina Fletcher Little has concisely summarized the pictorial achievements of William Matthew Prior: "it may fairly be said that he neither exhibited great artistic talent, nor excelled in imaginative composition. He could, however, execute portraits with a considerable degree of competence when occasion demanded. His flat likenesses are perhaps more interesting as examples of a conscious effort to give the public what it wanted at a price it was willing to pay, than for their inherent merit. Nevertheless, he was an able and varied craftsman, combining a knowledge of general decorating with commercial, portrait, and landscape painting, all of which he pursued throughout an active and colorful career." [39]

Sturtevant J. Hamblen was probably a pupil of his more eminent and successful brother-in-law, William Matthew Prior. Between 1841 and 1856 Hamblen exe-

43, 44, 45, 46 (left). Group of four watercolor portraits with hollow-cut faces, including a man, a woman, and their two children, artist unknown, c. 1835, New England, each 4″ x 6″. Silhouette artists utilized many techniques to fulfill their commissions. The unidentified maker of these portraits used the hollow-cut technique to create the faces and watercolors for the bodies, the costumes, and the decorative accessories. Portrait miniatures were as popular in New York as in New England, as evidenced by the following excerpt from the December 15, 1832, edition of *The New-York Mirror:* "There are no more graceful and precious relics of friendship or love than miniatures. They perpetuate the bloom of youth and the lustre of beauty. We become acquainted with those whom we never saw. We muse on the face we love, although peradventure in reality, an ocean rolls between us; and, by their aid, even death himself is forced to open his awful gates, and to suffer his victim once more to bless the eyes, although absent to the other senses of the bereaved survivors." (Private collection)

47 (above). *Self-Portrait of Jonathan Adams Bartlett* (1817–1902), oil on canvas, 1841, Maine, 33¼″ x 27¼″. Bartlett's self-portrait, executed when he was only twenty-four, is one of the great examples of American naïve painting. Its awkward simplicity provides a directness that few naïve paintings ever achieve. The artist wears a miniature painting of his wife, Harriet Glines Bartlett. (Abby Aldrich Rockefeller Folk Art Center)

48 (opposite). Theorem on paper, artist unknown, 1835–1845, New England, 15″ x 11″. Gray, black, and white theorems, such as this example, were among the most difficult to execute. If the artist made a mistake, it was impossible to correct. (Museum of American Folk Art; gift of Cyril I. Nelson)

49 (below, left). Theorem, artist unknown, watercolor on paper, c. 1835, New England, 14″ x 19″. It is interesting to compare this theorem with the example in the upper right corner. Although similar in composition, they are totally different because of the variation in execution. (Private collection)

50 (above, right). Theorem, watercolor on paper, artist unknown, dated 1825, New England, 17½″ x 22¼″. Countless watercolors of plaited baskets of fruit are known. When they were executed with stencils or "theorems," it was possible for less talented young ladies to achieve an instant success with their artistic efforts. The theorems were generally cut out of paper; thus they were inexpensive and easily accessible to nearly everyone. Theorems were especially popular when painting on velvet became the rage during the 1830s and 1840s. (Private collection)

51 (middle, right). Theorem by Caroline Bennett of Lunenburg, Massachusetts, watercolor on paper, c. 1835, 21⅞″ x 16½″. Naïve artists frequently included Staffordshire in their compositions. Perhaps they sought to elevate their efforts by painting exotic pottery and porcelain. (Greenfield Village and Henry Ford Museum)

52 (below, right). Theorem painting on velvet, artist unknown, 1830–1840, New England, 21½″ x 18″. This stylized composition must have been executed by someone thoroughly familiar with the theorem technique, for it is more complex in design than most. (Private collection)

cuted several competent portraits of New England gentry. Portraits of Mr. and Mrs. Aaron Jewett of Longmeadow, Massachusetts, indicate the artist's ability to create striking likenesses. These two small tempera paintings on academy board are signed on the reverse and include Hamblen's address and the date 1841.

Because Hamblen's work is so similar to that of his prolific brother-in-law, few of his paintings have been positively identified. The portrait of an *Unidentified Sea Captain* (plate 15) dramatically relates to a similar likeness of Captain Farnham of Farnham Point, Maine, attributed to Hamblen. The Farnham painting is now in the collection of Colby College, Waterville, Maine. It seems likely that many of the portraits associated with the Fall River–Sturbridge school of painting, previously attributed to Prior, were executed by Hamblen.

The similarities in the portraits of Captain Farnham and the *Unidentified Sea Captain* are interesting, for a detailed study of these two paintings might possibly prove that folk artists occasionally used stock bodies that they painted in advance and finished by dropping in a head. This idea has persisted since the appreciation of folk art began in the 1930s.

In the exhibition catalogue *American Folk Art, The Art of the Common Man in America 1750–1900*, published by The Museum of Modern Art in 1932, Holger Cahill wrote,

> The portrait-painting itinerants were the forerunners of American quantity production methods. In winter, when travel was difficult, they made sets of stock pictures, painting in the background, clothing, accessories, and hands. These pictures were usually in pairs, male and female. The clothing in the limner stock pictures was in line with the fashions of the period, with men's coats and waistcoats of a solid and conventional cut, and for the women dresses of rich stuffs decked with lace and ribbons. The backgrounds were usually arranged with pillars and decorative hangings. . . . The accessories were of vari-

53 (above). *Venice*, artist unknown, watercolor, *c.* 1840, probably New England, 14¾″ x 19¾″. Foreign places always sparked the imagination of the American folk artist. This architectural watercolor virtually teems with activity and life. (New York State Historical Association)

54 (above). *Allegorical Scene,* artist unknown, watercolor, first half of the nineteenth century, New England, 9″ x 9¾″. The symbolism in this fantastic watercolor is difficult to understand. The sailing ships all fly banners with multiple stars, and a dove with a sprig of olive is flying to a maiden seated in a stylized Windsor chair. Several other versions of this painting are known. (Mr. and Mrs. Jerome W. Blum)

55 (below) *Dexter, the Racehorse,* artist unknown, calligraphic drawing with watercolor, last half of the nineteenth century, New England, 14″ x 18″. A nearly identical watercolor is in the permanent collection of the New York State Historical Society at Cooperstown. The one difference is that the example at Cooperstown shows a rider seated on the horse. (Private collection)

56 (right). *Romantic Scene,* artist unknown, watercolor, first half of the nineteenth century, New England, 8″ x 11″. The painting could well be titled *The Rendezvous,* for what appear to be young lovers are secretly meeting under a tree. (Greenfield Village and Henry Ford Museum)

ous kinds, well-bound books with·Latin and French titles, newspapers, prayer-books, spectacles, and bouquets of flowers. With these accessories the painter usually tried to suggest the vocation of the sitter, using telescopes for sea captains, law books for lawyers, medical books for physicians, etc.

In the springtime the limner would set out with his lot of headless portraits and go from town to town hunting heads. The stock figure was one of the limner's best sales arguments, for what housewife could resist the fine dresses, the meticulously painted lace, and the lovely hands which the painter had prepared for her? This method of painting also had considerable influence upon the limner himself, for in preparing the stock figure in the absence of the sitter he became interested primarily in design. [40]

This point of view was originally supported by Jean Lipman: "The portraits were rarely painted strictly from life. The primitive artist typically allowed himself free rein in depicting pose, gesture, even details of costume, accessories, and background. In some cases, in fact, the bodies were prepared during the winter months and in the spring the itinerant limner set out with his stock of canvases to hunt for customers. As he had no specific model for his bodies, such a limner was apt thoroughly to indulge his liking for decorative silhouette, for the linear rhythm of ribbons and laces, or for the sweeping lines of a waistcoat." [41] Mrs. Lipman has since altered her opinion.

Through the years this idea was widely accepted; several leading authorities, however, refused to believe that it was true. Nina Fletcher Little maintains,

> This technique could not be verified by contemporary documentary references, nor had headless bodies been found in any quantity to support the theory. So it became the opinion of art historians, including myself, that this method had not been the usual one.
>
> However, as I also mentioned on page 4 of the Rockefeller Collection catalogue, artists occasionally repeated costumes and jewelry with which they were familiar. A few artists . . . are now known to have re-used the outlines of a given pose, then filled in colors, costume details, bonnets, and different personal accessories such as books or flowers, thus creating unexpectedly individual compositions. To my mind this procedure would have been a time-saving way of setting up a portrait at the beginning of its painting, but not the same thing as starting out with many pre-painted costumed bodies. [42]

The portraits of the *Unidentified Sea Captain* and *Captain Farnham* attributed to Sturtevant J. Hamblen may be instances in which the bodies and decorative accessories were prepainted. The head, the costume, and the accessories in the portraits are nearly identical. It would be possible to lift the countenance from one canvas and drop it onto the other without disturbing the composition in the slightest way. Furthermore, both paintings place the captain on board ship and for some inexplicable reason, behind the left shoulder of each figure is a hanging rope that has been painted out. If the artist had utilized this formula once and been disappointed with the composition, he might have painted out the rope and not reused it in another canvas. Thus it would appear that these two pictures were completed

without the heads, which were painted in at a later time. When the composition failed to satisfy the artist, he painted out the rope in both pictures.

As the nineteenth century progressed, better roads provided easier travel. Many folk artists journeyed about the countryside in wagons in search of commissions. William Matthew Prior, with various members of his family, is known to have made several such trips. After 1850 he traveled with a wooden chest, some 51 inches by 22 inches, which he on occasion loaded on a train. Over forty canvases were stored in the chest. These he kept at a central depot when he left the train. He would visit nearby communities and return to replenish his supply of canvases as required. Under such circumstances it would not be surprising that an artist could put to great advantage stock canvases that he had prepared at his leisure.

During the 1850s the daguerreotype forced most folk painters to attempt to earn their living in other ways. In 1856 Sturtevant J. Hamblen entered into a partnership for "Gents' Furnishings" with his brother Joseph. [43]

A detailed look at the life and work of another New England artist will reveal how advances in technology resulting from the Industrial Revolution altered the lifestyles and work patterns of the folk painter.

Erastus Salisbury Field (1805–1900) and his twin sister, Salome, were born in the tiny village of Leverett, Massachusetts, on May 19, 1805. By the time he reached the age of nineteen Field is thought already to have been working as a portrait painter, and in the summer of 1824 his efforts could have been seen by Samuel F. B. Morse when the older artist toured Connecticut and western Massachusetts.

Field, perhaps at the invitation of Morse, journeyed to New York City and for approximately three months during that year studied with the American master, who wrote to his wife shortly before Christmas, ". . . My two pupils, Mr. Agate and Mr. Field are very tractable and very useful. I have everything 'in Pimlico' as mother would say. I have begun, and thus far carried on, a system of neatness in my painting-room which I never could

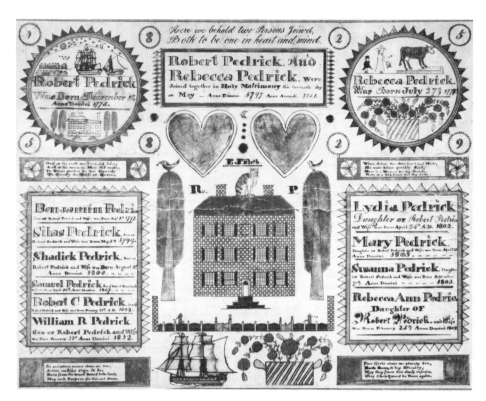

57 (opposite). Sewing box by Jane Otis Prior, maple and pine, 1822, Bath, Maine, W. 12″. The back of the sewing box is decorated with a "Sketch of Thomaston, Maine. Front Street." Written in ink on the bottom of the box is "Miss Sarah McCobb's, painted by Miss Jane Otis Prior March 1822. Remember your friend Jane when far distant from each other—when you look at this. J.O.P." The artist was one of four sisters of William Matthew Prior. Sarah McCobb, who owned the box, was the daughter of Denny McCobb, Collector of Customs for the District of Waldoboro, Maine. She and the artist visited the Prince family of Thomaston and are mentioned in the *Journals* of Hezekiah Prince, Jr. (Private collection)

58 (above). *Marriage and Birth Certificate for the Pedrick Family* by E. F. Firth, watercolor on paper, c. 1829, New England, 17″ x 21″. This highly elaborate family register contains many fascinating details. (Greenfield Village and Henry Ford Museum)

have with Henry. Everything has its place, and every morning the room is swept and all things put in order." [44]

Field returned to Massachusetts early in the spring of 1825 and traveled as an itinerant portrait painter for the next several years. Morse's influence caused Field's portraits from this era to be more finished, and there was a definite technical improvement between 1830 and 1840.

Field married Phebe Gilmur in 1831 and settled at Hartford, Connecticut. In 1832 their only child, Henrietta, was born. In 1833 he once again traveled extensively in search of commissions. By the mid 1830s Field had learned to paint with extraordinary speed, and portraits of the Reverend and Mrs. Frederick Marsh were completed on April 16 and 17, 1833, respectively.

Field's paintings were in many respects not as finished as those of Ammi Phillips (see pp. 74–78); therefore it is not surprising that his financial remuneration was somewhat smaller. In 1837 he began work on likenesses of the Ashley Hubbard family of Plumtrees,

Massachusetts. In February 1838 he presented his bill of $29, which represented the fee for five large portraits and six slightly smaller ones of the Hubbard children. While this might appear to be an inconsequential sum today, it must be remembered that in that year a night's lodging with breakfast could be had for 25 cents.

During the later 1830s Field executed some of his most beautiful portraits of children. His elfinlike subjects frequently stand on brilliant, multicolored carpets and are bedecked in elegant dresses trimmed with decorative embroidery and ribbons. These colorful paintings are almost blown-up details of the miniature watercolors executed by Joseph H. Davis, the artist who painted the double portrait of Asa and Susanna Caverly (plate 12).

About 1840 Field began to feel the intrusion of the daguerreotype portraitist. Commissions were fewer. Perhaps in order to improve his financial position, he moved his family to New York City, where from 1841 to 1848 he was listed as painter, portrait painter, and artist, at numerous addresses. In 1845 and again in 1847 Erastus Salisbury Field submitted oil paintings to the *Fair of the American Institute of the City of New York*. His wife also exhibited in the 1845 Fair and again in 1847, when the parents' artistic endeavors were accompanied by "one frame of Worsted-Work" executed by their fifteen-year-old daughter.

It was during Field's New York stay that his former teacher, Morse, experimented extensively with the daguerreotype, and it seems fairly safe to assume that the younger man learned the craft from him. While residing in New York, Field made at least one painting trip to Massachusetts.

In 1854 Field took painting rooms on the upper floor of the Cross Block at Palmer, Massachusetts. During this period he frequently placed his subject before a

59 (above). *New Bedford Harbor*, a scene from *The Whaling Voyage*, a panoramic painting by Benjamin Russell and Caleb Purrington, water-base paint on cotton sheeting, 1843, New England, 8' x 1300'. Benjamin Russell, a ship's carpenter, kept a sketchbook during a three-year whaling voyage out of New Bedford, Massachusetts. When he returned home, he persuaded Caleb Purrington, a local house-painter, to help him in the creation of a panoramic painting recording the daily activities and the landscapes he had seen on his travels. After mounting the enormous painting on rollers, Russell and Purrington had their initial showing in 1843. The partners took their work of art to many American cities. However, panoramas were an extremely popular form of entertainment in the mid-nineteenth century and *The Whaling Voyage* had strong competition from *Down the Mississippi* and *Burn Moscow*. Of these three panoramas only *The Whaling Voyage* is extant. (Old Dartmouth Historical Society Whaling Museum)

60 (left). *Compass Rose,* artist unknown, watercolor on paper, 1800–1830, New England, 15⅝" x 13⅛". Ship navigators occasionally executed decorative watercolor designs in compass-rose patterns, based on navigational charts. (Greenfield Village and Henry Ford Museum)

61 (below). Floor cloth by Captain Edwin Rumill, paint on sailcloth, *c.* 1900, Maine, 20" x 40". Captain Rumill is known to have executed several floor coverings with a nautical flavor. This carpet was said to have been made for his young wife, shortly after their marriage, while he was on a long voyage. The edges are hemmed with a sailor's needle, and the painted designs are symbolic of love, faith, hope, and the sea. (The Magazine *Antiques*)

62 (opposite, above). *Shooting the Polar Bear in the Arctic,* artist unknown, oil on canvas, late nineteenth century, New England, 20" x 24". In the background of this painting, a sailing vessel with steam capabilities is evident. Many New England captains are known to have sailed on Arctic missions during the late nineteenth and early twentieth century. (Private collection)

63 (below). *Outward Bound, Exchanging Signals at Sea, Homeward Bound,* and *Home Again* by Jas. D. L. Van Wagner, watercolor on paper, 1886, Massachusetts, 14½″ x 26½″. This charming record of marine activity is inscribed at the bottom: "Lively dreams of by-gone days/respectfully dedicated to the sailors snug harbor of Boston—by Jas. D. L. Van Wagner one of the inmates—1886." (Greenfield Village and Henry Ford Museum)

64 (above). *Sailing Vessel*, signed "Drawn by D.B.N. 1827," oil on board, Boston, Massachusetts, 16″ x 25¾″. (George E. Schoellkopf Gallery)

65 (above). *The "Prusia"* (*"Preussen"*) by William A. Lo, oil on canvas, c. 1907, New England, 35½″ x 37½″. This early-twentieth-century painting is an exciting example of pictorial design. (Mr. and Mrs. Michael Hall)

66 (below). *Fishing Boat* by A. D. Kent, oil on cardboard, c. 1970, Maine, 12″ x 16½″. Kent executed this painting at seventy-two years of age. He was a fish cutter who lost the use of his legs during the late 1960s and then began to paint. (Private collection)

camera and quickly took his photograph. He then painted the portrait from the photograph, thus freeing the subject from tedious hours of posing. Another advantage to the use of the camera was that posthumous portraits could be executed. Field also painted miniatures, and it is certain that his daguerreotype portraits were on occasion tinted to look more like paintings (fig. 33). Unfortunately, even though many of the paintings done after a daguerreotype are brightly colored, they tend to be mechanical and lack the spark so evident in his earlier work.

In 1859 Phebe Field, the artist's wife, died. Only a handful of portraits can be dated after this period. He and his daughter managed to farm the land and eke out a meager existence. Field turned to biblical and historical scenes, which must have provided a sense of accomplishment in his otherwise uneventful life. Few Yankees were willing to lay out cash for such pictures, and in time his source of income all but vanished.

During the summer months Field sometimes painted in a big barn behind an old tavern at Sunderland, Massachusetts. At other times he used a tiny shack, made from scrap lumber, as a studio. He probably wintered at Hartford, Connecticut. While plans were being formed for the Centennial celebration at Philadelphia, Field conceived the idea for his masterpiece—the *Historical Monument of the American Republic* (plate 32)—which he completed in 1876. The painting is permeated with nationalistic and abolitionist connotations.

During his later life, Field turned to engraved and printed sources for inspiration. Oftentimes he borrowed fragments from a print; at other times he completely copied a lithograph. His *Embarkation of Ulysses* is a direct copy of the print *A City of Ancient Greece* published at London in 1840 by J. W. Appleton. The conjecture is that this was Field's entry in the American Institute Fair in 1845.

Field's contributions to the genre of American folk art are extensive. Stuart Feld noted, "Although Field was remembered as 'an all-around painter of the old school' when he died at Plumtrees, Massachusetts, for many years his early portraits went unattributed. His identity was re-established in 1942; since then, nearly three hundred pictures have been attributed to him." [46]

A careful look at the watercolor artist Joseph H. Davis will provide an additional insight into the types of artistic creativity typical of New England throughout much of the nineteenth century. Though a large number of full-length watercolor miniature portraits are known by this artist, virtually no concrete information regarding his personal life has been discovered.

In an exhibition catalogue prepared to accompany the Three New England Watercolor Painters exhibition, first shown at The Art Institute of Chicago in 1974, Esther Sparks wrote, "There are no conclusive 'Vital Records,' no diaries, no trail of advertisements, no directories listing a painter of that name. Further, there are scores of Davises in New Hampshire and Maine where he worked and many Josephs to choose from. He may be identified as the voter in Dover in the 1850s, the confectionery of

67 (above). *Cape Cod Harbor*, artist unknown, oil on canvas, late nineteenth century, New England, 24″ x 30″. Though the artist responsible for this vibrant harbor view was relatively unskilled, his sense of design and his use of color were remarkable. This strong, vital painting is one of the best naïve pictures of the late nineteenth century. (Jay Johnson: America's Folk Heritage Gallery)

68 (right). *Ships in a Snowstorm* by J. O. J. Frost, oil on canvas, c. 1925. Marblehead, Massachusetts, 18¼″ x 23¼″. Frost is best known for his fishing harbors and seaport towns bursting with activity. The solitude expressed in this painting is rare among his works. (America Hurrah Antiques, N.Y.C.)

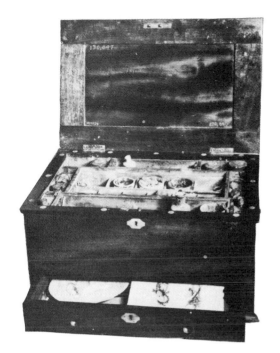

69 (above). Decorated box by Hannah Crowninshield (1789–1834), maple and mahogany, 1810–1815, Salem, Massachusetts, W. 12″. Hannah's mother's initials are on the front; two swans are on the top; and trophies of music and the arts are on the sides of this box. (The Peabody Museum of Salem)

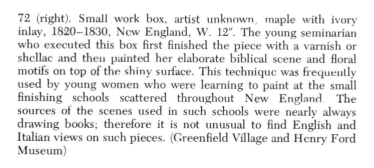

70 (above). Paint box that once belonged to Hannah Crowninshield, mahogany, c. 1800, American or possibly English, W. 18″. Hannah is known to have executed numerous watercolor portraits and scenes and to have fully restored a seventeenth-century portrait of Captain George Corwin of Salem. (The Peabody Museum of Salem)

71 (left), 71a (opposite). Drop-leaf table, artist unknown, maple, 1815–1835, Connecticut, W. 33″. The painting on this table is not as refined as that usually associated with academy or finishing-school work. Although the scene on the top, illustrated on the opposite page, looks as though it might be an actual location, it probably was derived from a print, a painting manual, or an exercise book. (Shelburne Museum, Inc.)

72 (right). Small work box, artist unknown, maple with ivory inlay, 1820–1830, New England, W. 12″. The young seminarian who executed this box first finished the piece with a varnish or shellac and then painted her elaborate biblical scene and floral motifs on top of the shiny surface. This technique was frequently used by young women who were learning to paint at the small finishing schools scattered throughout New England. The sources of the scenes used in such schools were nearly always drawing books; therefore it is not unusual to find English and Italian views on such pieces. (Greenfield Village and Henry Ford Museum)

73 (left). *Ishmael Being Driven Out*, artist unknown, watercolor on paper, first half of the nineteenth century, 11¾" x 15". The artist who executed this handsome watercolor placed the biblical scene in front of a New England house of the early nineteenth century. The naïve artist rarely thought about such inconsistencies. (Private collection)

74 (below). *God's Promise*, artist unknown, oil on board, mid-nineteenth century, Massachusetts, 16" x 22". After the deluge, the rainbow appeared in the sky signifying God's promise that he would never again destroy the earth by flood. (Private collection)

Dover, the landowner in Farmington in the 40s or the Davis in Farmington who bought 26 pounds of nails from Clark and Scruton in the last half of 1844." [47]

On the basis of a discovery of a likeness of Bartholomew Van Dame that was fully inscribed "Joseph H. Davis Left Hand Painter," Frank O. Spinney published an article in the October 1943 issue of *Antiques* Magazine ascribing a large group of profile portraits, set in brightly painted interiors with colorful painted and decorated furniture and gaudy floor coverings, to Joseph H. Davis. Not quite a year later, in the August issue of *Antiques*, he was able to publish additional information about Joseph Davis and to record a second signed painting by the artist.

This double portrait of Trueworthy Chamberlin and his wife, painted at Brookfield, New Hampshire, in May of 1835, is of particular interest, for it proves at least that Davis did not work up a supply of backgrounds and drop in portraits, as has been suggested in the case of Sturtevant J. Hamblen. On the reverse side of the Chamberlin picture is an unfinished pencil sketch that reveals how the artist approached his task. Obviously he worked first on the head and features of the subject, for they are recorded in detail in the sketch. Only a few lines suggest the pose and garments. It is easy to see that the artist began with blank paper and not a partially completed picture. Once the likeness was captured, the body, garments, and decorative accessories came easily. The details of the head and face were the only real problems that the artist faced with each new sitter.

Until recently it was thought that all of the Davis portraits had been executed in profile. The subjects were recorded while standing on vividly patterned floor coverings or while seated in brightly painted chairs drawn up to painted and grained tables. The likenesses were frequently strengthened with a pencil. More often than not a delightful variety of accessories provided additional interest; on occasion tiny miniature landscapes, mourning pictures, or maps hung on the walls and elegantly bound books and bountiful fruit and flower arrangements sat on tables, such as in the double portrait of Asa and Susanna Caverly (plate 12).

In the November 1970 issue of *Antiques* Nina Fletcher Little expanded the identified works by Davis. Her findings revealed that he had executed a three-quarter face portrait and a still life.

Dated works by Joseph H. Davis range between 1832 and 1838. By general consensus he was Pine Hill Joe Davis of Newfield, Maine. In 1832 Davis executed a portrait of Sally Chamberlin at Lebanon, Maine, and one of Sarah Ann Guppy at nearby Dover. In the years that followed, he appears to have radiated outward from Lebanon, and identified portraits have been found in small towns ranging from Brookfield, Maine, to Rye, New Hampshire. In 1836 dated pieces emanated from Wakefield, Maine, in the north to Epping, New Hampshire, in the south.

Esther Sparks believes that Davis was more than an itinerant artist and insists that there were many other

75 (above). *Girl Coming Through a Doorway* by George Washington Mark, oil on canvas, *c.* 1845, Greenfield, Massachusetts, 71½" x 56⅜". The artist was born in Charlestown, New Hampshire, in 1795 and moved to Greenfield, Massachusetts, in 1817. While serving as a sailor on a coastal schooner, he must have mastered the rudiments of painting, for in 1818 he advertised in the *Franklin Herald* that he had "commenced House Painting in its various branches and pledges that nothing on his part shall be wanting to give satisfaction." He closed the ad by indicating that he also did sign and fancy chair painting. Mark obviously continued to paint houses, for in January of 1820 he again advertised: "I would also inform those who are owing me small accounts, that my paint scraper is about worn out and they must pay me so I can get a new one." Mark wrote fluently and in one instance attempted to chide his neighbors and at the same time encourage business: "Having devoted some time in studying the recipes of the ancients and claiming some knowledge of the properties and affinities of paints, I have no hesitation in saying, that I think I can produce those delicate shades—those unfading tints and colors that give such celebrity to the Grecian Pencil. This has long been considered a desideration in modern painting, and the advantages of it in Coach, Sign and House Painting are obvious. At present I am in want of a quantity of Hog's Bristles, for which I will pay a liberal price, in any work in the line of my profession." [4] The doors in this life-size picture have been painted to simulate the popular grained decoration of the period. An ingrain carpet covers the floor. (Greenfield Village and Henry Ford Museum)

76 (left). *Portrait of a Young Woman* by Emily Eastman, watercolor on paper, *c.* 1820, New Hampshire, 10″ x 14″. Few small watercolor portraits have the style and presence this handsome picture possesses. (Peter H. Tillou)

77 (below). *Barnard Stratton* by Mr. Willson, watercolor on paper, 1822, New Hampshire, 15″ x 19½″. A number of works by Willson have been discovered in recent years. Time has altered the original appearance of this painting, and the paling of color and the aging of the paper have caused highlights that were not originally present when the picture was executed. (New York State Historical Association)

78 (opposite, above). *Family Portrait* by J. A. Davis, watercolor on paper, mid-nineteenth century, Rhode Island, 11¼″ x 14¼″. Stylized miniature portraits became obsolete when the camera provided a realistic likeness unobtainable from the folk artist. (Mr. and Mrs. William E. Wiltshire III)

79 (opposite, below). *Portrait of a Woman and Young Girl*, attributed to J. Evans, watercolor on paper, 1825–1840, New Hampshire, 9½″ x 13½″. This charming watercolor retains its original painted and stenciled frame. It is worth noting how the artist also used floral motifs to indicate a floor carpet. (Elise Macy Nelson)

things that he could have done while painting faces: "He could have been a writing-master or painted anything from mirror frames to barns. The paintings are redolent of craftsmanship, of a patient effort to master a formula and stay within its confines. His formula for perspective is common to most naive painting of the period. His formula for 'graining' furniture betrays more than casual knowledge." [48]

It seems evident that the success of nearly every itinerant artist was based upon the satisfied customer, for one commission led to another within the same family. Davis painted five groups of the Caverly family, recording for posterity three brothers, their wives, and their numerous children, nephews, and even their pets. In 1834 Fanny Libbey and her husband, Ira, stood for their portraits, and their daughter Sarah Ann and her husband, Joseph Emery, followed suit soon after.

Undoubtedly, one day a stroke of luck will firmly establish exactly who Joseph H. Davis was. In the meantime, the supposition that he was Pine Hill Joe Davis of Newfield, Maine, is supported by oral history taken in the tiny town, which revealed that Pine Hill Joe was not only a farmer and an incurable wanderer, but was "always dabbling with paints." [49] Perhaps he truly was the artist responsible for these watercolor-on-paper portraits that fall somewhere between the inexpensive black-faced silhouette and the much more costly oil portrait.

Joseph H. Davis's paintings are masterpieces of de-

80 (above). *Seaport Town*, artist unknown, oil on canvas, *c.* 1840, New England, 28″ x 36″. To the left of the road is a lighthouse. Its monumental scale indicates that the artist probably looked upon it as a very important structure in the bustling harbor. (Mr. and Mrs. Harvey Kahn)

81 (above). *Smelt Shacks at Bucksport, Maine*, by William P. Stubbs (1842–1909), pastel on paper, *c.* 1858, 23″ x 29″. The scene represented in this painting is in front of the Abel Stubbs cottage. Abel stands at the end of the house and his wife in the doorway. The shacks pulled up on the shore in the foreground were used in the winter for ice fishing. Some of the catch is being packed for shipment down the Penobscot River, and the boxes are marked "Boston" and "New York." (Private collection)

82 (left). *Samuel Chamberlain in Derby Square*, artist unknown, pastel on paper, third quarter of the nineteenth century, Salem, Massachusetts, 20″ x 29″. During the nineteenth century, Derby Square was Salem's market district. Several produce dealers, including Samuel Chamberlain, maintained stores there. Many of the old buildings seen in this view are still standing and are now part of Salem's historic district. (Private collection)

83 (right). *Falls at Vergennes, Vermont*, by S. H. Washburn, oil on canvas, *c.* 1875, Vermont, 29″ x 41″. S. H. Washburn is listed in *Walton's Register* for 1875–1876 as a painter. This view is similar but not identical to a lithograph of Vergennes printed by J. L. Giles & Co. in New York City and published by Sidney M. Southard of Vergennes. The lithograph is dated 1881. This picture is especially interesting for its documentation of early industry situated on the river. (Shelburne Museum, Inc.)

84 (above); 85 (right). Pair of paintings: *The Destruction of a Bath, Maine, Church* by John Heelings, oil on canvas, *c.* 1854, Maine, 18″ x 24″. This pair of pictures is one of five known sets depicting the burning of a Bath, Maine, church by a group known as the Know-Nothings during the 1850s. Though there are slight variations in design, it seems probable that all five sets were executed by the same artist. Once he had established a successful design concept, he simply reused it, much as William Matthew Prior is known to have painted and repainted reverse paintings on glass of George and Martha Washington on many occasions. Photographs courtesy *Maine Antique Digest.* (Berdan's Antiques)

86 (above). *Winter in Maine*, artist unknown, reverse painting on glass, 1875–1900, Maine, 20⅝″ x 24⅜″. This painting is inscribed "Winter in Maine." The small stone bridge over a frozen stream leads to a snow-covered cottage with high, peaked gables. Painting manuals and magazines of the period helped the do-it-yourself type master the techniques necessary for such artistic efforts. (Greenfield Village and Henry Ford Museum)

87 (opposite, above). *The Holy City*, artist unknown, oil on cardboard, *c.* 1880, New England, 14″ x 18″. (Private collection)

88 (opposite, below). *Oxen Sleigh Ride* by Rose Labrie, oil on canvas, 1970s, Portsmouth, New Hampshire, 40″ x 16″. Mrs. Labrie frequently incorporates into her bold, colorful paintings the wonderful New England homes that abound in her native state. (Jay Johnson: America's Folk Heritage Gallery)

By the mid-nineteenth century newspapers and magazines had become a much greater part of American life. Enthusiastic reviews of the art galleries and works of art included in the Great Exhibition of the Works of Industry of All Nations at the London Crystal Palace in 1851 and the World of Science, Art, and Industry at the New York Crystal Palace in 1853 sparked the American desire for more knowledge about art. Do-it-yourself manuals and art instruction books became increasingly popular, and as the various branches of artistic endeavor expanded, numerous publications dealing with specific types of painting reached the marketplace. Books on theorem painting, and especially floral painting, were snatched up by the Victorian amateur artist, who eagerly searched the printed pages for words of assistance and wisdom. Today enthusiastic collectors occasionally confuse poor Victorian art with folk art. Oftentimes the lines are thinly drawn.

New England has produced few great folk artists during the twentieth century. J. O. J. Frost (1852–1928) and James Crane (d. circa 1970) are among the best known. These two self-taught Yankee painters recorded the events of their daily lives in vital primitive styles.

J. O. J. Frost was born in Marblehead, Massachusetts, in 1852. In 1868, at the age of sixteen, he went to sea, where he remained for only two years: "It was not through fear of danger, but ambition spurred me on, to get into a better paid business so I could marry my sweetheart and establish a home. She became my compass to steer by, and we never parted after our marriage until her death in 1919." [50]

Frost began his artistic career in 1923 when a friend asked him to draw a picture of an old-time Grand Bank fishing vessel. In 1926 he opened his "new art building" to display his many paintings. While Frost is most celebrated for harbor scenes, his paintings of romantic vessels at sea, such as figure 68, are a high point in his oeuvre. in his oeuvre.

Little is known of James Crane's early years. It was not until late in life that he first attempted to paint. Crane, like many naïve artists, utilized whatever was close at hand. A bedsheet, a hunk of discarded plywood, or the back wall of a house was the canvas on which he laid some of New England's most poetic, vital landscapes and ship portraits. His colorful painting of the *Titanic* (plate 22) was executed on oilcloth. Crane's visual images are constructed from a multiplicity of perspectives and rely upon no single light source—both characteristics of naïve painting.

Rose LaBrie of Portsmouth, New Hampshire, has developed a flat, primitive, intensely personal style. Her nostalgic views of New England country life, such as the *Oxen Sleigh Ride* (fig. 88), reflect her interest in the fast-disappearing rural landscape. She is totally self-taught and has developed her technique by trial and error. When asked about her subject matter, she expressed the following point of view: "I paint primitives because I don't know how to paint any other way. The memories are my subjects."

sign, and their execution is far more meticulous and finished than most of the watercolors created by young women in finishing schools, or seminaries, that became popular with the rising middle class early in the nineteenth century. In nearly every town that boasted a significant population, the young woman's seminary played an important role in the cultural development of the family and the social growth of the community. Idealized representations of biblical scenes, romanticized depictions of literary heroes from the past, and landscapes derived from prints were some of the results of art training in the seminary. Mourning pictures and family records also resulted from seminary training; many are extraordinary for their bold design, their sensitive rendering, and their value as historical documents.

89 (above). *Seascape* by Ralph Cahoon, oil on board, *c.* 1967, Osterville, Massachusetts, 16¼″ x 11⅞″. Cahoon, an antiques dealer in Osterville, began, during the 1930s, to decorate old tin trays, lamps, and furniture. He ultimately developed a highly personal style and began to paint idealized scenes centering upon nautical themes. (Mr. and Mrs. Charles V. Hagler)

Plate 1 (above). *View of Boston* by John Smibert, oil on canvas, 1738, Massachusetts, 30″ x 50″. John Smibert, in his notebook entries from 1735 to 1740, records sixty-six paintings and in 1738 cites "a vew of Boston." In a letter written to Arthur Pound in London, dated Boston, April 6, 1749, he complained, "I grow old, my eyes have been some time failing me, but is still heart whole & hath been diverting my self with somethings in the Landskip way which you know I always liked." This view of Boston is from Camp Hill, Noddles Island, East Boston, and is believed to be the earliest known view of Boston in oils. (Childs Gallery)

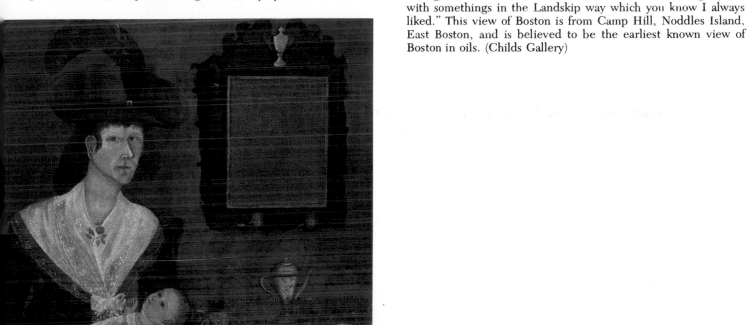

Plate 2 (left), *Mrs. Reuben Humphreys*, attributed to Richard Brunton, oil on canvas, *c.* 1800, East Granby, Connecticut, 44½″ x 40½″. Anna Humphreys (1758–1827), during her lifetime, bore twelve children. In this painting, she is depicted with her infant daughter, Eliza. Paintings that illustrate the furnishings of early homes are always interesting. Mrs. Humphreys is shown sitting in a Windsor chair; a Chippendale looking glass is supported on Battersea enamel knobs; and fashionable china tea equipage is set out on the table. (The Connecticut Historical Society)

Plate 3 (above). Overmantel, artist unknown, oil on panel, 1770–1775, Marblehead, Massachusetts, 23″ x 54″. Untrained artists who executed such pieces generally incorporated into the overall designs actual buildings. The structures in this painting might possibly be identified through extensive research. (Childs Gallery)

Plate 4 (below). Fireboard from a house built at South Sudbury, Connecticut, artist unknown, oil on board, c. 1820, 45¼″ x 34″. Fireboards were popular utilitarian objects used in early American homes to close off the fireplace when it was not in use. The recessed panels of this unusually fine example are decorated with graceful designs that include a blue urn with fruit and flowers. The urn is decorated with an eagle. Slits were cut into the bottom of the fireboard so that it could be set down over the andirons. (Private collection)

Plate 5 (right). Signboard, artist unknown, oil on wood, 1835–1840, Ackworth, New Hampshire, 35¾″ x 58″. Photograph courtesy George E. Schoellkopf Gallery. (Private collection)

Plate 6 (below). *A View of Mr. Joshua Winsor's House Etc.*, by Dr. Rufus Hathaway, oil on canvas, late eighteenth or first quarter of the nineteenth century, New England, 23¼″ x 27½″. Rufus Hathaway married Judith Winsor in 1795. The house in this painting was owned by her father, Joshua Winsor, who built the substantial dwelling in 1768 at Powder Point, Duxbury. Winsor had extensive commercial interests in the fishing industry, and the picture includes ships from his fleet of vessels, wharves, and his counting house. This painting is the only currently known landscape by Hathaway. The artist included a portrait of his father-in-law in the right foreground. Mr. Winsor is shown with a ring of keys in his hand. The view retains its original black painted frame, and Hathaway's inventory of 1822 included the entry, "carved work and picture hangings," perhaps referring to frame moldings.[1] (New England Historic Genealogical Society)

Plate 7 (above). *Picking Flowers*, artist unknown, oil on canvas, *c.* 1845, possibly Massachusetts, 27″ x 44″. There are several paintings that can, on the basis of stylistic similarity, be safely attributed to the painter who executed this handsome portrait of a young girl. Both Maine and Massachusetts abound with simple story-and-a-half clapboard cottages much like the one in the background of this painting. (New York State Historical Association)

Plate 8 (above). *Liberty in the form of the Goddess of Youth: giving Support to the Bald Eagle* by Abijah Canfield (1769–1830), reverse gouache painting on glass, *c.* 1800. Chusetown, Connecticut, 24³/₁₆″ x 18⁷/₁₆″. During the early Federal period, countless prints celebrating the growing strength of the young nation circulated both in America and in England. Some of the prints, aboard merchant ships, reached China, where they were freely copied, and paintings with designs identical to this example were painted by Oriental artists using the technique of reverse painting on glass. This is one of the very few known American examples, and the artist clearly states that his source of design was an engraving by E. Savage. The taste for reverse paintings on glass increased, and by the 1850s many of them were backed with gold or silver foil and called tinsel pictures. (Greenfield Village and Henry Ford Museum)

Plate 9 (left). Theorem painting on velvet by Susanna Hook, c. 1835, New England, 20″ x 22½″. The fad for theorem painting in America developed soon after the technique became popular in England, where it was introduced from China at the close of the eighteenth century. The English called theorem painting *Poonah* or *Oriental tintwork*. Most theorem paintings required several stencil sheets, which provided the basic shapes of the various parts. Theorem stencils were similar to patterns used to decorate furniture, tinware, and walls. (Mr. and Mrs. Charles V. Hagler)

Plate 10 (right). Fan with theorem painting by Delphina Paris, watercolor on paper with gold foil, 1825–1835, 6″ x 7½″. This is one of a pair of stick fans painted by Miss Paris at a female academy in Portland, Maine. (Private collection)

Plate 11 (above). *River and Townscape with Figures* by Prudence Perkins, watercolor and ink on paper, 1810, Rhode Island, 18½″ x 22¾″. During the last half of the eighteenth and the first half of the nineteenth century, it was fashionable for young women of upper-class families to attend local "seminaries" in which they were taught the polite arts, including music, needlework, and painting. Watercolor pictures, like this very beautiful example, were among the most popular seminary paintings, for the materials were more easily accessible and less expensive than those needed for oil paintings. (Peter H. Tillou)

Plate 12 (above). *Asa and Susanna Caverly* by Joseph H. Davis, watercolor on paper, 1836, New Hampshire, 11" x 14". This painting is inscribed "Asa Caverly. Aged 24. October 5th 1836. PAINTED AT STRAFFORD/BOW POND/AUGUST 9th/1836/Susanna Caverly. Aged 29. August 14th 1835." Asa Caverly was born on October 5, 1812. He was the son of Lieutenant John Caverly and lived on a farm at Strafford, New Hampshire, near the old Caverly homestead. On October 28, 1833, Asa married Susan Bunker from Strafford, who was born on August 14, 1807. Davis frequently inscribed the sitter's birth date on his portraits and the date that the portrait was executed on others. This watercolor records both. Dated works by Joseph H. Davis range between 1832 and 1838, and he is known to have painted in both New Hampshire and Maine. (Mr. and Mrs. Edwin Braman)

Plate 13 (right). *Basket of Shells,* artist unknown, watercolor on paper, 1830–1850, New England, 10¾" x 13⅝". Shells, fruit, and idealized romantic landscapes were favorite subjects of New England's young ladies, who painted them on paper or velvet to be framed and hung as pictures, as well as on furniture that had been made by local craftsmen especially to be decorated. (Private collection)

Plate 14 (left). *Unidentified Child* by William Matthew Prior, oil on canvas, 1830–1835, Portland, Maine, 27½" x 22". This painting is a large version of Prior's inexpensive "without shade" pictures and possibly cost the sitter's parents about $10, considerably more than the flat likenesses measuring approximately 10" x 13", for which the artist charged $1.25. Prior also executed reverse paintings on glass and is well known for his portraits of famous Americans like George and Martha Washington in this medium. In time, he developed a technical proficiency that enabled him to execute fine, fully representational portraits and well-conceived and well-executed landscapes. (Private collection)

Plate 15 (left). *Unidentified Sea Captain*, attributed to Sturtevant J. Hamblen, oil on canvas, *c.* 1830, Maine, 22" x 26". Much of Hamblen's work is difficult to distinguish from that of his more famous brother-in-law, William Matthew Prior. A picture nearly identical to this example is in the Colby College Museum of Art, Waterville, Maine. It is believed that Hamblen did indeed paint stock canvases during off months, which he completed by painting in the head of the sitter. It was generally believed that this practice was commonplace; however, in recent years, scholars have tended to discredit this theory. (Private collection)

Plate 16 (above). *Unidentified Gentleman* by Erastus Salisbury Field, oil on canvas, *c.* 1840, New England, 30½" x 25¼". Field, like many New England artists, was finally forced from his trade as a portraitist by the popular acceptance of the inexpensive daguerreotype, which caused the demand for painted portraits to decline dramatically after the 1850s. Though the artist utilized an often-repeated formula for the depiction of the body and the hand in this painting, the picture reveals in an uncompromising way the powerful, individual character of the sitter. (Private collection)

Plate 17 (above). *Eliza Anthony Brownell,* attributed to John S. Blunt, oil on canvas, 1828–1829, New Bedford, Massachusetts, 32¹¹/₁₅″ x 28⅛″. This painting is one of several that have been recently attributed to the Portsmouth, New Hampshire, and Boston, Massachusetts, artist John S. Blunt, who was born in 1798. He not only painted landscapes, seascapes, ship portraits, and genre pictures but is known to have executed decorative painting for several Masonic lodges in the Portsmouth, New Hampshire, area. In 1831 John Blunt moved to Boston, and until his death in 1835, he appears to have worked as an itinerant painter during the summer months throughout much of the New England coastal area. (Barbara Johnson)

Plate 18 (opposite). *Child with Cat*, attributed to Joseph Whiting Stock, oil on canvas, 1830–1840, Chicopee, Massachusetts, 27″ x 33″. Stock's recently published account book indicates that he was impressively prolific, sometimes executing several paintings within a single week. Like many New England artists of the period, he included several objects personally associated with the life of the subject, possibly an attempt to guarantee acceptance of the painting by the subject's family. This child wears a coral necklace, holds the family cat in her arms, and has a tasseled purse over her right wrist. The doll's cradle and the decorated basket further personalize this handsome painting. (America Hurrah Antiques, N.Y.C.)

Plate 19 (right). *Phoebe Hoyt*, artist unknown, oil on canvas, *c.* 1840, Connecticut, 35½″ x 28″. (America Hurrah Antiques, N.Y.C.)

Plate 20 (below). *Freeport, Maine*, by G. J. Griffin, oil on canvas, dated October 1886, New England, 21″ x 39″. The artist was a house painter in Freeport. He finished the picture on a platform that he built in a tree on a hill across from the town. All of the buildings actually existed as shown in the painting, and many of them still survive, although modern structures make it nearly impossible to get the same view of the town today. The reds, the mauves, and the maroons used by the artist are typical of High Victorian taste. (Private collection)

Plate 21 (above). *The Crucifixion* by Frank Baldwin, oil on canvas, twentieth century, Pittsburg, New Hampshire, 40″ x 48″. Baldwin had been a tremendously successful businessman who literally owned much of the town of Pittsburg, New Hampshire. He gave up his business and became a hermit who lived in a visionary world. (David B. Wiggins)

Plate 22 (below). *The Titanic* by James Crane, oil on oilcloth with paper collage, *c.* 1968, Ellsworth, Maine, 20″ x 28″. Crane's special vision enabled him to record a subject from many perspectives at the same time. In this painting, one views the ship from above and from the side. (Private collection)

NEW YORK and
NEW JERSEY

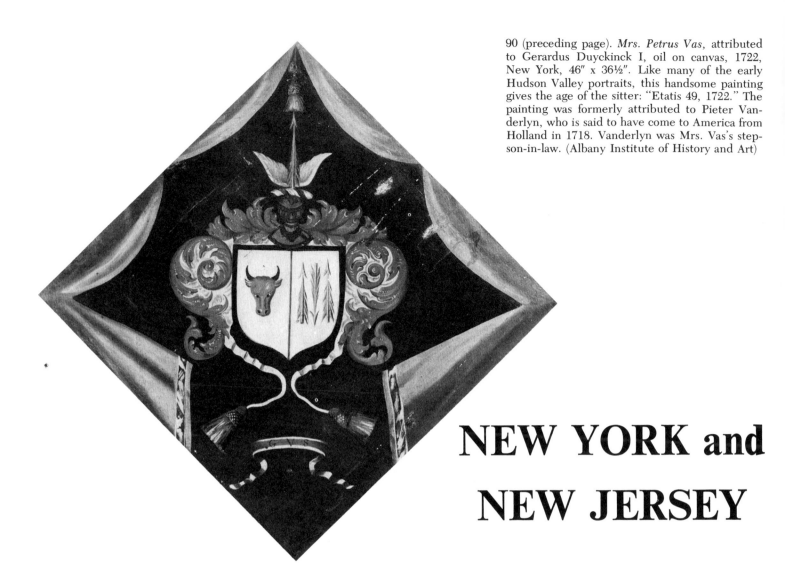

90 (preceding page). *Mrs. Petrus Vas*, attributed to Gerardus Duyckinck I, oil on canvas, 1722, New York, 46″ x 36½″. Like many of the early Hudson Valley portraits, this handsome painting gives the age of the sitter: "Etatis 49, 1722." The painting was formerly attributed to Pieter Vanderlyn, who is said to have come to America from Holland in 1718. Vanderlyn was Mrs. Vas's stepson-in-law. (Albany Institute of History and Art)

NEW YORK and NEW JERSEY

The Hudson River, with its many tributaries, doubled as a lifeline for trading and as an inexhaustible stimulant to painters. Portraits were among the earliest canvases executed in the Hudson Valley. This is not surprising, for the American Dutch left behind in their homeland the largest middle-class population in the world, one which loved both education and culture. Because of extensive commerce and trade, seventeenth-century Holland was a wealthy, creative melting pot for the world.

In America, Dutch immigrants continued to be prosperous traders, thus attracting people with commercial inclinations to their settlements. At New Amsterdam the population was made up of Walloons, Normans, Germans, Scandinavians, English, and Dutch. The tiny town

of less than ten thousand harbored people speaking eighteen different languages. When the English seized control of the colony in 1664, their influence for a very extended period of time was political and little more. The Dutch continued to live comfortably and surrounded themselves with refinements only dreamed of in other colonies. In 1730 Captain Dean, a lumber merchant and sloop captain, owned thirteen pictures, as well as books, a tea table, a looking glass, a mahogany table, and extensive silver.

Interest in painting was inherited from the Old World, where during the seventeenth century, canvases by skilled artists were sold in open-air markets in nearly every city in Holland. Undoubtedly Dutch paintings

91 (above). *Van Schaick Hatchment*, artist unknown, oil on canvas, first half of the eighteenth century, New York, 31¼″ x 31⅛″. Hatchments are funeral emblems that were often hung on or in houses and churches and were carried in burial processions. Hatchment design was based upon heraldic devices associated with the family of the deceased, and their use is recorded in New England and the South as well as in New York. (Albany Institute of History and Art)

92 (opposite). *Mrs. David Ver Planck*, attributed to the Schuyler Limner, oil on canvas, *c.* 1717, Albany County, New York, 79⅝″ x 47½″. Ariaantje Coeymans Ver Planck was an imposing woman, and her presence dominates this painting. The background in the picture can be traced to a mezzotint of Lady Bucknell executed *c.* 1686 after Kneller. Awkward, overpowering, and ruthlessly honest, Ariaantje inherited a large fortune from her father in 1716. At fifty-one, a spinster, she married David Ver Planck, who was twenty-three years her junior. (Albany Institute of History and Art)

93 (above). *Van Bergen Overmantel*, artist unknown, oil on wood, *c.* 1735, New York, 18″ x 87″. This overmantel is one of the earliest American landscapes extant. It originally was a panel over the fireplace of the parlor in the Van Bergen homestead. Rich in detail, it offers a comprehensive view of the Van Bergen farm, its owner and his family, Indians, slaves, livestock, architecture, activities, fences, and the natural landscape. (New York State Historical Association)

were brought in great numbers to New Netherland.

In New Amsterdam, soon after the mid-seventeenth century, Jacob Strijcker painted a likeness of himself, and Henri Couturier, a Frenchman, is known to have painted portraits before 1663.

No early body of work from this area is as well known as that executed by several members of the Duyckinck family: Evert Duyckinck I; a son Gerret; grandsons Evert III and Gerardus I; and a great-grandson Gerardus II. Each was described in contemporary documents as "painter" or "limner." [51] Evert Duyckinck, like nearly all painters at the time, was a craftsman of many talents. He is known to have engraved glass, and on occasion he decorated fire buckets with the arms of the city as well.

Jacob de Lange, a barber-surgeon in New York, had in his home sixty-one paintings; many of these were portraits. Other types of art were included, however, and landscapes, a seascape, still lifes with flowers and fruit, a genre picture, and a study of Abraham and Hagar taken from the Bible were among them.

One of the earliest Hudson Valley genre pictures was executed sometime between 1733 and 1735 by an unknown artist on a farm owned by Marten Van Bergen at Leeds, Green County, New York. This painting served as an overmantel in the Van Bergen house until the structure was demolished. The overmantel was reused in the house that was built to replace the original Van Bergen home. Appearing in the painting are numerous members of the Van Bergen family, including three adults, nine young people, four black slaves, two white servants, and two Indians, of either the Catskill or the Esopus tribe. The picture also illustrates the farm, livestock, and pets and provides a document for the study of Hudson Valley architecture of the period. The artist,

in typical genre painter fashion, included nearly everything he saw. A farm wagon stands before the mill (a similar conveyance is evident in the portrait of Abraham Wendell, fig. 100). The hay barracks, peculiar to this area, was constructed so that the roof and floors could be raised and lowered to protect the hay. Prototypes for this ingenious device are known in Europe. The Van Bergen house was constructed of stone, with a tile roof over the main structure and shingles over the kitchen wing. Small dormers and a wooden gutter, a front stoop, and windows with solid wooden blinds further illustrate the architecture of the Hudson Valley Dutch. Slave holding in the valley was occasionally encountered during the period, and it has been documented that Mrs. Van Bergen received a slave as a wedding present from her father. It is believed that the elderly seated figure is that woman.

In this picture and in the painting *The Old Plantation* (fig. 234), the naïve artists have concerned themselves with many small details. Such works of art deserve study, for they are reliable sources of information for both the general historian and the art historian.

Louis C. Jones, in his essay "The Genre in American Folk Art," speaks about the importance of folk genre pieces. He indicates that many might be "greater as a document than as a work of art and it should be recognized as a supplement to the written word, as an historical source. All social history is weak when it comes to the habits, work, dress, attitudes, play and religious life of the lower classes in *any* society and this is very true of Americans. People who work with their hands keep few diaries, write few letters, and until recently have seldom been a subject of concern to the scholar." Jones further observed, "The naïve artist's lack of discipline in composition and his tendency to 'get it all in' leads to

94 (above). *Southwest View of the City of New York*, artist unknown, oil on panel, late eighteenth century, New York, 34″ x 52″. The view on this panel was taken from Brooklyn with the Rutgers family brewhouse evident in the foreground. The *trompe l'oeil* frame is actually part of the painting. (Private collection)

95 (left). Kas, pine, 1690–1720, found in Saugerties, New York, W. 43″. This piece is embellished with grisaille and polychrome decorations, which include cherubim, pears, apples, and grapes. (Mrs. Mitchel Taradash, on loan to Van Cortlandt Manor, Sleepy Hollow Restorations)

96 (below). Room interior from the Winterthur Museum, which includes a painted and decorated kas of more elaborate design than the one shown above. The Dutch often embellished simple forms with bright paint to enliven their domestic interiors. (The Henry Francis du Pont Winterthur Museum)

97 (above). *Two Boys with Pets*, artist unknown, oil on canvas, 1730, New York, 31½" x 39". The Dutch in the Hudson Valley were especially fond of elegant clothing and rich, sumptuous furnishings for their homes. Their love of opulence is evident in this revealing document, which includes a bowl heaped with fruit, an imported parrot, and a family cat and dog. (Philadelphia Museum of Art; the Edgar William and Bernice Chrysler Garbisch Collection)

the inclusion of details a more sophisticated painter might well reject." [52]

As in New England, many of the earliest painters arriving in New York were at least moderately well trained. Edgar P. Richardson, the art historian, noted, "Dutch painters of skill and fame found their way to Dutch colonies in Brazil or in the Indies. But New Amsterdam was very small and very poor, compared with the East Indies; and the human race is careless, destructive, and governed by fashion in what it keeps or throws away. Very little has come down to us. Yet the important thing is that the craft of painting was established in the New Netherland province, and by the early years of the next century there were already native-born painters at work along the Hudson River." [53]

Robert G. Wheeler, one of America's most eminent scholars of the Dutch in the Hudson Valley, confirms this idea:

98 (above). *Portrait of a Woman*, artist unknown, oil on canvas, second half of the eighteenth century, Staten Island, New York, 24″ x 30″. Pets were an intimate part of family life in the Hudson Valley. This woman holds her favorite bird. (Private collection)

99 (opposite). *Portrait of a Woman*, attributed to Gerret Duyckinck, oil on panel, 1690–1710, New York, 31½″ x 24¼″. Expensive imported carpets were never used on the floor during the early eighteenth century; they were reserved for table tops. This custom was not confined to the Hudson Valley but is evident in early eighteenth-century portraits from New England and the South as well. (The Henry Francis du Pont Winterthur Museum)

Beginning with the first decade of the eighteenth century American painters were at work in the Hudson Valley. Their portraits—known generally as the "patroon portraits"—and their religious subjects represent "the earliest significant development of native-born talent in American painting." These portrait subjects included members of the leading families of the Hudson Valley: Beekmans, Van Cortlandts, Van Schaicks, De Peysters, Schuylers, Wendels, and Van Rensselaers.

The basic painting style of these artists was broad, flat, and decorative. Background features, as in the portraits of the three Van Cortlandt boys and Ariaantje Coeymans, often were borrowed from English mezzotint engravings. While the patroon artists of the Hudson Valley (none of whom, with the possible exception of Pieter Vanderlyn, have been identified as yet) painted with imagination and an occasional gay verve, they achieved firm statements of mood and character. They generally portrayed individuals of Dutch background who typified the strength of body and soul necessary to settle a wilderness, flourish, and retain the Dutch traits of tolerance, thrift, and forthrightness for over a century.[54]

Extensive study has enabled researchers to divide the canvases executed in the Hudson River Valley during the early eighteenth century into several distinct groups. Together they are commonly recognized as the first indigenous school of art in America. They have been subdivided and classified as the work of the Schuyler Limner and his followers (fig. 92), the Gansevoort Limner and his followers (plate 24), and the Aetatis Suae paintings (fig. 90). There also is a large body of anonymous portraits and a charming group of religious paintings. Almost none of the early Hudson River paintings has been positively attributed to specific painters. The still unidentified paintings confirm the observations of Dr. Alexander Hamilton, a traveler to Albany in 1744, who observed the women in the community and recorded, "in general, both old and young, are the hardest favoured ever I beheld. Their old women wear a comical head-dress, large pendants, short petticoats, and they stare upon one like witches."[55]

By the mid-eighteenth century "a new wave of immigrants" and a "new generation of native-born talents"[56] added their contribution to the Hudson Valley school. Portraits became more technically proficient, and the flat decorative style of the previous century started to give way to a careful, more realistic rendering of the people and their community.

Pieter Vanderlyn (1687–1778) was once credited with painting the portrait of his stepmother-in-law, Mrs. Petrus Vas, now at The Albany Institute of History and Art. Vanderlyn is believed to have come to America

100 (below); 100a (right). *Abraham Wendell,* artist unknown, oil on ticking, *c.* 1740, New York, 35¾" x 29½". This portrait was executed when the subject was twenty-two. The mill in the background of the painting was located on Beaver Creek and was included on a map of Albany in 1794. It is one of the few instances where such a structure is documented in an eighteenth-century painting. Of special interest is the horse and wagon that stands in front of the mill. This vehicle, peculiar to the Hudson Valley, is included in the Van Bergen overmantel, figure 93, as well. The mill was bequeathed to Abraham in his father's will. (Albany Institute of History and Art)

101 (opposite). *Pau de Wandelaer,* attributed to the Gansevoort Limner, oil on canvas, *c.* 1725, Albany County, New York, 44¾" x 35¼". The youthful de Wandelaer was the son of a prosperous trading family of Albany, which owned property both there and in New York City. (Albany Institute of History and Art)

102 (above). *Johannes Schuyler and His Wife Elizabeth Staats*, attributed to John Watson, oil on canvas, first half of the eighteenth century, New York, 53½″ x 71″. Mrs. Schuyler is portrayed sitting in an upholstered William and Mary armchair. Her left hand rests on a Bible, which is supported by a tasseled cushion. Hudson Valley painters who executed pictures like those on the opposite page freely borrowed and adapted illustrations in Bibles. (The New-York Historical Society)

103 (right). Engraving from a 1702 Dutch Bible that contained the Schuyler family genealogies. (Albany Institute of History and Art)

104 (opposite, above). *Crowning of King Jereboam*, artist unknown, oil on canvas, first half of the eighteenth century, probably Albany County, New York, 27″ x 37½″. The similarity of design between the engraving from the Bible, figure 103, and this picture is striking. The painting is inscribed at the bottom center "1 Kon XII 20" (1 Kings 12:20). (Albany Institute of History and Art)

105 (opposite, below). *Belshazzar's Feast*, artist unknown, oil on canvas, first quarter of the eighteenth century, probably Albany County, New York, 31½″ x 41″. The design of this picture is very similar to an engraving included in the van Rensselaer family Bible printed in Holland in 1702. On the table are plates and tankards that are typical of pieces created by New York silversmiths Jan Van Niewkirke and Benjamin Schaats, who worked in the first quarter of the eighteenth century. (Albany Institute of History and Art)

Genef. 41. Vs. 42.
Joseph met Pharaos ringh, fyne linnen kleederen, en gouden keten verciert, rydt op den tweeden wagen.

106 (above). *Susanna Truax*, attributed to the Gansevoort Limner, oil on canvas, dated 1730, Schenectady, New York, 37⅞" x 32⅞". Miss Truax, who was born in 1726, was four years old when this portrait was executed. She is shown eating a sweet from a small scroll-footed tea table, which holds chinaware and a silver teapot. There are several portraits of children that were obviously executed by the same limner, for they all wear similar dresses. (Edgar William and Bernice Chrysler Garbisch)

from Holland in about 1718, settling first at Albany and later moving to Kingston. He was the grandfather of the famous Federal artist John Vanderlyn (1755–1852). The painting of Mrs. Vas, one of the most sensitively executed portraits of the entire group, has been recently attributed to Gerardus Duyckinck I.

Because of their devout beliefs, many of the settlers in and around Albany adorned their walls with religious paintings. These biblical pictures were usually adapted from engravings found in locally owned Bibles, most of which were actually printed abroad. Several of the biblical paintings shown at The Albany Institute of History and Art in the 1959 exhibition "Hudson Valley Paintings 1700–1750" were accompanied by an engraved print source. Two of them were obtained from Dutch Bibles printed in Amsterdam and Dordrecht in 1702. Because these religious paintings tend to be relatively crude, it seems likely that they were created by the same native-born, self-trained artists who executed the patroon portraits.

Many merchants located in the city of Albany were sloop owners as well. Despite a 1703 law that provided for roads to connect the cities of Albany and New York on both sides of the Hudson, it was not until 1785 that a stage line was actually run on a regular basis on the east shore of the river between the two cities. Throughout the entire eighteenth century and well into the nineteenth century, the river was the major highway, and the broad-beamed, shallow draft Albany sloops, evident in the portrait of Pau de Wandelaer by the Gansevoort Limner, carried the traveler, the trader, and the merchandise between these bustling cities.

Albany merchants enjoyed the advantage of being near the junction of the Hudson and the Mohawk rivers, which provided a gateway to Canada and the west. Via the Hudson it was possible to reach Lakes Champlain and St. Lawrence and via the Mohawk, the Great Lakes. As Cadwallader Colden observed in 1838, "By means of these lakes [the Great Lakes] & the Rivers which fall into them, Commerce may be carried from New York, through a vast Tract of Land, more easily than from any other Maritime Town in North America."[57]

Most of the patroon paintings have always remained in the Hudson River Valley, where they have been collected by The Albany Institute of History and Art and several sister institutions. They are among the greatest examples of American Colonial painting.

By the mid-eighteenth century Holland's strong influence in the New World had all but spent itself. Like the rest of the country, hopeful native artists turned to England for their inspiration. The vigorous toughness displayed in the blunt, sometimes awkward, and yet incredibly vital pictures of the earlier period was replaced by a more elegant and urbane style.

Robert G. Wheeler has written, "Among those migrant painters in this first half of the 18th Century were men who typified an era of wandering artists seeking patrons and commissions. They brought with them from Europe a knowledge of form and a solid craftsmanship. They brought a new mode, a fashionable manner, and found eager sitters."[58]

John Watson, a Scot, arrived in America in 1714, worked in the Hudson Valley, and finally settled in New Jersey. This artist was one of the first immigrants to arrive in America who left behind a body of work that has been positively identified. Though his paintings display such technical faults as incorrect highlighting and sketchy anatomical knowledge, his naïve representations contain a power and honesty that was transmitted to numerous native-born artists who immediately followed him.

Landscape painting was especially popular with the Dutch colonists. Inventories abound with a surprising number of references to "landskips." By the mid-eighteenth century landscape painting continued to grow in popularity, and men like Lawrence Kilburn, an artist traveling from London, could expect to earn a living as an art teacher in New York. Kilburn announced, "LAWRENCE KILBURN, Limner, from London. Intends during the Winter Season, to instruct Gentlemen in the Art of Drawing Landskips, Faces, Flowers, &c. on very reasonable Terms, and at such hours as will be most suitable to those Gentlemen. N.B. He lodges at Mr. Schuyler's next Door to Mr. Henry Holland's near Coenties Market."[59]

Few artists could earn their living by remaining in a single location. When the Hudson River thawed in the spring of 1761, Lawrence Kilbrunn announced his intentions of heading north to Albany: "As my Business calls me up to Albany in about three Weeks Time, I desire therefore all who are indebted to me, to settle with me; and all who hath any Demands on me, to send in their Accounts that they may be settled. And as my Affairs may Keep me in Albany all next Summer, I shall therefore be glad that if any Gentlemen or Ladies who might incline to have their Pictures drawn by me, to apply speedily, at my lodgings in Bayard-Street, at Mr. John Lansing's. LAWRENCE KILBRUNN." [60]

Stephen Dwight, who advertised in *The New-York Mercury* on May 2, 1763, indicated the vast number of artistic activities that might augment the income of the painter:

STEPHEN DWIGHT, Begs leave to acquaint the Publick, that he continues Portrait and History Painting, as usual; and begs such Gentlemen and Ladies who incline to employ him in the Portrait way, that they would be speedy in their Application, as the present Season is most suitable for that work. He likewise intends the ensuing Week to open a school for the Instruction of Youth in the several Branches of Drawing; the Hours of Drawing at School will be from 1 to 2, and from 5 to 6 in the Afternoon, at 6 Shillings per Week; if it should suit any Persons he will attend from 5 to 6 in the Morning, he proposes not to take above 6 or 8 Scholars. N.B. Said Dwight also continues to Carve all Sorts of House, Ship and cabinet Work in the best Manner.

The technique of reverse painting on glass was well established by the mid-eighteenth century. No examples from this early date have been positively identified; however, a careful survey of newspapers of the period indicates that many artists practiced this difficult technique. An advertisement in *The New-York Gazette or The Weekly Post-Boy* on July 9, 1753, indicates,

107 (below). *The William Denning Family* by William Williams, oil on canvas, 1772, New York, 35¾" x 52". The merchant William Denning; his wife, Sarah Hawkhurst; and their children, William (b. 1768) and Lucretia Anne (b. 1766), were painted in the garden of their house on Wall Street, New York City. Mr. Denning sits in a low-back splay-legged Windsor chair. The style of costume and the inclusion of the Classical urn indicate that the artist was familiar with Continental ideas of fashion and design. Inevitably people who lived close to the major seaports were painted in a more modish dress than those living in rural isolation. (Mr. and Mrs. William Denning Harvey)

108 (above). *Mary Bontecou Lathrop* by John Durand, oil on canvas, second half of the eighteenth century, New York, 35½″ x 27⅝″. (The Metropolitan Museum of Art; gift of Edgar William and Bernice Chrysler Garbisch)

PAINTING ON GLASS.—By a Person lately arrived in this Town. Painting upon Glass (commonly call'd burning upon Glass) is performed in a neat and curious Manner so as never to change its Colour; Perspective Views neatly colour'd for the Camera Obscura. N.B. Young Gentlemen and Ladies are instructed in either of the above, so as to be capable to perform it themselves in a little Time, at a reasonable Rate. By the same Person, Land survey'd designs for Buildings, Plans and Maps neatly drawn. Enquire at Mr. John Ditcher's, Tallow-Chandler and Soap-Boiler in the Sloat.

Numerous art manuals and instruction books divulging the secrets of reverse painting on glass were readily available. Perhaps the most popular book relating to this technique was Carrington Bowles's *The Artist's Assistant in Drawing, Perspective, Etching, Engraving, Mezzotinto Scraping, Painting on Glass, in Crayons, in Water Colours, and on Silks and Satins, the Art of Japanning, etc.* Records indicate that this book was included in several American libraries soon after its first release in 1750 and that it went through as many as six editions.

The technique of reverse painting on glass was revived in the second and third quarters of the nineteenth century.

John Durand (active between 1766 and 1782) is believed to have been born in France. Durand is known as a portrait painter; however, an entry in *The New-York Gazette or The Weekly Post-Boy* for April 11, 1768, indicates that he, like Stephen Dwight and other artists of the day, attempted to master the art of history painting as well:

JOHN DURAND.—The Subscriber having from his Infancy endeavoured to qualify himself in the Art of historical Painting, humbly hopes for the Encouragement from the Gentlemen and Ladies of this City and Province, that so elegant and entertaining an Art, has always obtain'd from People of the most improved Minds, and best Taste and Judgement, in all polite Nations in every Age. And tho' he is sensible, that to excel (in this Branch of Painting especially) requires a more ample Fund of universal and accurate Knowledge than he can pretend to, in Geometry, Geography, Perspective, Anatomy, Expression of Passions, ancient and modern History, &c. &c. Yet he hopes, from the good Nature and Indulgence of the Gentlemen and Ladies who employ him that his humble Attempts, in which his best Endeavours will not be wanting, will meet with Acceptance, and give Satisfaction; and he proposes to work at as cheap Rates as any Person in America.

To such Gentlemen and Ladies as have thought but little upon this Subject, and might only regard painting as a superfluous Ornament, I would just observe, that *History*-painting, besides being extremely ornamental, has many important uses. It presents to our View, some of the most interesting Scenes recorded in ancient or modern History; gives us more lively and perfect Ideas of the Things represented, than we could receive from an historical account of them; and frequently recals to our Memory, a long Train of Events, with which those Representations were connected. They shew us a proper Expression of the Passions excited by every Event, and have an Effect, the very same in Kind, (but stronger) than a fine historical Description of the same Passage would have upon a judicious Reader. Men who have distinguished themselves for the good of their Country, and Mankind, may be set before our Eyes as Examples, and to give us their silent Lessons, and besides, every judicious Friend and Visitant shares with us in the Advantage and Improvement, and increases its Value to ourselves. John Durand, near the City-Hall, Broad-street.

Durand traveled to Connecticut in 1769 or 1770 and in June of 1770 departed for Virginia, where he executed several portraits. During the late 1770s Durand seems to have disappeared. In 1781 he resumed painting in Virginia and in 1782 he vanished again.

During the remaining years of the Colonial period many portrait artists of varying capabilities flocked to the cosmopolitan capital at the mouth of the Hudson River, where they attempted to earn their livelihood by executing portraits. Many were of native stock; however, the more successful, nearly without exception, were of European extraction or had at least studied in Europe.

Ezra Ames (1768–1836) was probably the most successful portrait artist working in upstate New York during the first third of the nineteenth century. Because he painted so many of the prominent politicians who resided, for the most part, in and around Albany, he has been called the "official New York State portrait painter." Ames was born in Framingham, Massachusetts, and settled at Albany by 1793. While residing in the state capital, he executed some five hundred portraits. His work is important because folk painters like Ammi Phillips (see p. 91) were greatly influenced by his polished style.

Theodore Bolton, in his introduction to *Ezra Ames of Albany*, relates Ames's work to that of the more prominent American artists: "In New England during the 18th century there had been an uninterrupted development of portrait painting from Smibert to Feke, to Copley, and to John Trumbull. In Pennsylvania and Maryland, likewise, a development may be traced, beginning with Engelhardt Kühn and Gustavus Hesselius, and extending to John Hesselius and Charles Willson Peale. But in New York State, until 1800, there had been no continuous tradition of painting as there had been in New England, Pennsylvania, and Maryland. After 1800 in New York State, however, a development of portrait painting began which flourished principally in New York City; and of the numerous artists in this movement

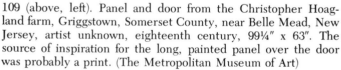

109 (above, left). Panel and door from the Christopher Hoagland farm, Griggstown, Somerset County, near Belle Mead, New Jersey, artist unknown, eighteenth century, 99¼″ x 63″. The source of inspiration for the long, painted panel over the door was probably a print. (The Metropolitan Museum of Art)

110 (above, right). Detail of painted walls from the Carroll Stairhall from East Springfield, New York, by William Price, 1831. Itinerant muralists traveled throughout much of New York and New England during the first half of the nineteenth century. Quite probably these were rural efforts to simulate the expensive, imported French wallpapers that were being used in the more elegant mansions of the time. The decorative scenes in the Carroll House paintings include a romantic landscape of waterfalls, rivers, and hills; Classical ruins; steamboats, plantation houses; giant-sized fruit trees; and modishly dressed ladies and gentlemen. (The Henry Francis du Pont Winterthur Museum)

111 (below, right). Paneled door, artist unknown, first half of the eighteenth century, New Jersey, H. 72″, W. 37″. This door is painted on both sides, and simulated graining surrounds the pictorial elements of a vase of flowers and a man on horseback. (Rutgers University Fine Arts Collection)

112 (above). Stenciled room from a small, frame, slate-roofed structure built at Sherburne, New York, c. 1790. The elaborate stenciling was probably executed about 1820 and was included on the wallboards of the small entrance hall and two rooms on either side of it. Stenciling generally was executed on plaster walls, and its use on the wood walls of this house is unusual. Some elements of the designs are similar to documented work by Moses Eaton (1753–1833), who was one of the most prolific itinerant artists working during the period. Examples of his stenciling have been found in New York, New England, Ohio, and Indiana. (Shelburne Museum, Inc.)

John Wesley Jarvis, Henry Inman, and Charles Loring Elliott were, successively, the most distinguished. Outside of New York City, Ezra Ames achieved in upper New York State a position of similar importance in this trend." [61]

John Vanderlyn (1755–1852) was the grandson of the primitive limner Pieter Vanderlyn. As a youth he studied drawing with Archibald Robertson and around 1794 began to copy portraits by Gilbert Stuart. Aaron Burr was much impressed by these copies and made it financially possible for the artist to receive further instruction from Stuart. In 1796 he was sent to Paris to study, and upon his return to New York in 1801 he produced several striking portraits. In 1803 he again traveled to Europe, where he executed numerous commissions until 1808, when Napoleon awarded him a gold medal for his history picture *Marius Among the Ruins of Carthage*. In 1815 Vanderlyn returned to America, where, for the rest of his life, success eluded him.

In a letter dated September 9, 1825, Vanderlyn not

113 (above). *Battle of Lake Erie*, artist unknown, oil on canvas, nineteenth century, New York, 30″ x 36″. This painting records Captain Perry's victory on Lake Erie. (New York State Historical Association)

114 (left). *The Train Wreck* by the "Utica artist," watercolor on paper, 1870–1890, New York, 8½″ x 10½″. During the last quarter of the nineteenth century, a still-unidentified artist working in Utica, New York, executed some 200 watercolors depicting local architecture, scenes, and incidents. The train wreck portrayed in this small painting occurred on the New York and Boston line. (Private collection)

115 (opposite, above). *Fort Ontario* by Colonel R. L. Kilpatrick, watercolor on paper, 1869, Oswego, New York, 11⁷/₁₆″ x 19⅞″. Colonel Kilpatrick executed two watercolors that record daily life at Fort Ontario. In the background, the building to the right is the commanding officer's quarters; the building to the left is the officers' quarters. (Greenfield Village and Henry Ford Museum)

116 (opposite, below). *Zouaves at Astor House, New York City*, artist unknown, oil on composition board, *c.* 1860, New York, 26″ x 32⅜″. During the Civil War, training units costumed in colorful Oriental-style garments emulated the French infantry. (New York State Historical Association)

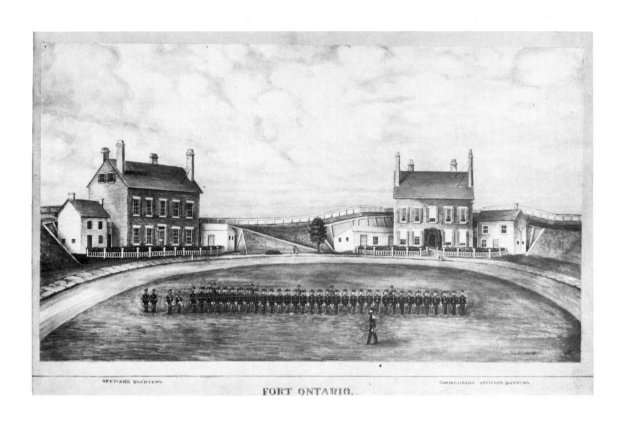

FORT ONTARIO.

OFFICERS QUARTERS.   COMMANDING OFFICERS QUARTERS.

117 (opposite). *Mr. and Mrs. Sherman Griswold Salting Sheep* by James E. Johnson (1810–1858), oil on canvas, *c.* 1837, Spencertown, New York, 85¼″ x 49″. The Griswolds are shown on their substantial estate, which included a handsome house, spacious barns, and a multitude of animals. The artist might have been familiar with Sir Thomas Gainsborough's portrait of Robert Andrews and his wife painted about 1755, for the composition is strikingly similar. Mr. Griswold was a wool merchant; therefore it is not surprising that he would be painted with his own sheep. In 1837 Griswold sold ten farms, including the Hatfield spread pictured in this portrait. He invested his money in the Hudson and Berkshire Railroad, which went into bankruptcy in 1841. (Columbia County Historical Society; gift of Mr. and Mrs. Charles L. Rundell in memory of Mrs. Frank Rundell)

118 (above). *The Hobby Horse*, artist unknown, oil on canvas, *c.* 1840, probably New York, 40¾″ x 40″. Country painters were quick to include objects that were part of the everyday lives of their sitters. Rocking horses were frequently utilized. In 1800 Charles Swift of Philadelphia bought from Charles and William Wigglesworth, local toy dealers, "one middle-size Hobby-horse" for $27. (National Gallery of Art; gift of Edgar William and Bernice Chrysler Garbisch)

only mentioned the work of the younger artist Ammi Phillips but indicated to his nephew and namesake the prestige afforded the artist in America:

I heard with pleasure that you had made some very clever attempts in portraits where you are and which have given much satisfaction. A couple of years more spent in N. York must improve you in this occupation if you pay the least attention to it and in being only a little superiour to the Philips (*sic*) who was here some years since, you may gain more money than you could by any Mechanical business, which you must know, is far more labourious and less genteel and considered. Were I to begin life again, I should not hesitate to follow this plan, that is, to paint portraits cheap and slight, for the mass of folks can't judge of the merits of a well finished picture, I am more and more persuaded of this. Indeed, moving about through the country as Philips did and probably still does, must be an agreeable way of passing ones time. I saw four of his works at Jacobus Hardenburgh's the other day painted a year or two ago, which seemed to satisfy them—it would besides be the means of introducing a young man to the best society and if he was *wise* might be the means of establishing himself advantagiously in the world,—property is after all, the most important thing in the country particularly, fame is little thought of, money is all and everything.[62]

In his final years Vanderlyn returned to Kingston, New York, his native town, where he died penniless in a rented room.

By the close of the eighteenth century appreciation for art had become a status symbol, and the subjects that the fine artist and folk artist might paint had greatly expanded. An advertisement in the *Columbian Gazetteer* of February 24, 1794, offered a large group of paintings for sale. The themes are revealing, for they indicate the broad range of topics that were popular at the time. The collection consisted of

upwards of fifty elegant Portrait Paintings (drawn from the life) and several fine historical subjects and fancy pieces . . . amongst which are the President of the United States, E. Randolph, present Secretary of the United States; C. Thompson, Secretary to the Continental Congress during the American War; T. Pinckney, present American Plenipotentiary at London; D. Humphreys present American Consul at Algiers; B. Hawkins, a present Senator in Congress from North Carolina, D. Caroll of Maryland, General Milandor of Pennsylvania; H. Williamson of North Carolina; S. Chace of Maryland; J. Wilkes or Wilkes and Liberty, 1745; the late Duke of Norfolk; Alderman Beckford of London; David Garrick; Vandike, an ancient celebrated painter, Phillis Wheatley, the celebrated

119 (opposite). *Captain Jonas Holland,* artist unknown, watercolor, first half of the eighteenth century, New York, 12½″ x 7½″. Captain Holland was registrar and treasurer of Union College, Schenectady, New York, and captain of the Second Regiment, U.S. Light Dragoons in the War of 1812. The artist framed the top of the painting with a border of floral motifs and a scalloped edge. (Munson-Williams-Proctor Institute; gift of Charles Childs)

120 (above). *The Prodigal Son Taking Leave of His Father,* one of a set of four watercolors depicting the story of the prodigal son by Mary Ann Willson, watercolor on paper, 1810–1825, Green County, New York, 7½″ x 5″. The story of the prodigal son fascinated Old Testament readers in the young nation. Little is known about the artist except that she and another spinster lived together in Green County. Her friend farmed the land while Mary Ann peddled her watercolors "way to Canada and clear to Mobile."[5] (National Gallery of Art)

View of the Genesee Falls, when Sam Patch took his last leap in 1829.

African Poetess of Boston; that excellent and much admired painting of a mad woman in chains; Mrs. Howard of Maryland; Mr. S. Hacket of Baltimore; Miss Smith of Baltimore; Helena, the wife of Constantine; Mary Queen of Scots, Mrs. Rubens; Mrs. Prichard, a late celebrated actress; the late Dutchess of York. The Dutchess of Devonshire; an Egyptian fortune-teller; a sleeping Venus; an original Drawing by Mr. Pine, of that celebrated and much admired print of America; an original drawing of Canute the great, reproving his courtiers; Time clipping cupids wing; Cupid and Somnus, Earl Warren, a fine historical subject; a Pastoral concert; Maternal instruction, a print of Belisarius, after he was reduced to a beggar, where he is seen receiving alms; several fruit pieces and landscapes &c. &c. any one of which may be purchased separately, the prices are from one to one hundred dollars.

A detailed look at the life and work of Ammi Phillips is now possible because of the great scholarly research and attention that his paintings have attracted in recent years. It is worth studying many of the known facts about this highly gifted artist since his experiences are undoubtedly similar to and typical of those experienced by countless numbers of other self-taught American folk painters of the first half of the nineteenth century.

Ammi Phillips was the son of Samuel Phillips, Jr., and Milla Kellogg Phillips of Colebrook, Connecticut. In the 1800 census the Phillips family consisted of Samuel Phillips and nine members. Ammi, then aged twelve, was the third or fourth among seven brothers and sisters. In the 1810 census he was still recorded as a member

125 (below). *Cabin in the Adirondacks* by William Fellini, oil on canvas, twentieth century, New York, 28″ x 32″. Fellini was a New York City house painter and decorator who died around 1965. A family friend recalled: "He was so poor he could not afford to buy any canvas and would often buy used canvas for 25¢ and paint on the reverse side."[6] (Private collection)

121 (opposite, above). *Suspension Bridge at Niagara Falls*, artist unknown, oil on canvas, nineteenth century, New York, 30¼″ x 39″. (Museum of Fine Arts, Boston; M. and M. Karolik Collection)

122 (opposite, below). *View of the Genesee Falls When Sam Patch Took His Last Leap in 1829*, artist unknown, charcoal on marbledust paper, nineteenth century, New York, 13″ x 18¼″. Sam Patch, the famous nineteenth-century Falls jumper, is visible on the platform built on the slip of land between the two waterfalls. (Private collection)

123 (top, right) *The Mighty Hudson*, artist unknown, oil on canvas, second half of the nineteenth century, New York, 13½″ x 19⅝″. This view of the Hudson near West Point was undoubtedly copied from a print. (Private collection)

124 (middle, right). *Lake George*, artist unknown, oil on canvas, second half of the nineteenth century, New York, 20¼″ x 23⅜″. (Private collection)

of the household. One year later, in 1811, he signed and dated two portraits of Massachusetts residents, probably indicating that he had left home and was working as an itinerant portrait painter.

Information about his initial painting efforts is relatively obscure. In his early work it is possible to see evidence of familiarity with other painters working in western Connecticut and New York. Reuben Moulthrop, Nathaniel Wales, Uriah Brown, and Samuel Broadbent all probably influenced the young artist in one way or another. Their influence brought about such drastic changes in style that until recent years various segments of his work have been attributed to different people at different times.

During the 1820s Ammi Phillips's portraits became much more realistic than those of the earlier period, perhaps because of the influence of the Albany artist Ezra Ames. The two artists covered much of the same territory on their itinerant trips. It seems evident that the trained portrait painter greatly influenced his country counterpart, who had to have seen Ames's more finished, sophisticated portraits in villages along the Hudson. The Ames portraits provided a formula that Phillips could readily utilize.

Phillips was listed as a Troy, New York, resident in the United States Census of 1820. Evidently his artistic

Residence of Mrs. Catherine Snyder, Hallsville, N.Y.
to Wickham Griswold, Schenevus,
Otsego Co., N.Y.

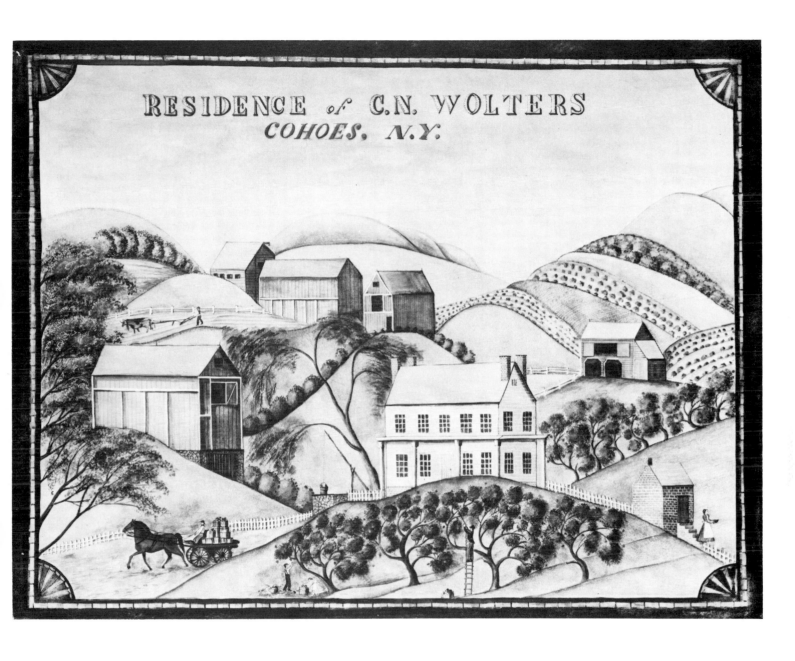

126 (opposite, above). *Annekje Jans Farm on Lower Manhattan with a Family Tree of the Jans-Bogardus Family*, artist unknown, ink on paper, nineteenth century, New York, 30″ x 22″. This painting was executed during the early nineteenth century to be used as evidence in a court battle between the Annekje Jans descendants and Trinity Church. The names of many of New York City's "first" families are included on the family tree. (Mr. and Mrs. Edwin C. Braman)

127 (opposite, below). *Residence of Mrs. Catherine Snyder, Hallsville, New York*, by Fritz G. Vogt, pencil, crayon, and watercolor on paper, second half of the nineteenth century, New York, 24½″ x 37″. Over 100 examples of Vogt's work are known. He lived in Upstate New York, where he recorded numerous farmsteads. (Mr. and Mrs. Richard Dubrow)

128 (above). *Residence of C. N. Wolters, Cohoes, N.Y.*, artist unknown, watercolor on paper, c. 1850, New York, 23″ x 29″. This marvelous watercolor is not only beautifully designed and executed but is also full of many fascinating details of rural life. Photograph courtesy Thos. K. Woodard: American Antiques & Quilts. (Kinnaman-Ramaekers Gallery)

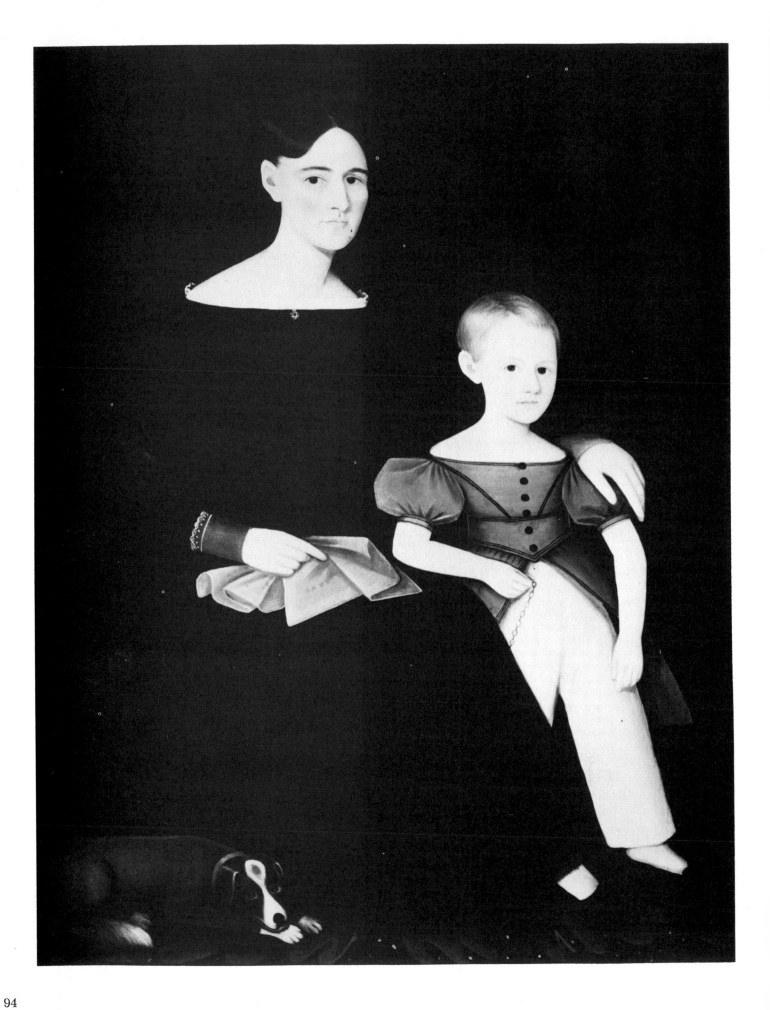

129 (opposite). *Mrs. Ostander and Son Titus* by Ammi Phillips, oil on canvas, *c.* 1838, New York, 58″ x 44″. This painting is one of the greatest examples known of Phillips's work. (Mrs. Jacob M. Kaplan)

130 (below). *Twenty-two Houses and a Church*, artist unknown, oil on canvas, mid-nineteenth century, New York, 24″ x 30″. (National Gallery of Art; gift of Colonel Edgar William and Bernice Chrysler Garbisch)

131 (above). *Ludlam Homestead, West Shore Road,* by Martin, watercolor and pencil, *c.* 1856, New York, 26″ x 39″. (Raynham Hall)

endeavors were not limited exclusively to portraiture, for a history of Orange County published in 1881 mentions an inn sign executed at Goshen, New York, in 1824, "painted by Phillips, the artist, with an eagle on each side."[63]

The first group of portraits by Phillips to elicit admiration were exhibited at a small summer fair in Kent, Connecticut, in 1924. For this show the local residents pulled from parlors and attics many portraits that had been painted in the area during the previous century. Five of the pictures that had been shown at Kent were again shown in 1925 at the International Studio, where they were attributed to the "Kent Limner."

Agnes Halsey Jones, in *Rediscovered Portraits of Upstate New York 1700–1875,* published in 1958, illustrated a group of paintings, now known to be by Phillips, which she attributed to the Border Limner, for the identified subjects lived in hamlets on both sides of the Massachusetts–New York State line. At one point several of the Kent portraits were attributed to John Bradley, a New York City and New Jersey artist. It was not until The Connecticut Historical Society show in 1965 that the entire body of work, representing several styles of painting, was considered to be the result of a single man's painting efforts.

Appreciation for the works of Ammi Phillips has been universal. The Holdridges, writing in 1969 in a catalogue for an exhibition at The Museum of American Folk Art, New York City, and at The Albany Institute of History and Art, praised the folk art master:

By almost any standard, Phillips is the best, the most prolific, and the most inventive American country portrait painter of the 19th century. The outside influences on his early style appear to have come from the last of the great generation of 18th-century Connecticut painters who raised folk art from a craft to a profession. His style was modified by seeing the work of Ezra Ames and may have been further influenced by John Vanderlyn's portraits. He was himself a clear influence on the pose and costume seen in portraits by Erastus Salisbury Field, who worked a territory slightly east of Phillips and, in part, concurrent with that of the older painter.

Influences aside, Phillips is the nearly perfect example of the self-taught painter who experimented to find solutions to his own painting problems. For him, figures presented difficulties from first to last. In his Border period he made his limitations work

132 (left). Page from a sketchbook executed by the Pennsylvania artist Lewis Miller while on a visit to New York, watercolor on paper, 1864, 7″ x 9″. Miller was fascinated with Central Park and illustrated many fashionable women enjoying themselves there. (Greenfield Village and Henry Ford Museum)

133 (below). *Fields at Ludlam Homestead Looking Toward Oyster Bay* by Martin, watercolor and pencil, *c.* 1856, New York, 26″ x 39″. (Raynham Hall)

for him and the lumpy coats, gangling arms, huge hands, wooden arms—even the tables tilted at crazy angles—were all part of well composed and beautiful portraits. . . .

It is easy to think of Phillips as a poor, struggling country craftsman, but the image is faulty. In his old age his life was certainly a simple one, but more often than not his galleries were the great houses and mansions of the valleys of the Hudson and the Housatonic. The countenances of his rural subjects show that patron and painter met on nearly equal ground.[64]

Phillips's pictures were generally mounted upon strainers in contrast to stretchers. A stretcher may be keyed to tighten or loosen the canvas; the strainer is rigid. Ammi Phillips secured his strainers at the corners with wood dowels, nails, or screws.

Phillips spent the last six years of his life in a small house at Curtisville, Berkshire County, Massachusetts. There are several well-painted pictures from this era. Many of them strive toward a realism that could be achieved only by the camera. Phillips, like Field, certainly must have felt the economic impact of photography, and commissions were probably fewer in his last years. In 1863 he drew a will, which indicated that his real and personal property was valued at $850.

Ammi Phillips painted four portraits of members of the Carter family of Stockbridge, Massachusetts. He was paid $10 each for three likenesses of young girls. These sums were substantial for the time. It is safe to believe that Phillips was a well-respected, much-patronized artist and could continue to earn his living in a rural setting long after most academically trained portrait painters in major cities, like New York, had been forced by the new art of photography to turn elsewhere to earn their livelihood.

European visitors to the New World often were severely critical of native artists. Frances Trollope, the indefatigable traveler, recorded in her acid-etched portrait of America her evaluation of self-taught artists like Ammi Phillips:

For a great part of this day we had the good fortune to have a gentleman and his daughter for our fellow-travellers, who were extremely intelligent and agreeable; but I nearly got myself into a scrape by venturing to remark upon a phrase used by the gentleman, and which had met me at every corner from the time I first entered the country. We had been talking of pictures, and I had endeavoured to adhere to the rule I had laid down for myself, of saying very little, where I could say nothing agreeable. At length he named an American artist, with whose works I was very familiar, and after having declared him equal to Lawrence, (judging by his portrait of West, now at New York), he added, "and what is more, madam, he is perfectly *self-taught*."

I prudently took a few moments before I answered;

134 (above). Engraving after a painting titled *American Harvesting* by Jasper F. Cropsey, published by the American Art Union, New York City, in 1851, 7″ x 10″. The engraving was done by James Smillie. The American Art Union circulated numerous engravings after works by its members, which served as sources of inspiration for the many folk artists who executed the paintings on this and the accompanying page. (The New York Public Library)

135 (opposite, middle). Painting based on the engraving of *American Harvesting* by Jasper F. Cropsey, oil on canvas, second half of the nineteenth century, 24½" x 29¼". (Private collection)

136 (opposite, below). Painting by M. J. Tanner based on the engraving of *American Harvesting* by Jasper F. Cropsey, oil on canvas, 1856, 28" x 35". Photograph courtesy America Hurrah Antiques, N.Y.C. (John Spiers and Sheri Safran)

137 (above). Painting based on the engraving of *American Harvesting* by Jasper F. Cropsey, oil on canvas, second half of the nineteenth century, 28¾" x 35½". (Cary F. Baker, Jr.)

138 (right). "Sandpaper" painting based on the engraving of *American Harvesting* by Jasper F. Cropsey, published by American Art Union, New York City, in 1851, New York, mid-nineteenth century, 15" x 11". The artist of this piece on marbledust board is unknown. (Jack T. Ericson)

139 (above). *Spuytenduyvil* by P. A. Hunt, oil on canvas, 1912, New York, 15¾″ x 21¾″. Spuytenduyvil is the waterway that separates Manhattan from the northern mainland. A coach drawn by four horses and a high-wheel bicycle probably indicate that the artist based his painting on memories of his youth. (Museum of American Folk Art; gift of Cyril I. Nelson)

140 (below). *Rebecca at the Well*, artist unknown, oil on canvas with watercolor and wool embroidery, 1830–1850, New York, dimensions unavailable. The background of this picture is painted with oil on canvas; the hands and the faces of the two figures are cut-out pieces of paper that have been highlighted with watercolor; the trees and the foreground are worked in several embroidery stitches with silk and wool threads. (Current whereabouts unknown)

141 (opposite, above left). *Knickerbocker Hall* by W. Seamen, oil on canvas, *c.* 1850, New York, 28½″ x 35¾″. The horse-drawn carriage provided transportation between Broadway, Bleecker Street, and Eighth Avenue in the north to the South Ferry at the tip of Manhattan. (The New-York Historical Society)

142 (opposite, above right). *The Inventor Incessantly at Work for 17 Years to Complete the Cherished Labor of His Life* by Joseph Bruce, oil on canvas, nineteenth century, New York, 102″ x 114″. Circus-banner, advertising, and promotional paintings provided a means of attracting potential customers before the days of radio and television. It is not clear what this banner was originally intended to convey. (Private collection)

143 (opposite, below). *Church of the Ascension, Syracuse, New York*, by the Reverend Dr. Graziani, oil on canvas, 1885, New York, 41¼″ x 51¼″. Note the horse-drawn trolley cars in the foreground. (Herbert W. Hemphill, Jr.)

for the equalling our immortal Lawrence to a most vile dauber stuck in my throat; I could not say Amen; so for some time I said nothing; but, at last, I remarked on the frequency with which I had heard this phrase of *self-taught* used, not as an apology, but as positive praise.

"Well, madam, can there be a higher praise?"

"Certainly not, if spoken of the individual merits of a person, without the means of instruction, but I do not understand it when applied as praise to his works."

"Not understand it, madam? Is it not attributing genius to the author, and what is teaching compared to that?"

I do not wish to repeat all my own *bons mots* in praise of study, and on the disadvantages of profound ignorance, but I would willingly, if I could, give an idea of the mixed indignation and contempt expressed by our companion at the idea that study was necessary to the formation of taste, and to the development of genius. At last, however, he closed the discussion thus,—"There is no use in disputing a point that is already settled, madam; the best

144 (above). *Main Street, Paterson, New Jersey*, signed A.B.M. Ward and dated 1870, watercolor on paper, New Jersey, 17″ x 23″. The carriage and horses are tied outside of the Passaic County National Bank, which has, on the street level, an office of the New York Express. (Mr. and Mrs. Samuel Schwartz)

145 (opposite, top). *J. and R. Fisher's Bloomingdale Flint Glass Works* by B. Whittle, oil on canvas, 1837, New York, 18″ x 24″. The Fisher establishment was located at the foot of West Forty-seventh Street in New York City. None of their products has been positively identified as yet. (The New-York Historical Society)

146 (opposite, middle). *Fraktur Marriage Certificate* for Francis Stanger and Elizabeth L. Campbell dated March 11, 1803, artist unknown, watercolor on paper, New Jersey, 8⅞″ x 6¾″. The Stanger family founded the second glasshouse in New Jersey. Several other New Jersey Frakturs are known. (Greenfield Village and Henry Ford Museum)

judges declare that Mr. H——g's portraits are equal to that of Lawrence."

"Who is it who has passed this judgment, sir?"

"The men of taste of America, madam."

I then asked him, if he thought it was going to rain? [65]

By the mid-nineteenth century vast numbers of European immigrants began to pour into the young nation. Their goal was a better way of life, to be achieved through employment, and political freedom. With them came new infusions of traditional European peasant design, which only occasionally became rooted in the new nation. Understandably the immigrant attempted to cast aside his former language and lifestyle; he strove toward Americanization.

Nearly everyone who could trekked to New York City in 1853 to see the much-touted New York Crystal Palace. At this international exposition, the first to be mounted in America, visitors were exposed to "accepted" European art exhibited in a specially constructed art gallery at the rear of the edifice. In the ensuing years there existed a climate in which the Italians, the French, and the English painters with their classical traditions dominated the American art scene; the folk artist gradually faded. To be sure, during the second half of the nineteenth century in New York there were Victorian theorem painters, there were schoolgirl artists, and there were the Sunday painters. It was not, however, until the opening of the twentieth century that naïve, self-taught artists zealously recorded the bustling city and town life centered at Albany, the head of the Hudson River, and the thrill of the hustle-bustle of Manhattan,

147 (below). Advertising sign for the Orient Delights Candy Factory, Hoboken, New Jersey, artist unknown, house paint on board, c. 1920, New Jersey, 36" x 72". (Herbert W. Hemphill, Jr.)

148 (above). *Sailing Ship Skulda, Course N. by East 15° East* by R. Johnson, oil on window shade, *c.* 1960, New York, 29½″ x 43″. Born in Sweden about 1898, Johnson was a merchant seaman who lived in the Bronx, New York, for most of his life. He died in 1977. Eight of Johnson's nautical paintings survive from a total of about fifty that he based on his memories of sixty years of sailing all over the world. The paintings contain many collage elements, and the frames are crafted from rope decorated with sailor's knots. (America Hurrah Antiques, N.Y.C.)

150 (above). *Pride of Our Lake* by P. S. Downes, watercolor on paper, *c.* 1890, New York, dimensions unavailable. Downes celebrates in this watercolor his romance with "schoolmarm" Rose L. Benedict of Potter Center, New York. Several paintings by Downes are known and are variously inscribed "By an old soldier and sailor," "77 years of age and 48 years at sea," "11 times wrecked on the Blue Ocean," "Now land wrecked among Christian friends." (Current whereabouts unknown)

149 (opposite, below). *Commonwealth* by James Bard, oil on canvas, *c.* 1854, New York, 35¾" x 58". This painting bears the following two inscriptions: "Built by Messrs. Lawrence and Foulks. NY." and "Picture drawn and painted by James Bard, NY/162 Perry St." Photograph courtesy George E. Schoellkopf Gallery. (Private collection)

Brooklyn, and the Bronx, where the river empties into the Atlantic.

Few contemporary artists have enjoyed the great popularity and almost national reverence afforded Anna Mary Robertson Moses, better known as Grandma Moses. She was born in Greenwich, New York, in 1860 and lived a full century and a year. Grandma Moses wrote in a letter to the art dealer Sidney Janis, "When I was quite small, my Father would get me white paper by the sheet. It was used in those days for newspaper. He liked to see us draw pictures, it was a pennie a sheet, and it lasted longer than candy. For myself I had to have pictures and the gayer the better. I would color it with grape juice or berries, any thing that was red and pretty in my way of thinking. I dabbled in oil paints and made my *lamb scapes* as my Brother said I called them. Then long years went by." [66] At seventy-seven Grandma Moses once again took brush in hand and until the end of her life produced nostalgic memories on canvas. Perhaps no contemporary naïve painter, with the exception of Mattie Lou O'Kelley from Maysville, Georgia, and Tella Kitchen from Adelphi, Ohio, has created greater pictures in the American homespun style.

151 (below). *Krueger Cafeteria, Brooklyn,* by Joseph Fracarossi, oil on canvas, *c.* 1960, New York, 16″ x 20″. Fracarossi was born in Trieste in 1886 and came to Brooklyn in 1914. He worked as a baker, and after losing his right eye in an accident, he obtained a job stamping patterns on women's dresses. The artist is best known for his detailed renderings of New York City scenes. He was especially fond of the amusement park at Coney Island, which he recorded several times in various pictures. (Patricia L. Coblentz)

Contrasting with these down-to-earth, able artists are the European immigrants who have so clearly affected the traditional attitudes toward folk art.

Morris Hirshfield was born in Russian Poland in 1872 and came to America some eighteen years later. His efforts at earning a living in the women's garment industry ultimately led to retirement in 1937, when he began to paint. He recalled, "It seems that my mind knew well what I wanted to portray, but my hands were unable to produce what my mind demanded. After working five months on one and then the other I put them to one side, coming back again to them in 1938. I worked on them for about five or six months . . . muchly improved, they still did not satisfy me. I took them up again in 1939 [and] brought them out to my entire satisfaction." [67]

The art historian Barbara Novak has made observations about Morris Hirshfield's work that are thought-provoking and deserve consideration: "the primitive can work . . . aiming hard for realism . . . and yet end up

152 (left). *The Witch Doctor* by Inez Nathaniel Walker, crayon and colored pencil on paper, 1974, New York, 18″ x 22″. Inez Nathaniel Walker began painting while incarcerated in the Bedford Hills Correctional Facility in New York. Her much-sought-after works are generally portraits. She explained: "I don't look at nothing to draw by. Just make 'em myself. I can't look at nobody and draw. Now that's one thing I wished I could do. But I can't. I just draw by my own mission. I just sit down and start to draw."[7] (Private collection)

153 (below, left). *Children's Children Are the Crown of Old Men, and the Adornment of Children Are Their Fathers* by Harry Lieberman (b. 1877), oil on canvas paper, *c.* 1977, New York, 14″ x 18″. This painting was executed the year Lieberman was 100 years old. When asked about the significance of his work, Lieberman replied, "I don't believe there is a life Upstairs. The life I got now is the heavenly reward because when I die, my paintings will be here and people will enjoy."[8] (Private collection)

154 (below, right). *Frolicking Horses* by Lawrence Lebduska, pastel on paper, *c.* 1963, New York, 18″ x 24″. Lebduska is best known for his Fauve-like colors. His paintings inspired Abby Aldrich Rockefeller to begin her collection of great American folk art. (Private collection)

155 (above). *The Iceman Crucified* by Ralph Fasanella, oil on canvas, 1958, New York, 25″ x 36″. (Ralph Fasanella)

156 (below). *The Black Cat* by Vestie Davis, oil on canvasboard, 1964, New York, 12″ x 16″. (Private collection)

with something that is much truer to his mind's eye than to anything his physical eye has perceived. It is almost as though that outer eye were turned off, rendered oblivious to light and air. And the two-dimensionality of that inner image prevails. This is, of course, frequently explained by a reference to technical inabilities. . . . But . . . the problem is more complex, having to do with the nature of artistic vision and with points along a possible spectrum in the conditioned development of perception." [68] Miss Novak's comments about Hirshfield might well be applied to many of the naïve artists of the twentieth century.

Harry Lieberman, the Polish-American artist, was born in 1877 and immigrated to the United States in 1906. He did not begin painting until his late seventies. One day at the Golden Age Club in Great Neck, New York, his chess partner stood him up, so he joined the painting class. Since as a youth he had prepared for the rabbinate, his canvases relate directly to his study of the Talmud, the Gemara, and other Yiddish literature. Contemporary naïve painters have earned the unabashed respect of art critics and teachers alike. Mr. Lieberman could not have known that his teacher, Larry Rivers, was destined to be one of America's most significant innovational artists. He recalled the incident: "I noticed the teacher, Mr. Larry Rivers, was going around to all the others and talking about what they were doing. But to me, he never came. I felt a little disturbed. Am I so bad? So one day I went to him. 'Mr. Rivers,' I said, 'why is it you go to everyone and you don't come to me? What is it? Have I got chicken pox or something, you're afraid?' 'No, Mr. Lieberman,' he says, 'Only, to you, I can't teach you more than what you are already doing.' 'So,' I said, 'Mr. Rivers, you want I should teach you, then?' He says to me, 'Mr. Lieberman, some things I can do that you can't do. But some things you can do, I can't do. What you do is right the way it is.' " [69]

Another European-American to achieve recognition for his naïve painting is Lawrence Lebduska (1894–1966), who as a youth was taken to Europe, where he studied the craft of stained-glass making and decorating. Upon returning to the United States in 1912 he worked as a decorative mural painter and in spare hours painted childhood recollections. Lebduska and his work faded from national prominence during the 1940s. When collectors once again began to appreciate naïve painting in the 1960s, his pictures attracted significant attention.

Joseph Fracarossi (1886–1970), who was born in Trieste, arrived in Brooklyn in 1914. For nearly four decades he worked as a baker and a textile pattern stamper. It was not until 1957, when he visited the open-air art show in Washington Square in New York City, that he began to paint. Ill health forced him to leave his beloved adopted city, and finding small-town life unbearable, he painted from memory some of New York's greater architectural monuments.

Ralph Fasanella was born in 1914 and grew up in New York City's Greenwich Village. Though he now lives in the suburbs, his love for the city serves as a source of inspiration for his art. He believes, "There's no

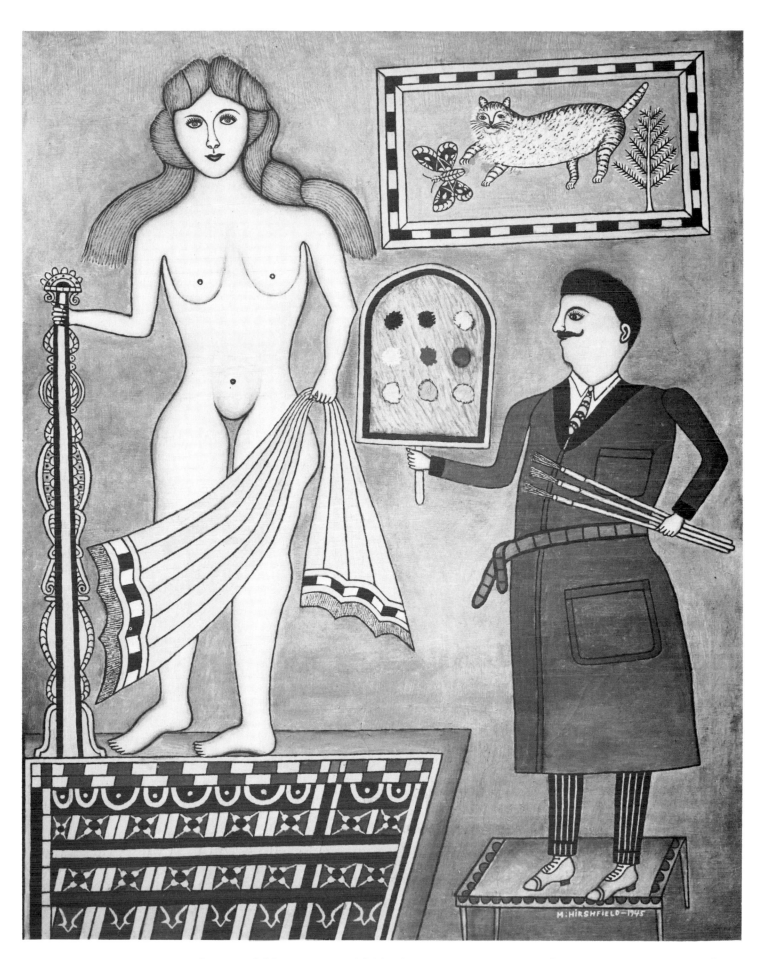

157 (above). *The Artist and His Model* by Morris Hirshfield, oil on canvas, 1945, New York, 43½″ x 33¼″. (Sidney Janis)

158 (above). *Hoosick Falls in Winter* by Grandma Moses, oil on canvas, 1944, New York, 18″ x 21⅜″. Though many art commentators have remained critical of Grandma Moses's contribution to the field of American folk art, she is still one of the most popular of the twentieth-century naïve painters. (Abby Aldrich Rockefeller Folk Art Center)

159 (opposite). *Thousand Islands, New York,* by Peter Contis, tempera on artist's board, 1950, 18″ x 20″. Contis was a Greek immigrant who settled in Pittsburgh, Pennsylvania, where he owned a restaurant. He began painting when he retired. Most of his pictures are memory pieces recalling places that he and his family had visited. His pointillist style has a Mediterranean feeling. The artist was a perfectionist who did not let anyone see his work until it was completely finished and framed to his liking. (Gene and Linda Kangas)

place like New York, and I wanted to get it all, hug it all, everything. I make a portrait of every window. Every face is a person I know. I painted in memory my mother, my old man, working-class Italian families. Marcantonio, injustice: Italians, Jews, Blacks, Puerto Ricans. I wanted the cars, the movement, the streets that pour people into sweatshops, the McCarthy era—the Rosenbergs . . . I wanted to show that the city goes on anyway." [70]

Malcah Zeldis was born in New York in 1931 and grew up in Detroit, Michigan. Her Sunday-painter father discouraged her early efforts to paint, and she did not attempt it again until she was sixteen. During the 1970s, after her family was raised, she began to pursue an artistic career in earnest. "Suddenly all the years of waiting have been erased and the emotional depths from which my paintings arise give me a great sense of fulfillment. The world is infused with greater meaning. I feel I have undergone a profound transformation. It is though I am a vessel waiting for the experiences of my life, the lives of others, the meanings of the universe to come into my being as visitors telling me about the wonder of their existences. All my life seems to have taken on a mystery and beauty for which I am deeply grateful." [71] The Zeldis pictures teem with vitality. Bold, raw pigments laid onto the canvas in a deceptively simple manner disguise the masterly draftsmanship possessed by the artist. Malcah Zeldis is an urban painter, and her complex city views, such as *The Bond's Store at Times Square, New York City* (plate 30), are among the most interesting examples of her work. She is also preoccupied with the allegorical figures of the Bible and with America's political leaders.

Inez Nathaniel Walker's childlike drawings, executed in pencil, crayon, and felt-tipped marker, have a directness, a strength, and a vitality that is frequently disguised by the childlike quality of her portraits, which she confides are "all about bad girls." [72]

While incarcerated in the Bedford Hills Correctional Institution, New York's state prison for women, she began to pursue an artistic career as an escape from the reality of the situation. She explains, "Lordy, a woman got to keep her head around her! There were all those bad girls talking dirty all the time, so I just sit down at a table and draw." [73] Speaking of her work to Michael Hall, she confided, "I just sit down and go to drawing. You know—the more I draw the better I get. I don't look at nothing to draw by. Just make 'em myself. I can't look at nobody and draw. Now that's one thing I wished I could do. But I can't. I just draw by my own mission, you know. I just sit down and start to drawing." [74]

Perhaps because of their great sense of humor, the nudes of Gustav Klumpp have attracted considerable attention. Klumpp, a German, was born in 1902 and in 1923 came to America, where he was employed as a compositor and linotype operator until his retirement in 1964. His unabashed enthusiasm for the nude female figure ties directly to his ideas of art: "My philosophy of art painting which is expressed in the visualization of painting beautiful girls in the nude or seminude and in fictitious surroundings including some other paintings of dreamlike nature. This is one reason I love to paint and I was trying to accomplish something particular at the golden age and as an inspiration to other Senior Citizens or the younger generation. To beautify and enhance the place where it is displayed." [75]

The New York folk painters of the seventeenth and eighteenth centuries would not understand the New York naïve paintings of the twentieth century. Their early portraits were social and economic icons that provided security and a sense of propriety in a land that was full of known and unknown threats. The naïve painters of the twentieth century are a different breed of cat. They paint for fun, they paint for enjoyment, they paint for the satisfaction that being creative can bring. And while their oftentimes brightly colored pictures do not serve the same social ends, they do impart a sense of joy to the lives of dwellers in the mechanized world.

160 (above). *Positive Thinking* by Andy Kane, acrylic on canvas, 1977, New York, 30″ x 36″. (Museum of American Folk Art; gift of the artist)

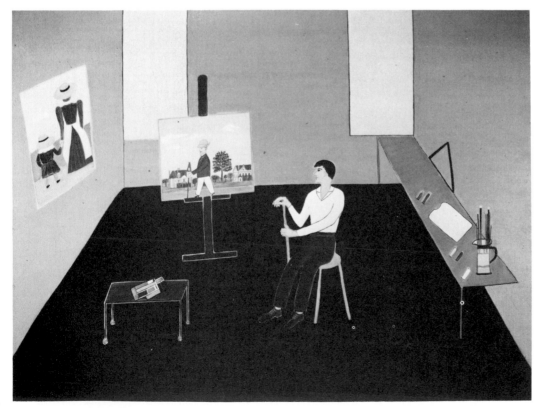

161 (left). *The Artist in His Studio* by Antoinette Schwob, oil on canvas, *c.* 1975, New York, 28″ x 30″. Mrs. Schwob's husband was also a painter, and she shows him here with two of his paintings. (Private collection)

Plate 23 (above). *The Hunting Party,* artist unknown, oil on canvas, late seventeenth century, overmantel painting from the Van Horne family house, Communipaw (now Jersey City), New Jersey, 25½" x 47". This action-filled painting was probably seen by the famous American man of letters Washington Irving when he stopped as a guest at the home of John Van Horne during 1839. It might well have served as a source of inspiration for portions of his essay, "A Conspiracy of the Cocked Hats," which retold the story of the English occupation of New Amsterdam. Photograph courtesy The Metropolitan Museum of Art. (Mr. and Mrs. Samuel Schwartz)

Plate 24 (right). *Magdalena Douw* (Mrs. Harme Gansevoort), artist unknown, oil on canvas, *c.* 1740, Albany County, New York, 51¹/₁₆" x 33". Magdalena Douw was the daughter of Peter Jonas and Anna Douw of "Wolven Hoecke." She married the merchant and brewer Harme Gansevoort of Albany in 1740, when this portrait was probably painted. The broad, flat, decorative style evident in this striking painting is typical of the basic approach to portraiture practiced by the early eighteenth-century American painters in the Hudson Valley. The beautiful Magdalena Douw quite possibly was the toast of Albany, for Dr. Alexander Hamilton, who visited the modern city on the Hudson in 1744, noted that the female members of the community "in general, both old and young, are the hardest favoured ever I beheld. Their old women wear a comical head-dress, large pendants, short petticoats, and they stare upon one like witches."[2] (The Henry Francis du Pont Winterthur Museum)

Plate 25 (above). *View of the Cannon House and Wharf* by Jonathan Budington, oil on wood panel, signed, dated, and inscribed in the lower right, "Jonathan Budington Pinxt/John Cannon/1792," New York, 44″ x 80″. Budington was listed in the New York City directories from 1800 to 1805 and again from 1809 to 1812. He was also active in Connecticut, where he probably painted the four other works that bear his signature—portraits that are dated 1800, 1802, and 1806. This picture was probably painted for John Cannon (born 1725), son of Captain John Cannon, Jr. (1703–1761), who was one of the most prominent merchants in New York, and who owned Cannon Wharf in lower Manhattan. Although traditionally described in the Cannon family as a view of John Cannon, Jr.'s, house and wharf in New York, the painting was actually executed after the elder Cannon's death and probably represents the home and fleet of his son. The picture is one of the most important American views of the eighteenth century. Photograph courtesy Hirschl & Adler Galleries, Inc. (Richard Dietrich)

Plate 26 (right). *Portrait of a Young Man,* artist unknown, oil on canvas, late eighteenth or early nineteenth century, originally found in a stone house in Kinderhook, New York, 29″ x 24½″. Several paintings by this yet unidentified artist have come to light in eastern New York and western Connecticut. This painting, which includes a mounted sphere and several books, is strikingly elegant. Photograph courtesy Allan Daniel. (George E. Schoellkopf Gallery)

Plate 27 (opposite, above). *Portrait of a House and Farm Buildings,* artist unknown, watercolor on paper, *c.* 1875, Westernville, New York, 22″ x 28″. This marvelous watercolor sums up several of the best qualities found in American folk art: strong design, beautiful color, and fascinating details. (Mrs. Jacob M. Kaplan)

Plate 28 (opposite, below). *View of West Point* by Thomas Chambers, oil on canvas, mid-nineteenth century, New York, 22″ x 30″. Several other identical views of West Point were executed by Chambers. Almost certainly they are copies of the print done after an original painting by Bartlett. (Minneapolis Institute of Arts; The Julia B. Bigelow Fund)

Plate 29 (overleaf, above left). *Miss Tweedy of Brooklyn*, artist unknown, oil on canvas, *c.* 1840, New York, 41″ x 33″. Several additional paintings by this still unidentified artist have come to light in recent years. In every instance, they are double portraits of young people who appear to be members of the same family. (The Detroit Institute of Arts; gift of Mrs. Edith Gregor Halpert)

Plate 30 (overleaf, above right). *The Bond's Store at Times Square, New York City,* by Malcah Zeldis, acrylic on Masonite, *c.* 1970, New York, 40″ x 40″. Zeldis celebrates contemporary American urban life. Although many find her color schemes harsh, they vividly portray the world that surrounds her. (Private collection)

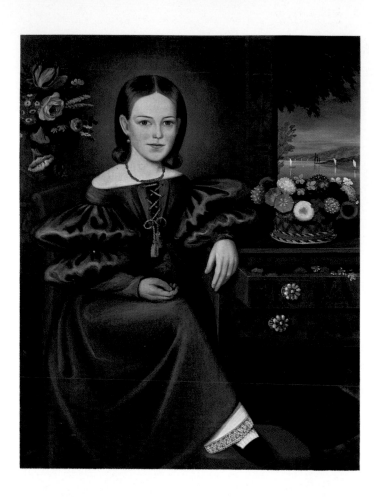

Plate 31 (bottom). *Reclining Nude* by Gustav Klumpp, oil on canvas, *c.* 1970, New York, 14" x 20". Klumpp was fascinated with the female figure and executed well over twenty paintings of nudes. (Private collection)

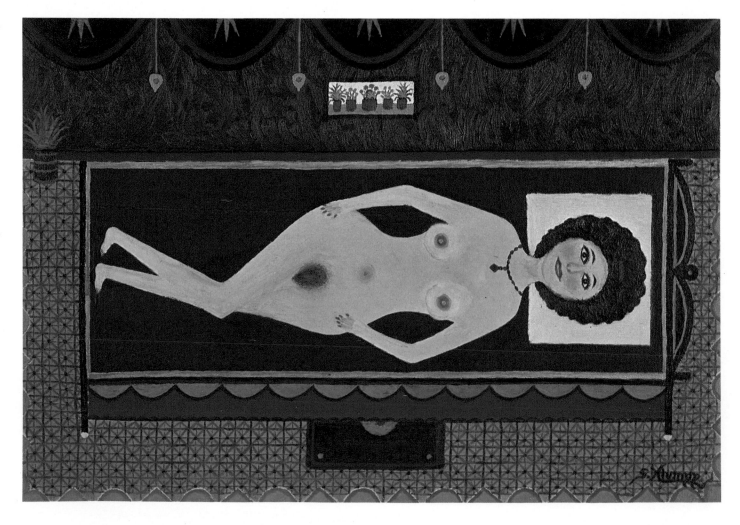

PENNSYLVANIA

162 (preceding page). *Heisse dein Schifflein* by the Reverend Daniel Schumacher, watercolor on paper, 1775, Pennsylvania, 7½″ x 12¼″. (Rare Book Department, Free Library of Philadelphia)

163 (below); 163a (above). *South East Prospect of the City of Philadelphia,* signed "Peter Cooper, Painter," oil on canvas, *c.* 1720, Pennsylvania, 20¼″ x 87″. This painting is the earliest known existing American panoramic cityscape executed in oil. (The Library Company of Philadelphia)

PENNSYLVANIA

By the time Philadelphia was settled toward the end of the seventeenth century, other cities, such as Boston and New York, had become major urban centers with populations large enough to support numerous professional artists who journeyed from city to city and colony to colony in search of patrons. On March 4, 1681, in payment of a debt owed Sir William Penn by King Charles II, William Penn, Sir William's son, received a charter to establish a colony that was to lie north of Maryland and west of Delaware.

The young man, a Quaker, came to look upon his planned colony as a "Holy experiment" where religious and personal freedoms might flourish. Penn instructed his agents to plan Philadelphia, the center of his colony, so that it might always be "a greene countrie towne which will never be burnt, and always wholesome."[76] Penn sailed to America in 1682 aboard the ship *Welcome* and, after arriving inside the Delaware capes on October 24, proceeded, probably by barge, from Chester to Philadelphia.

Because of its religious freedom, Pennsylvania soon began to attract a large multinational immigration that made it, like New York, its sister colony to the north, a prototype of the American melting pot. A population census taken in 1700 would undoubtedly have included Swedes, Finns, Englishmen, Welshmen, Dutchmen, and Germans, who had come in large numbers and were the vanguard of the great German migration to Colonial Pennsylvania.

It is not surprising that the self-taught artist should emerge from such a cosmopolitan city as Philadelphia, for academically trained artists from England and Europe are known to have been working there before the close of the seventeenth century. In fact, in 1696 the governor boasted that "Philadelphia in 14 years is become equal to the city of New York in trade and riches."[77]

The South East Prospect of the City of Philadelphia, executed by Peter Cooper about 1720, indicates that this mushrooming city was already lined with "brave, brick houses."[78] Cooper's meticulously detailed *Prospect* is similar to Thomas Leitch's panoramic drawing of New York City. Leitch boasted, "so exact a portrait of the town as it appears from the water that houses in view will be distinctly known."[79]

Despite the polyglot nature of Philadelphia, Penn's capital city, for the most part it remained English in character. Benjamin West, one of America's foremost Colonial painters, was born there in 1738. He began to paint at the age of eight and only seven years later received his first commission for a portrait. At the age of twenty-two West set up in Philadelphia as a professional sign and portrait painter, and his work from this period clearly indicates an awareness of engravings after English portraits. While by no stretch of the imagination can West be considered a folk painter, his youthful efforts, filled with experimentation, might well be the experiments duplicated by countless numbers of naïve painters who never achieved West's technical ability.

In time West traveled to Europe and ultimately became historical painter to the English king George III. This American-born artist, first to win international fame,

164 (above). *Landscape* by Benjamin West, oil on panel, *c.* 1750, Pennsylvania, 26″ x 49½″. This picture shows the beginning efforts of the young West. William Dunlap, in his *History of the Rise and Progress of the Arts of Design in the United States*, published in 1834, noted: "In the building erected to receive 'The Healing in the Temple' presented by West to the Pennsylvania Hospital, may now be seen two of those juvenile performances painted on panel. The largest is his own composition, and consists of a white cow, who is the hero of the piece, and sundry trees, houses, men, and ships, combined in a manner perfectly childish; the other is a sea-piece, copied from a print with a perfect lack of skill, as might be expected." (Pennsylvania Hospital)

165 (below). *Family in a Landscape* by Robert Edge Pine, oil on canvas, second half of the eighteenth century, Pennsylvania, dimensions unavailable. Pine's earliest pictures were crude at best. The artist is most famous for his *Signing of the Declaration of Independence*, which was frequently copied by young artists who had gained possession of the many prints that were done after Pine's original work of art. (Current whereabouts unknown)

opened his London studio to fellow countrymen who were the foremost American painters during the first years of the nineteenth century.

In an attempt to encourage colonists to settle in the rural areas of Pennsylvania, Penn's agents visited the Rhineland during the latter part of the seventeenth century. Religiously persecuted Protestants were attracted to the New World. These early settlers, inaccurately referred to as Dutch, were often members of the Lutheran and Reformed churches. The Amish and the Mennonites from Switzerland came as well.

Craftsmen played an important role in the newly established farm communities. They furnished all of the articles needed for comfortable living, often embellishing them with designs and decoration remembered from the homeland. Consequently the Pennsylvania German decorative and folk arts were at first nearly indistinguishable from European prototypes. Frances Lichten, noted scholar in the field, described their efforts: "Originality was not expected of the folk decorator; he adhered to motifs which his forebears had used for centuries, therefore his art has a timeless quality. The less skilled decorators copied freely from their betters, and in so doing, achieved a naivete which we today find appealing." [80]

In time memory faded and a simplification of line and decoration became evident. From about 1760 through 1830 the Pennsylvania German artisans produced distinctive pieces that have a unique place in the history of the American decorative arts.

Painting in the Pennsylvania German communities tended to be traditional. For the most part the colonists preferred to maintain their own language and looked askance at any neighbor who patronized an English-speaking itinerant artist.

Portraiture in such circumstances was virtually nonexistent. In its place the Fraktur or illuminated manuscript enjoyed a great popularity as a record of important family events and as a pictorial decoration for the wall. The birth and baptismal certificate, or *Taufschein*, was used by members of the several Protestant sects that practiced infant baptism. These highly ornamented, hand-drawn, and colored records were created by an educated elite—the schoolmasters or clergymen.

Vorschriften, or writing models, were also created by these skilled men for their pupils. Many of the *Vorschriften* are inscribed with the names of the instructors and their hopeful students.

Haus-Segen, or house blessings, reminded the family of the ever-present spirit of the Almighty in the home.

The Fraktur artist, like the portrait painter in New England, was also itinerant. Unlike most of his New England counterparts, he often prepared his documents in advance and filled in spaces as required by his customers.

Traditional motifs abound. Unicorns, stags, decoratively drawn mermaids, heraldic lions, and an endless variety of birds, including the dove, the peacock, the distelfink, and the parrot, appear in a vast body of work that includes painted and decorated furniture as well.

Like its prototype, the medieval manuscript, the early Fraktur was executed entirely by hand.

Probably the earliest known American Frakturs were created by members of the religious community founded at Ephrata Cloister, Lancaster County, Pennsylvania, in 1728. Schools in German communities throughout Pennsylvania continued to teach manuscript illumination and Fraktur writing well into the nineteenth century. In fact, many of them were still instructing their pupils in the ancient craft of Fraktur writing at the time of the establishment in the 1850s of the English school system, which virtually ended the Fraktur art. As the printing press became more widely used during the second quarter of the nineteenth century, the Fraktur maker was ultimately forced from his trade. From this point forward printed, ready-made certificates intended to be colored by the amateur at home and filled in as required were mass-produced. Hand-executed examples were simply too expensive to compete.

It is not difficult to distinguish the early Frakturs, for the materials used to obtain the dark colors frequently destroyed the very paper they were laid on. The Bucks County Historical Society at Doylestown, Pennsylvania, owns a schoolmaster's Fraktur painting box, which contains the materials and the tools the typical Fraktur artist used for his work: "In it are goose quill pens and cat's-hair brushes, small bottles containing colors that were once liquified with whiskey, and cherry gum varnish which was occasionally used, diluted

166 (below). Printed page from the *Ephrata A B C Book* executed in 1750 by a member of the Spiritual Order of The Solitary. The Cloister at Ephrata, Pennsylvania, was a fountainhead for Fraktur artists. The *A B C Book* served as a book of style for *Frakturschriften* at the writing school. (Ephrata Cloister)

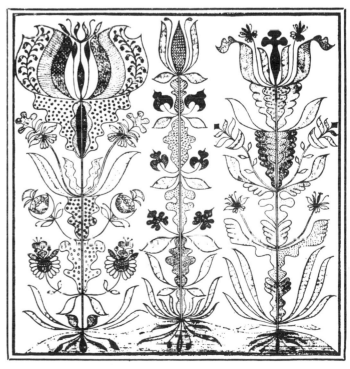

117

167 (above). Birthday greeting for Jacob Van Vleck, artist unknown, watercolor on paper, 1795, Bethlehem, Pennsylvania, 10″ x 8″. Van Vleck was a minister and musician in the Moravian Church at Bethlehem, Pennsylvania. (Moravian Historical Society)

168 (above); 169 (left). Four book pages (front and back) by Susanna Sibbel, watercolor on paper, 1808, Pennsylvania, each page 6½" x 3¾". Susanna Sibbel was familiar with the standard Fraktur motifs; however, her primary concerns were in depicting the world that surrounded her. Many of her visual images are shown in profile, a convention often encountered in folk painting. (Mr. and Mrs. William E. Wiltshire III)

with water, to add a shining finish to the colors. The paints—golden yellow, blood red, soft blue and delicate green—were homemade from dyes concocted by the artist according to old recipes. Using pen and ink, he carefully lettered the inscriptions and drew the outlines of the accompanying designs; he then filled in the illuminated initials and design motifs with flat washes of color." [81]

Numerous Frakturs from the second half of the eighteenth century have come to light in recent years. None has been as impressive as those executed in 1784 by Ludwig Denig of Chambersburg, Pennsylvania. They include an album of biblical scenes, quotations from the Bible, Fraktur writings, and numerous pieces of music.

Little is known about the personal life of Denig, but his incredibly beautiful watercolors are one of the high points of Fraktur art. His simple, straightforward paintings are permeated with religious fervor.

Denig's searing depictions of biblical scenes have a more quiet counterpart in the work of Jacob Maentel, who was born in Cassell, Germany, in 1763. Maentel

170 (above). *The First Fruits* by John Valentine Haidt, oil on canvas, *c.* 1760, Pennsylvania, 41½" x 50½". *The First Fruits* is one of the most significant paintings in the history of the Moravian church. The idea behind the composition was based upon Count Zinzendorf's conviction that in every country throughout the world there were potential converts eagerly awaiting the Gospel. This conviction led to global missions of the Moravian church. Note particularly the Indian in the feathered headdress in the lower right-hand foreground. This figure is intended to represent Franceso, from Florida. (The Moravian Archives)

171 (opposite, above). *Birth and Marriage Record for Joseph Rhodes and Frances Brown*, artist unknown, pen and ink with watercolor, *c.* 1803, probably Pennsylvania, 7⁵/₁₆" x 8³/₁₆". This Fraktur is one of a large group recording family statistics for the Rhodes family. Of special interest is the building on the left, which prominently displays a Masonic compass and square and other fraternal insignia. (Greenfield Village and Henry Ford Museum)

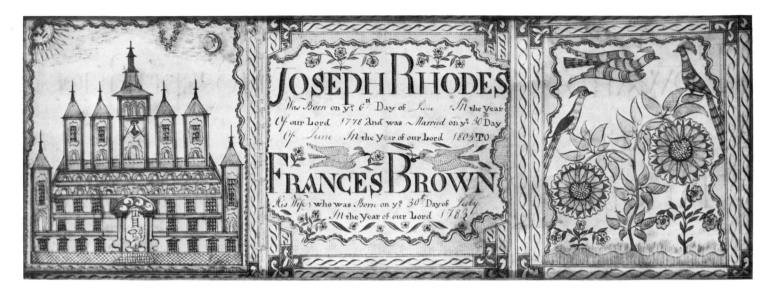

172 (below). Religious text, attributed to George Geistweite, ink and watercolor on paper, 1801, Pennsylvania, 12⅜″ x 15⅛″. Traditional Pennsylvania German motifs such as the tulip, the carnation, the parrot, the rampant lion, and the peacock abound on this handsome Fraktur. Several other versions that appear to be by the same hand are known. (Philadelphia Museum of Art)

173 (above). *Celebrating Couple: General Jackson and His Lady*, artist unknown, pen and wash, nineteenth century, Pennsylvania, 10¼″ x 7⅝″. The couple depicted in this Fraktur might possibly have been celebrating their wedding, for the man is passing to the woman a celebrant bowl. (Museum of Fine Arts, Boston; M. and M. Karolik Collection)

174 (opposite). *Mrs. Calmes IV* by J. Frymire, oil on canvas, 1806, Pennsylvania or Kentucky, 27½″ x 22″. Frymire included imported porcelain in the portrait. This probably was intended to indicate the upper economic stratum of the sitter, who was married to Marquis Calmes IV. (Chicago Historical Society)

123

175 (right). Birth certificate of Maria Statler, artist unknown, ink and watercolor on paper, c. 1810, Pennsylvania, 13⅛″ x 16¼″. The unicorn as a decorative motif appears not only on Pennsylvania Frakturs but on painted chests as well. As a symbol, this mythical creature is often used to represent the incarnation of Jesus and His sinless life. (Peter H. Tillou)

176 (below). Birth certificate of Abraham Killian, watercolor on paper, 1812, Lancaster County, Pennsylvania, 13″ x 16″. Several birth and marriage certificates by the unidentified Fraktur artist who executed this piece are known. (Greenfield Village and Henry Ford Museum)

177 (opposite, above). Fraktur by Francis Portzline, watercolor on paper, 1838, Pennsylvania, 17″ x 13½″. The concept of placing birds in a facing position was used not only by the Fraktur artist, who worked in the freehand tradition, but also by printers, who executed block-printed Frakturs designed to be filled in by the customer. Typical of Portzline's work is the inclusion of a heart motif as wings on the birds. (Philadelphia Museum of Art)

178 (opposite, below). Crucifixion Fraktur, artist unknown, ink and watercolor on paper, first half of the nineteenth century, Pennsylvania, dimensions unavailable. Though biblical scenes were of keen interest to the Pennsylvania Germans, birth and marriage certificates far outnumber them. (The Metropolitan Museum of Art)

is thought to have served Napoleon as a secretary. He came to Pennsylvania sometime early in the 1800s and in 1841 moved west to New Harmony, Indiana. This man, by profession a farmer, was also a prolific portraitist. By the time of his death in 1863 he had finished hundreds of small watercolor portraits. For years Maentel's work was ascribed to Samuel E. Stettinius (1768–1815), another immigrant who had arrived in Pennsylvania about 1791. A signed and dated likeness of a child inscribed by Maentel permitted Mary Black, then director of the Museum of American Folk Art, to reattribute nearly one hundred portraits to him.

The traditions that nurtured the Pennsylvania German Fraktur artist waned after the first half of the nineteenth century. The watercolor artist Margarette Phipps of Lancaster worked in a traditional manner during the 1830s using designs and motifs that had permeated the Pennsylvania German decorative arts from their very beginning. Burnt reds, yellows, bright blues, and greens give her paintings a vivid character. By the 1860s Victorian ideas had intruded into her world, and the delicate watercolor floral renderings that she produced thereafter could have been executed by anyone at any place in the United States. The increasing availability of books, newspapers, and publications like the ever-present *Godey's Lady's Book* pierced cultural barriers and ultimately diluted traditional, inherited European folk expressions.

One of the earliest known Pennsylvania folk portrait painters to leave a large body of work was Jacob Frymire, who was born in Lancaster County, Pennsylvania, sometime between 1765 and 1774. The bustling town of Lancaster boasted a population of some four thousand people, which made it the largest inland town in America and a stopping-off point for budding young artists like Benjamin West who sought commissions from its prosperous citizenry.

Art seemed to flourish everywhere in the busy Pennsylvania communities, for as one astute observer noted, "The portraits of half the Kings of Europe, of many warriors and statesmen, and of numerous things, animate and inanimate, made the streets an outdoor picture gallery." [82]

It seems reasonable to believe that Frymire had the benefits of at least some professional instruction, for unlike the materials of his contemporary Reuben Moulthrop in New England, Frymire's materials were of good quality.

Frymire usually painted life-sized, half-figure portraits in oil on canvas; however, to satisfy those with more modest budgets, he also executed miniature portraits in watercolor on ivory. Frymire traveled into the hinterland between 1799 and 1805; he is known to have worked in Winchester, Alexandria, and Warrenton, Virginia, during the spring, summer, and fall. In 1806 he traveled into Kentucky and in 1807 returned to Pennsylvania, where he was described as a limner on the tax lists.

In 1814 Jacob Frymire was taxed in Cumberland County, Pennsylvania, for a house, a lot, and a cow. Upon

179 (opposite, above). *Scene in a Quaker Meeting House*, artist unknown, oil on canvas, *c.* 1790, Pennsylvania, 25″ x 30″. This painting is based on a print of a Quaker meeting by Egbert von Heemskirk of London, *c.* 1670, now in the Quaker Collection, Haverford College, Haverford, Pennsylvania. Heemskirk executed many Quaker meeting scenes. (Museum of Fine Arts, Boston; M. and M. Karolik Collection)

180 (opposite, below). *Noah's Ark* by Edward Hicks, oil on canvas, 1848, Pennsylvania, 26″ x 36″. Paintings by Hicks are among the most sought after of all American folk art. The artist was a Quaker who is known for his many paintings illustrating biblical stories. (Philadelphia Museum of Art)

181 (above). *Picnic on the Wissahickon*, artist unknown, oil on canvas, *c.* 1845, Pennsylvania, 25¹¹/₁₆″ x 34⅛″. This was executed after a print by William Croome. The house in the background was built on the side of a hill, a popular Pennsylvania method of construction. (Greenfield Village and Henry Ford Museum)

182 (above). Fraktur, artist unknown, watercolor and ink, 1800–1820, eastern Pennsylvania, H. 13". This piece may be of Mennonite origin. (The Henry Francis du Pont Winterthur Museum)

his father's death in 1816 the artist received a substantial estate, including a farm outside of Chambersburg. Although Frymire was well established by the time he died in 1822, only some thirty paintings remain today. His handsome, straightforward representations of Pennsylvanian and southern gentry have earned for him a permanent place in the history of American folk art.

The most celebrated of all Pennsylvania folk painters is Edward Hicks, who was born in the village of Attleborough, now Langhorne, Bucks County, Pennsylvania, on April 4, 1780. He was the son of a Quaker father and an Episcopalian mother who died when he was an infant. Because of severe financial losses, Hicks's father was unable to support young Edward and placed him with the Twining family.

At thirteen years of age Edward Hicks entered apprenticeship with a coachmaker. Soon after the turn of the nineteenth century he became a partner in a Milford, Pennsylvania, coachmaking and painting business and in time painted street signs and shop and tavern signs. A jack-of-all-trades, he also executed decorative paintings on furniture, fireboards, and even clock faces. Later his success was such that he required assistance, and when wriitng his memoirs, he noted, "I am now employing four hands, besides myself, in coach, sign and ornamental painting, and still more in repairing and finishing carriages, and I think I should find no difficulty in doubling my business." [83]

183 (below). *The Gettysburg Blues*, artist unknown, oil on canvas, *c.* 1850, Pennsylvania, 25½" x 41⅛". This picture belonged to Colonel C. H. Buehler, Commander of the Blues in 1850. It shows the local military company parading in front of wonderful stone and brick houses. Many of the buildings still stand today in historic Gettysburg. (Greenfield Village and Henry Ford Museum)

184 (above). *General Hospital, Chestnut Hill, Pennsylvania,* artist unknown, oil on canvas, 1862–1870, 14½″ x 24″. The hospital in this painting was built in 1862 and was an important facility during the Civil War. (New York State Historical Association)

Hicks, a deeply religious Quaker, was accepted into the ministry. Wherever he traveled, he attracted large gatherings, and because of his great empathy with others, he was especially popular. He devoted an inordinate amount of time to painting historical and religious scenes. Like many American folk painters Hicks relied upon prints and biblical illustratons as a chief source of inspiration. He frequently repeated a composition that pleased him. Hicks seems never to have tired of the idea that the wild beast and civilized man could peacefully coexist in God's world. In his lifetime he executed over one hundred versions of *The Peaceable Kingdom.* Painting ultimately became an obsession, and on one Sabbath in a Quaker meeting, he exhorted the congregation about the importance of art in life. The conservative parishioners were upset and appointed a committee to express condemnation of his testimony. For them the idea of the constant pursuit of beauty was akin to consorting with the devil.

Hicks became well known for his artistic endeavors, and a friend, Abraham Chapman, an attorney who lived nearby, encouraged the artist: "Edward, thee has now the source of independence within thyself, in thy peculiar talent for painting. Keep to it, within the bounds of innocence and usefulness, and thee can always be comfortable." [84]

Travelers to America frequently recorded their impressions at a later date. Paul Petrovich Svinin, a young Russian diplomatic secretary who in 1811 sailed for the

185 (above). *Farmstead with Fences,* artist unknown, watercolor on paper, mid-nineteenth century, Pennsylvania, 18″ x 23⅞″. This exciting painting is a textbook example of the folk artist's delight in design and pattern for their own sake coupled with an almost complete disregard of perspective. (Museum of Fine Arts, Boston; M. and M. Karolik Collection)

186 (above). *The Tibby Brothers Glassworks* at Sharpsburg, Pennsylvania, by W. Heerlein, oil on paper, *c.* 1880, 14¼″ x 22⁷/₁₆″. The Tibby Brothers manufactured several kinds of glass, including bottles for H. J. Heinz Co., famous for their 57 Varieties. (Greenfield Village and Henry Ford Museum)

187 (left). *View of Darby, Pennsylvania, After the Burning of Ford's Mill* by J. D. Bunting, 1840–1850, Pennsylvania, 42″ x 51¼″. A flat-bed wagon, a covered wagon, and an open sulky are included in this documentary painting. (Museum of Fine Arts, Boston; M. and M. Karolik Collection)

188 (above); 189 (right). Pair of painted screens, artist unknown, oil on canvas, 1860–1880, Philadelphia, 52″ x 52″. These paintings were executed for the Order of United American Mechanics through their Office of the State Council of Pennsylvania. They were probably commissioned from a local artist who was charged with the creation of teaching or demonstration aids that could be used by union members in their recruiting efforts. This organization was one of many that, during the nineteenth century, attempted to represent the working class in its struggle to achieve for the common man a sense of dignity, independence, and a measure of security. The shipyard was probably located in Pennsylvania, and the landscape in the background would represent New Jersey. The comfortable interior, with its painted window shade, would have inspired workingmen to seek a better way of life for their families. (Private collection)

190 (above). *View of the Montgomery County Almshouse Buildings* by Charles C. Hofmann, oil on canvas or tin, 1878, Pennsylvania, 32″ x 45½″. John Rasmussen, Louis Mader, and Charles C. Hofmann all painted scenes of the almshouse located in Berks County, and they are known as the Pennsylvania almshouse painters. Vivid colors and meticulous attention to detail are characteristics of the works of these three artists. Of special interest in this picture is the canal, where one boat bears the name *Reading* and the other is marked *Centennial-Fright* [sic] (*Canada*). During the nineteenth century, canals played a very significant role in the development of the area. (Abby Aldrich Rockefeller Folk Art Center)

United States, where he remained through the spring of 1813, has left one of the best eyewitness reports of the Federal period. Though attached to the Consul General Andrey Dashkov based in Philadelphia, he traveled extensively, journeying as far north as Niagara Falls and as far south as the Natural Bridge in Virginia. He was especially qualified to comment on the state of the art in America, for he was a member of the Academy of Fine Arts of St. Petersburg. Upon his return to Russia, he reported in a magazine article that portrait painting in America "has been brought to the highest degree of perfection . . . portrait painters are constantly in demand and are very well paid. The most wretched paint slinger receives no less than twenty dollars for a bust portrait, and some men get as much as a hundred dollars. It must be noted, however, that the painters here are forced to charge such prices because of the high cost of living and artists' materials. A piece of canvas for a bust portrait costs about three

dollars in Philadelphia; a good brush is one dollar; and the prices of other items are proportionately high. . . . In every city there is bound to be a miniature portrait painter, but none may lay claim to the name of a good artist." [85]

No traditional Pennsylvania German artist is more interesting than the carpenter Lewis Miller, who was born at York, Pennsylvania, in 1796. For forty years he lived in York and executed some two thousand water-color genre drawings of his neighbors and friends. Miller's lively sketches record the beginning of the great transition from a nation of farmers and craftsmen to one of factories and mechanized power. Miller was a self-taught artist and his vibrant drawings are full of life and rough humor. His work contains hundreds of individual portraits of the citizens of York.

Lewis Miller lived a long life and on a trip to New York City recorded the newly created popular attraction, Central Park (fig. 132). Several of his sketches from this trip have been included in the chapter devoted to New York and the Hudson River Valley.

The Pennsylvania German folk artist might one day execute a *Taufschein*, the next day a *Haus-Segen*, and on the following day be asked to paint bold, colorful "hex" signs on barns or traditional motifs in bright colors on gaily painted furniture. Dotted throughout the Pennsylvania countryside were huge red barns with vivid hex symbols that were probably derived from ancient magical emblems. In Berks, Lebanon, Montgomery, and Lehigh counties, numerous examples of this barn art still remain. Legend indicates that the wide circular medallions, sometimes several feet in diameter and centered with vibrant geometric designs, were originally intended to protect the structure from lightning and the livestock within from witches. Arches were painted above the doors and windows so that evil spirits attempt-

ing to fly through the window or ride through the door on the backs of the cattle would bump their heads and be sent sprawling.

While the witch story is a popular one and is tenaciously clung to by German descendants today, it seems likely that these designs were intended merely as decorations. The idea of barn decorating first became popular in the 1830s or 1840s, and at first the farmers themselves were the artists. In time itinerants much like those who executed wall murals in New England houses came upon the scene. These wandering painters, many of whom specialized in barn decoration, have left behind enough examples of their work so that their route of travel can be determined. While some artists are known to have used stencils, most sketched the design with chalk and a string or sometimes a wooden compass and then filled it in. Barn designs were traditional, and the

191 (below). *Berks County Farm Scene* by John Rasmussen, oil on tin, *c.* 1880, Berks County, Pennsylvania, 27" x 36". Rasmussen is listed as a painter in the *Reading Pennsylvania Directory* from 1867 to 1879, when he was committed to the Berks County Almshouse for his "intemperance." Almshouse records indicate that he was born in Germany and that he died in the institution in 1895. The use of tin, which provided a smooth, hard surface, enabled Rasmussen and the other Pennsylvania almshouse artists to execute very detailed work. (Mr. and Mrs. William E. Wiltshire III)

192 (above). *Rampant Lions* by Johann Henrich Otto, watercolor on paper, *c.* 1780, Lancaster County, Pennsylvania, 8³/₁₆″ x 13⅛″. Otto, one of the best known Fraktur artists of the eighteenth century, relied heavily upon inherited European design motifs in his art. In this watercolor, he used confronting parrots and an eight-petal, star-shaped flower flanked with rampant lions. (Greenfield Village and Henry Ford Museum)

193 (right). Birth certificate for Susan Yockey by Samuel Jackson, ink and watercolor on paper, *c.* 1820, Pennsylvania, dimensions unavailable. During the eighteenth century, Fraktur artists almost always executed the inscriptions on their birth and marriage certificates in German. As better communications and transportation opened isolated communities to the outside world, the inscriptions began to appear in English. This situation increased as the nineteenth century progressed. (Mr. and Mrs. Jerome Blum)

196 (below). Floral painting by Margarette R. Phipps, watercolor on paper, 1841, Pennsylvania, dimensions unavailable. (Current whereabouts unknown)

194 (above). Certificate of birth and baptism for Emma Sibella Ort by Henry Young (1792–1861), watercolor on paper, Union County, Pennsylvania, approx. 10″ x 8″. Emma was the daughter of Henry and Hannah Ort and was born in Derry Township, Mifflin County, Pennsylvania. (Mr. and Mrs. Jerome Blum)

195 (above, right). *Distelfink* by Margarette R. Phipps, watercolor on paper, c. 1830, Pennsylvania, 5″ x 7″. This drawing and figure 196 were found with over 100 watercolors pasted in a scrapbook. Miss Phipps, who probably grew up in a rural farming community, used traditional designs in her earliest work. By the time she executed the floral piece below in 1841, she had obviously been influenced by early Victorian periodicals and she no longer resorted to the artistic conventions that she grew up with. (Private collection)

pomegranate; the flower; Solomon's Temple, a symbol of prosperity and fertility; and geometrically constructed heart designs were among the most popular motifs.

Traditional motifs were part of furniture decorations as well. Though at first the designs used on decorated chests and other furniture forms were traditionally significant, by the mid-eighteenth century they were probably primarily treasured for their decorative qualities. Like nearly all Germanic folk artists the furniture decorator used the tulip most frequently. This variation of the lily had three petals, which stood for the Trinity. The mermaid was also a popular symbol, for it represented the dual nature of Christ. There is a great similarity between Fraktur designs and the painting found on dower chests and other case pieces. Lions, griffons, crowns, the tree of life, and the pomegranate are frequently encountered. The unicorn (the guardian of virginity) and the heart (symbolizing love and joy) were especially popular for bridal chests.

After the struggle for independence had been won

and the loosely knit colonies joined together to form a nation, the traditional nature of furniture decoration began to fade. At times it was combined with patriotic symbols and mottoes, further suggesting that the German tradition was waning. Eagles, flags, and even depictions of George Washington abounded.

By the early nineteenth century needlework was being replaced as a popular pastime by theorem painting.

While "fancy paintings" of elegant floral arrangements and still lifes of fruit were especially popular in New England with instructors at young girls' finishing schools, the Pennsylvania folk painters created similar pieces.

Theorem paintings were often executed on velvet in watercolors or oil paints through the use of a set of numbered stencils, or theorem sheets, which created various areas of the picture. Once the stencils had been traced, the outlines of the basic shapes were then filled in or shaded. This technique was similar to that employed by furniture and tin decorators, who used pow-

197 (opposite). *Still Life with Parrots,* artist unknown, watercolor on paper, 1830–1850, Pennsylvania, 18″ x 22″. As the nineteenth century progressed, the use of traditional design motifs began to fade. The Classical urn might well be considered an intrusion into the Pennsylvania German culture. (Jay Johnson: America's Folk Heritage Gallery)

198 (left). *Still Life* by David Ellinger, watercolor on velvet, *c.* 1960, Pennsylvania, 20″ x 26″. David Ellinger is the best known of the contemporary artists who execute still-life and floral pieces on velvet. Many of his works have found their way into significant private collections and museums. They are frequently so well painted that they pass through the marketplace as nineteenth-century examples. (Private collection)

199 (below). *Still Life,* artist unknown, reverse painting on glass backed by metal foil, second half of the nineteenth century, Pennsylvania, 20″ x 24″. Tinsel pictures were often executed in the home by "artistic" young women. Fashionable feminine publications, such as the *Godey's Lady's Book,* included articles about this form of art and suggested numerous designs that could be utilized. (Greenfield Village and Henry Ford Museum)

200 (above). *Taufschein* printed by Moses and Peters, watercolor on paper, dated 1826, Carlisle, Pennsylvania, 16" x 13". Printed records such as this served as a source of design for decorators in the Mahantango Valley. The desk below has a pair of facing angels on the drop-front lid, and the drawer fronts of the four-drawer chest have birds that quite probably were copied from such a document. (Philadelphia Museum of Art)

201 (above). Chest of drawers, artist unknown, dated 1836, Mahantango Valley, Pennsylvania, H. 52½". (Private collection)

202 (above, right). Desk, artist unknown, *c.* 1835, Mahantango Valley, Pennsylvania, H. 44". This desk is most unusual in that it is one of only two known examples of Mahantango furniture where the decoration is painted on bare wood rather than on a painted surface. (Private collection)

203 (below); 203a (above). Fireman's parade hat, artist unknown, oil on leather, *c.* 1840, Pennsylvania, H. 6″, brim, 13½″ x 12″. (Howard and Catherine Feldman)

204 (above). *Manchester Valley* by Joseph Pickett, oil with sand on canvas, 1914–1918, Pennsylvania, 45½″ x 60⅝″. Pickett began painting late in life, and his total output includes six or seven known paintings. He invented his own technique of mixing sand with house paints. (The Museum of Modern Art, New York)

205 (opposite, below). *John Brown Going to His Hanging* by Horace Pippin, oil on canvas, 1942, Pennsylvania, 24″ x 30″. Pippin's paintings are beautifully designed, meticulously executed, and forceful cultural records of America's social development.(Pennsylvania Academy of the Fine Arts; Lambert Fund Purchase)

206 (above). *Crucifixion* by Peter Charlie, oil on canvas, mid-1960s, Pennsylvania, 28″ x 36″. Three sources of inspiration affected the Armenian immigrant artist Peter Charlie: traditional Armenian motifs, scenes from American history, and ideas relating to the space age, including space travel and visitors from other planets. (Jay Johnson: America's Folk Heritage Gallery)

207 (below). *Windmill and Traction Engine* by J. C. Huntington, watercolor on paper, *c.* 1960, Pennsylvania, 19½″ x 42½″. Huntington began painting when he retired from working on the railroad. His use of the flat Fraktur style well into the twentieth century is unusual. (Mr. and Mrs. Michael Hall)

dered bronze instead of paints. Still life subjects like the wonderful example executed by Susanna Hook (plate 9) were most popular, and the skillful artist could obtain surprisingly professional results.

Originally theorem painting was called *Poonah painting, formula painting,* or *India tint work.* Theorem painting was Chinese in origin and consisted of precisely executed stencil pictures on a white, pithy substance that resembled velvet but probably was rice paper: "The old stencils were cut from horn paper, which was nothing more nor less than drawing paper coated with linseed oil and varnished." [86]

The heyday of theorem painting in America was between 1800, when its popularity spread from England, and 1850, when colorful, inexpensive Victorian floral prints made it no longer necessary to execute decorated pictures for the home. By the 1830s the upper class began to look disparagingly at theorem painting and *The Young Ladies' Assistant in Drawing and Painting,* published in 1833 in Cincinnati, Ohio, noted, "Velvet painting was a few years ago very fashionable for young ladies because they thought it could be learned without study or knowledge of drawing. Then every miss could become an artist with $3.00 for six lessons. Frightful specimens multiplied until it has dropped into oblivion and is scarcely mentioned except in the country where painting has not made great progress." [87] In spite of such derision, the theorem art continued to flourish for yet another twenty years.

Charles C. Hofmann (1820–1882), a German immigrant who came to America in 1860 at the age of forty, settled at Reading, Pennsylvania, and between 1865 and 1881, a year before his death, executed large landscapes on canvas and zinc that depicted Berks County, Montgomery County, and Schuylkill County almshouses. Not unlike those of his contemporaries, the painter John Rasmussen and the woodcarver Wilhelm Schimmel, much of Hofmann's life was spent as a vagrant. In 1872 he committed himself to the Berks County almshouse and through the years returned there for the shelter it provided from the hostile world outside. The almshouse register indicates, "Occupation, painter; Habits, intemperate; Cause of Pauperism, intemperance," [88] a modest appraisal for one of America's greatest folk artists.

Joseph Pickett (1848–1918) was born at New Hope, Pennsylvania. During his early youth he worked with his father repairing canal locks: "Although he had this early training and did a great deal of manual work, there is good evidence that he was not a master-craftsman; still he was an ingenious man with ideas and ability to carry them out . . . he built two houses, made a pair of calfskin boots, a chest of drawers elaborately patterned in marquetry, and a homemade barber chair, crude but inventively made." [89] Joseph Pickett was a wandering man; he traveled as a concessionaire with carnivals, where he maintained shooting galleries. At the age of forty-five he married and settled in his home town, where he began painting pictures with house paints. In time he learned about conventional artists' supplies. He also mixed sand with "store-bought" paints to create a three-

dimensional texture. Though there are very few works by this extraordinary artist, they are a high point in the history of twentieth-century American naïve painting.

Perhaps no modern folk painter has enjoyed more success than John S. Kane, a Scotsman born in 1870. At the age of nineteen he came to America, where he worked for the railroad and as a miner, a steel mill worker, and finally a freight car painter and house painter. Kane's *Self-Portrait,* painted in 1929, just five years before his death, is one of the true masterpieces of American folk painting. In his homespun way Kane advised future artists, "The best thing in the world for a young artist would be to hire himself out to a good painting contractor." [90]

An equally famous artist, born in West Chester, Pennsylvania, in 1888, was Horace Pippin, a black painter. After moving about the country as a youth, he joined the army in 1917 and was wounded in action during World War I. Though he suffered paralysis in the right arm, he supported it with his left hand. Pippin began to paint in 1929 and in a letter revealed, *"How I paint . . . the colors are very simple. . . . The pictures which I have already painted come to me in my mind, and if to me it is a worth while picture, I paint it. I go over that picture in my mind several times and when I am ready to paint it I have all the details that I need."* [91] Horace Pippin's *John Brown Going to His Hanging* is probably his greatest painting.

Patrick J. Sullivan was born in Braddock, Pennsylvania, on March 17, 1894, of Irish parents. His father died when Patrick was two, and his mother, who was also very ill, was forced to stay at the Pittsburgh hospital for an extended period of time. She placed the baby in an orphanage, where he remained until the age of fifteen. Sullivan recalled later in life, "In the orphan home I worked in the printing shop. This work first gave me the idea of dabbling in painting, but I never gave much time to it other than sketching what everyone thought meaningless stuff." [92]

Folk painters frequently record their personal experiences in their art. Others, like Peter Charlie, illustrate their subconscious fears of the past, present, and future. Peter Charlie immigrated to America from Armenia before World War I. He returned to his native land to fight in the war and came back to Leechburg, Pennsylvania, to settle permanently. This house painter and general handyman rented a garage behind a local hardware store, where, until his death in the late 1950s, he painted in secret. His complex, intensely symbolic canvases are permeated with invaders from other planets.

The traditional Pennsylvania folk idiom of the eighteenth and nineteenth centuries prevailed well into the twentieth century, especially in the work of J. C. Huntington, a retired railroad worker from Sunbury, Pennsylvania. His watercolor renderings are spiritually akin to the much earlier Frakturs. Huntington's deceivingly simple compositions of rural life, in muted pastel shades, are the exact opposite of the bold, vibrant paintings by Jack Savitsky.

Savitsky, a coal miner throughout his life, was born

208 (right). *Recess Time* by Clarence (Pa) Perkins, oil on canvas, 1977, Pennsylvania, 20″ x 24″. The artist's rendering of the baseball game in the left-hand corner of the painting is highly unusual. (Private collection)

in 1910. When he found himself out of a job in 1959, his son suggested that he once again resume his former pastime of painting. He replied, "What the hell. Why not? I sold my early paintings for a few dollars, now I get a good price. I like to do my oils on masonite, and to work with crayons, pen and ink, charcoal, colored pencils. I never took a lesson. Figured everything—mixing paint, glazing with varnish—myself."[93] Savitsky's rugged miners in garish colors exude the raw strength of the men they portray.

The painting Perkinses—Ruth Hunter Perkins and her husband, Clarence Perkins—bring to their work a sense of nostalgia and an intense interest in experimentation. Ruth Perkins was born in 1911 in Jamestown, Mercer County, Pennsylvania, and has painted ever since childhood, when she first "did maps in school."

Clarence (Cy) Perkins grew up in Gustavus Township, Trumbull County, Ohio, where he was born in 1906. Unlike his wife, he did not paint as a child: "I was never able to do anything in painting—absolutely nothing—school painting or drawing maps. I graduated second highest in my class, but could not draw a thing. One day in 1976 I just sat down with some paper and tried, and amazed myself."[94]

Before embarking upon "serious painting," the Perkinses were in business together preparing and serving chicken dinners; Cy Perkins was in the front, meeting people, and Ruth was in the kitchen, doing the "hard work." "When we went down the street, he was always recognized, but I was not,"[95] complains Mrs. Perkins.

When asked about her painting, *Original Garage Sale—Body Parts and Apples,* Ruth Perkins replied that because her husband had always been the prominent one in the chicken dinner enterprise, she was a little aggravated when he started to paint: "I was a bit resentful that my husband was going to take away the chance I had to do something on my own; and besides that, he was better than I was!"

Painting has added a new dimension to the lives of the Perkinses. Each claims to be the other's most severe critic; at the same time they are immensely proud of one another's pictures.

Contemporary folk painting is in itself a study in contrasts and the work defies consistent classification. Folk art seems to spring from many wells, each with its own particular flavored water.

209 (above). *The Christmas Tree* by Ruth (Ma) Perkins, oil on canvas, 1977, Pennsylvania, 20″ x 24″. (Private collection)

210 (below). *The Dog World* by Justin McCarthy, oil on tiles, c. 1970, Pennsylvania, 16″ x 22″. McCarthy's semiabstract style grew out of his highly personal vision. (Private collection)

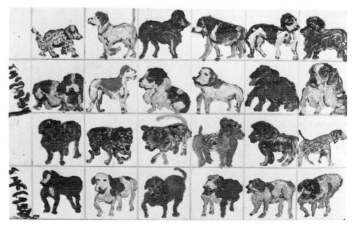

211 (above). *An Historical Event* by Patrick J. Sullivan, oil on canvas, 1937, Wheeling, West Virginia, 24¼″ x 25″. Sullivan, who was born in Pennsylvania in 1894, first worked in a sheet-iron mill and then became a house painter. This inspired him to try painting on wrapping paper and window blinds. In a letter to art dealer Sidney Janis, he stated: "I never took an art lesson in my life. I just like to paint and from now on I shall paint things that come to mind—powerful stuff that will make people think." He describes *An Historical Event* as ". . . the heart of the ex-king [Edward VIII]. . . . 'Wally' and Edward like the twins are inseparable—part them and it means the end of both." (Sidney Janis Gallery)

212 (left). *Covered Bridge in My Hometown* by Mary Lou Robinson, acrylic on canvas, 1979, Pennsylvania, 22″ x 28″. (Private collection)

144

Plate 32 (above). *The Peaceable Kingdom* by Edward Hicks, oil on canvas, *c.* 1847, Newtown, Pennsylvania, 26″ x 29½″. This lovely painting, one of the many variations on the theme made famous by Hicks, includes in the left background William Penn's treaty with the Indians. It pictorializes Isaiah's words from the Old Testament, "The wolf also shall dwell with the lamb, and the leopard shall lie down with the kid; and the calf and the young lion and the fatling together; and a little child shall lead them." (Private collection)

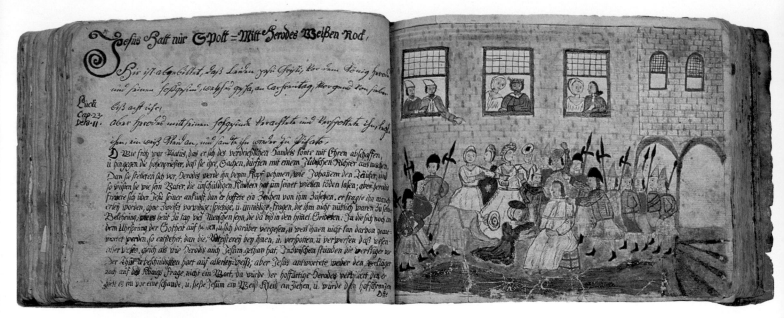

Plate 33 (above); plate 34 (left). Illustrations from an album by Ludwig Denig, 1784, Chambersburg, Pennsylvania. Each page measures 6½″ x 8½″. This unique Fraktur book of biblical scenes contains 59 pictures, 114 pages of script, and several pages of music. The vase of flowers at the left appears on another of the pages. (Mr. and Mrs. Samuel Schwartz)

Plate 35 (right). *The Nativity* by John F. W. Stahr, watercolor on paper, March 15, 1835, Pennsylvania, 15⅞″ x 12⅝″. (Private collection)

Plate 36 (opposite). Birth and baptismal record of Elizabeth Eyster, artist unknown, watercolor and ink on paper, dated 1776, York County, Manchester Township, Pennsylvania, 8¾″ x 6¾″. This is an especially appealing Fraktur landscape. (Private collection)

Elisabeth - Geboren Im
Jahr Christi 1776 Den 25t Februar Im Zeichen
Gelauft vom Dern pfarer
Tauf Zeige Warren Peter spiess und Magdalena Eyster ledig
Elisabeth ist geboren In Der provinz Pensylvania
In York Caunt In Manchester Taunschip Der Vatter
Deist Georg Eyster Die muter Eysterin gehorne
Allklandin Deülle Zieh Du Zartte Seelle
Aluß Der Sinden Finstern Hoelle Durch
Die Tauf Deraußgefirt Hall Dich Hinfort
Zu Den Fromen, So Wirst Du Die
Cron Bekomen Womitt Gott Die
Seinen Ziert

Homestead of Jacob H. Landis,

From a sketch taken by Jacob Stauffer, July 17, 1879, during a visit, in company with Dr. S.S. Rathvon, and enjoyed the kind hospitality of their host and his family. Presented in commemoration of that day by the humble delin or, not as a matter of skill or beauty—but as a token of fond memories.

July 22ᵈ 1879, aged in his 71 Year of Age, Lancaster, Pa.

Plate 37 (opposite). *The Apothecary* by Jacob Maentel, watercolor on paper, *c.* 1840, Pennsylvania, 16⅝″ x 10½″. Tradition indicates that this is the portrait of Christian Bucher of Schaefferstown, Lebanon County, Pennsylvania. (Private collection)

Plate 38 (above). *Homestead of Jacob H. Landis* by Jacob Stauffer, watercolor and ink on paper, dated July 17, 1879, Lancaster County, Pennsylvania, 9⅞″ x 13⅜″. All of the buildings depicted in this painting are still standing. (Private collection)

Plate 39 (left). *Unidentified General*, artist unknown, watercolor and ink on paper, 1810–1820, Pennsylvania, 8″ x 6½″. This stylized portrait of a military man is in a frame that is decorated with carved motifs and split balusters. (Peter H. Tillou)

Plate 42 (opposite, above). Taufschein of Johannes Meyer, artist unknown, watercolor on paper, dated 1809, Berks County, Pennsylvania, 8¼" x 13½". Photograph courtesy George E. Schoellkopf Gallery. (Howard and Catherine Feldman)

Plate 43 (opposite, below). Fraktur, artist unknown, ink and watercolor on paper, 1800–1840, probably eastern Pennsylvania, 12⁹/₁₆" x 15⁷/₁₆". The painting has a narrow painted border, a device used many times by the Fraktur artists. This highly stylized and rhythmical basket of tulips is a major example of Pennsylvania German folk art. Note how the curly-maple frame contributes strongly to the liveliness of this splendid watercolor. (The Henry Francis du Pont Winterthur Museum)

Plate 40 (above). Birth and baptismal certificate for Johannes Dottern (born December 25, 1831) by the Northampton County artist, watercolor and ink on paper, c. 1835, Pennsylvania, 15" x 11⅞". The inscription on this beautiful Fraktur reads: "One bird in the hand is worth two in the forest." Photograph courtesy George E. Schoellkopf Gallery. (Private collection)

Plate 41 (right). Fraktur, artist unknown, ink and watercolor on paper, c. 1810, southeastern Pennsylvania, 8½" x 4¾". This delightful Fraktur portrays a pipe-smoking gentleman walking among giant tulips. (Free Library of Philadelphia, Rare Book Department)

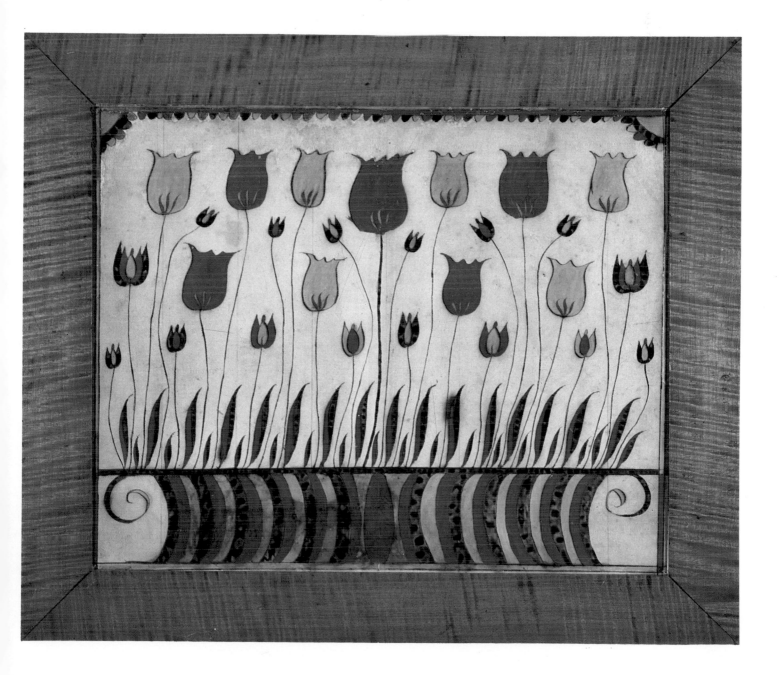

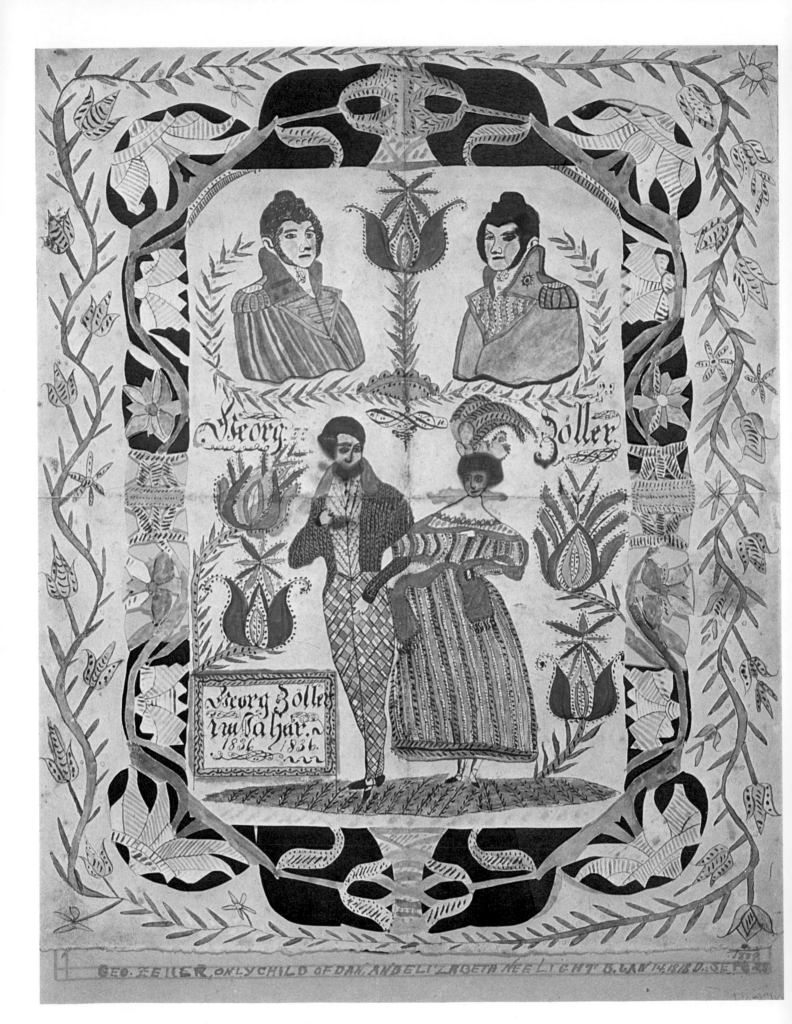

Plate 44 (opposite). Fraktur cutout, signed George Zoller and dated 1836, watercolor on paper, Pennsylvania, 16½″ x 13½″. The traditional tulip motif is repeatedly used on this unusual watercolor. (Mr. and Mrs. James O. Keene)

Plate 45 (above). Fraktur from Jacob Schmidt's hymn book, artist unknown, watercolor on paper, dated May 5, 1833, Washington Township, Franklin County, Pennsylvania, 5½″ x 3½″. Photograph courtesy America Hurrah Antiques, N.Y.C. (Private collection)

Plate 49 (right). *Portrait of Frank Peters, the Tailor* by Joseph P. Aulisio (1910–1974), oil on canvas, 1965, Pennsylvania, 28″ x 20″. Aulisio worked in a dry-cleaning establishment and did not begin to paint until late in life. He once said: "I paint because I love it. Winning a top prize in a regional show at the Everhart Museum in Scranton encouraged me to paint more."[3] (Museum of American Folk Art; gift of Arnold Fuchs)

Plate 50 (below). *Sunrise* by Jack Savitsky, oil on board, dated 1964, Pennsylvania, 24¾″ x 49″. Savitsky titled this painting twice. On the back of the painting he has written: "Sun rise / Sun rise in the coal region/ I went to school/ I went to church/ I went to work/ And on pay day, I went out and got drunk. Jack Savitsky 1964." (David Davies)

THE SOUTH

213 (preceding page). *Mrs. Mordecai Booth* (neé Joyce Armistead), attributed to William Dering, oil on canvas, 1745–1749, Virginia, 50″ x 39½″. William Dering, a dancing master, was established in Philadelphia by 1735. By 1745 he had apparently turned to portraiture as a way of increasing his income and until 1750 worked in and around Williamsburg, Virginia, where he executed stylish portraits of the South's most prominent citizens. Photograph courtesy Museum of Early Southern Decorative Arts. (Mr. and Mrs. R. Lawson Miles, Jr.)

215 (below). Fireboard inscribed "View of the Castle of Montgomery," artist unknown, oil on canvas, 1830–1840, South Carolina, 41½″ x 55½″. Until the mid-nineteenth century, decorated fireboards were constructed of either battened boards or canvas stretched on a light frame. They covered hearth openings when fireplaces were not in use. This fireboard is one of two identical versions painted by an unknown artist for homes near Spartanburg, South Carolina. The source of the composition is unknown; probably it was derived from a print or a book illustration. (New York State Historical Association)

214 (above). Overmantel from Morattico, Richmond County, Virginia, oil on wood, *c.* 1715, 20¹/₁₆″ x 91¾″. Built by Charles Grymes about 1715, Morattico was destroyed during the 1920s through erosion of the banks of the Rappahannock River. This panel from the elaborate mansion is framed in marbleized moldings. A similar panel, which might have served as the inspiration for this piece, was found in the Wilsley House, Cranbook, Kent, England. It was executed around 1690. The owners of most large southern mansions regarded the overmantel as a status symbol, and in a letter dated October 12, 1756, Henry Laurens asked Richard Shubrick's help in obtaining "handsome Landscapes": "Our brother Elias Ball who has lately finished & got into his new house is desirous of compleating the decorations within by adding two handsome Landscapes of Kensington & Hyde Park which will just fill up two vacancys over the Chimney pieces in the Hall and a large Parlour, & we must now beg the favour of you to procure such for him & send them out by the first good opportunity. . . . He would have handsome Views of those two places with the adjacent Woods, Fields, & Buildings & some little addition of Herds, Huntsman, &ca., but not too expensive in the Painting. Suppose they may cost two or three Guineas each. Will it not be best to have the Canvass rolled up & the frames pack'd for putting together here as they will take the less room, 'tho great care should be taken to prevent the paint from sticking when it is rolled up."[9] (The Henry Francis du Pont Winterthur Museum)

THE SOUTH

Some of the earliest representations of America are contained in the works by Jacques Le Morgues Le Moyne (died 1588), who recorded René de Laudonnièrc's (died c. 1586) expedition in Florida in 1564, and John White (working 1585), who documented Sir Walter Raleigh's colonial venture in Virginia in 1585.

Le Moyne, a French watercolorist, is the earliest known artist to have visited and worked in what is now Florida, Georgia, and the Carolinas. He was one of the few survivors of the disaster-plagued Huguenot settlement at Fort Caroline on the St. Johns River, which was destroyed by the Spanish in 1565. His American watercolor scenes of the expedition were engraved and published with a narrative.

Le Moyne ultimately settled in London, where he became a "servaunt to Sir Walter Raleigh."[96] He produced numerous watercolors of England's flora and fauna prior to his death in 1588.

Le Moyne's *Indians of Florida Collecting Gold in the Streams Flowing Out of the Apalachy Mountains* is generally believed to be the first oil painting depicting an American scene. The artist probably painted it in London using sketches that he had executed earlier in the New World. Though crude in execution and dark because of extensive oxidation of the paint, it is a striking document in the history of America.

After Le Moyne's death, Theodore De Bry purchased his American watercolors, drawings, and narrative journal, which he published and illustrated with copper engravings under the title *Brevis Narratio eorum quae in Florida Americae provicia Gallis acciderunt*, generally known as the *Voyages*.

In 1585 John White, an English watercolorist, visited Sir Walter Raleigh's colony at Roanoke Island, where he recorded the natural curiosities, including the native Americans. In 1587 he returned to the colony as the second governor. His married daughter accompanied him and later gave birth to Virginia Dare, the first English child born in America. White returned to England in 1587 and remained there until 1590, when he traveled once again to Roanoke, this time finding no trace of the colony.

Several of White's views of Virginia were engraved by the German Theodore De Bry and published in *A*

Briefe and True Report of the New Found Land of Virginia in 1590.

Almost as soon as permanent settlements took root in the New World, the portrait painter appeared.

Henrietta Johnston (died 1728/9) was one of the first pastel artists and possibly the first woman to work in America. Mrs. Johnston came to America about 1707 with her husband, the Reverend Gideon Johnston, commissary of the Bishop of London in South Carolina and rector of St. Philip's at Charleston. She augmented the family income by executing pastel portraits of the local gentry. Mrs. Johnston is believed to have made at least one trip to New York around 1725 in search of commissions.

While Henrietta Johnston's surviving pictures indicate no great artistic talent, her efforts were probably as successful as those of the many itinerant English artists who traveled throughout the South in search of painting commissions.

For most of the eighteenth century, folk art that grew out of inherited European peasant traditions that were passed from generation to generation, such as the folk art of the Pennsylvania Germans, did not really exist in the South. Countless immigrants, many armed with the benefits of at least rudimentary art education, struggled to eke out a living.

Settlements established by the Spanish and the French tended to be of a different nature from those set up by English colonists, who, from the very first, attempted to build homes and establish communities and trade with the mother country.

The Spanish and the French looked upon their New World possessions as a source of wealth and upon the conversion of the Indians as a way to propagate Catholic beliefs.

Of the many Spanish and French settlements in the American South, St. Augustine, New Orleans, Natchez, and Mobile were among the most important.

It is little wonder that the English and finally the Americans became possessors of the land, since the problem at New Orleans, so vividly described by Father Charlevoix in 1718, prevailed in most of the other settlements. Charlevoix recorded, "Two hundred people have been sent here to build a city, and are encamped on the great river, where their only thought has been to protect themselves from the elements while waiting for someone to draw up a plan and build houses for them. M. de Pauger has just shown me his idea of a plan; it is indeed handsome, and most orderly, but it will not be as easy to execute as it was to trace on paper." [97]

The Mobile area was first explored by the Spaniards in 1519, and successive expeditions occurred in 1528, 1540, 1558, and 1559. French colonists, under Jean Baptiste le Moyne, sieur de Bienville, established the city of Mobile at its present site in 1711. Because it was situated on the Gulf of Mexico, the city played an important role in the settlement of the South. Mobile was the capital of French Louisiana until 1720. In 1763 the British assumed control, and during the American Revolution Spanish forces captured the city.

216 (above). *Indians of Florida Collecting Gold in the Streams Flowing Out of the Apalachy Mountains* by Jacques LeMoyne, oil on canvas, 1564, England, 31¼" x 42". The composition of this picture is identical to Plate 41 of Theodore DeBry's *Voyages.* This painting is believed to be the first oil painting that exists of an American scene. (Sotheby & Company, London)

217 (opposite). *Indian Village of Secoton* by John White, watercolor, 1585, England or America. The artist was an English watercolorist who specialized in botanical objects. In 1585 he went to Roanoke, Virginia, where he joined Sir Walter Raleigh's colony. Over sixty drawings and watercolors by White are now in the British Museum. (The British Museum)

The United States occupied Mobile in 1813 and acquired the busy port city in the Florida Purchase of 1819. Throughout the antebellum days Mobile was one of the leading ports in the cotton trade.

Numerous English and French artists of reputation attempted to establish themselves in the bustling community, and those of lesser talent often traveled to outlying plantations in search of portrait commissions. Many of the southern paintings that today are classified as folk art are from the brushes of the itinerants.

Colonization in South Carolina began with the settlement of Charleston in 1670. An excellent harbor, which proved to be the most defensible one between Virginia and Florida, provided security for the town, which was systematically laid out in streets and lots around 1672. Throughout the Colonial period the colony grew, and outlying plantations sprang up along natural intracoastal waterways. By the mid-1670s rice-growing was introduced, and in time Charleston became the center of industry in this southern British colony.

Contact with the mother country and with sister colonial settlements in the West Indies, Barbados, and other parts of British America was strong. Charleston's wealthy farmers and merchants considered London their primary city and frequently journeyed there to transact business, to buy furniture and elegant accessories, and to have their portraits taken. The practice of looking to London in matters of style and taste had already been established in other southern colonies, for Mr. Fitzhugh of The Virginia Company wrote to London in 1681 requesting a "feather bed & furniture, curtains & vallens.

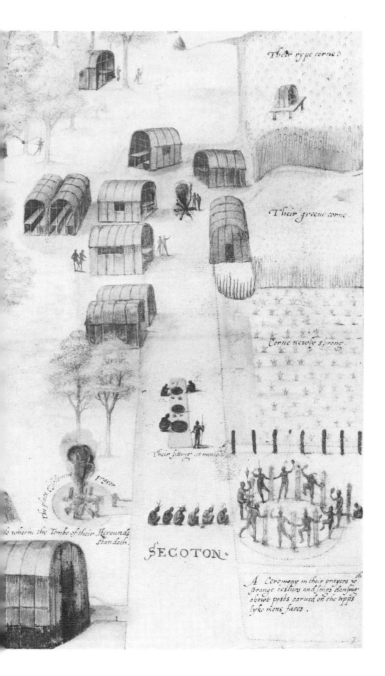

The furniture, Curtains, & Vallens, I would have new, but the bed at second hand, because I am informed new ones are very full of dust." [98]

English artists visited the colony and were favored with extensive patronage by Colonials who were eager to demonstrate their sophistication by sitting for Old World artists rather than the local painter.

The taste for English lifestyles permeated every aspect of South Carolina life. Architecture was patterned upon English models, buildings were furnished with English goods, and Colonials dressed in clothes made from English textiles and were best satisfied with paintings executed by Englishmen or other Europeans. In such a climate the American naïve painter was slow to develop.

Jeremiah Theus (1719–1774) was probably the most popular artist working in the South during the Colonial period. Born in Switzerland, he came to America with his family at the age of sixteen. By the time Theus was twenty-one, he advertised in the *South-Carolina Gazette*

as a limner: "landskips of all sizes, crests and Coats of Arms for Coaches or Chaises. . . . Likewise for the Convenience of those who live in the Country, he is willing to wait on them at their respective Plantations." [99]

Some four years later the artist attempted to expand his activity and offered "to all young Gentlemen and Ladies inclinable to be taught the Art of drawing, that an Evening school for that Purpose will be opened . . . where every Branch of that Art will be taught with the greatest exactness by Jeremiah Theus, limner." [100]

At the time of Theus's death, the *South-Carolina Gazette* reported that he had been "an ingenious and honest man . . . who had followed the Business of a Portrait Painter here upwards of 30 Years." [101]

Natchez, the oldest settlement on the Mississippi River, was founded by the French. The site was first selected around 1700 as a military post, one in a chain designed to halt the westward penetration of the British.

Actual settlement occurred in 1716, and the city remained French until 1765, when it was ceded to Britain at the conclusion of the French and Indian War. Numerous Loyalists who were forced to flee East Coast colonies during the preliminary stages of the American Revolution sought refuge in this British outpost.

In 1779 the town was captured by the Spanish, who retained control until 1795. In 1798 Natchez became the first incorporated town and the first capital of the territory of Mississippi; it was soon the commercial and cultural center of a vast, rich, cotton-producing area.

Ties with France remained strong, and much of the early nineteenth-century folk art from the Natchez area reveals traces of Gallic inspiration.

New Orleans, the Crescent City, the crown jewel of the French in America, was situated about one hundred miles from the mouth of the Mississippi River. Originally founded as the city of La Nouvelle Orleans, it was established by the French governor of Louisiana, Jean Baptiste le Moyne, sieur de Bienville, sometime around 1718. In 1727 most inhabitants still lived in rude cabins fashioned from split cypress boards and roofed with cypress bark.

Although there was little domestic use for the art of painting, the artist received patronage from the church. Two squares on the riverfront close to the center of the city were set apart for the ecclesiastic and military establishment, and it was here in a monastery erected by the Capuchin monks in 1726 that southern French folk painting probably had its beginnings in America. A group of Ursuline nuns came to New Orleans in 1727, and that same year Jesuits arrived and settled on a large tract of land near Bienville.

The territory west of the Mississippi River changed hands several times and came under both Spanish and English control prior to the Second Treaty of Paris in 1783. This treaty confirmed Spain to be the possessor of the territory and granted the United States free and open navigation on the Mississippi River.

The opening of the river hastened the development of the American interior, and in 1795 the Treaty of Madrid allowed the United States access to the port

218 (below). *Ann Broughton* (Mrs. John Gibbs) by Henrietta Johnston, pastel on paper mounted on wood panel, 1720, South Carolina, 11⁵/₁₆" x 8⅜". Johnston is the first artist in America known to have executed pastels. (Yale University Art Gallery; The John Hill Morgan Collection)

219 (right). *Archer Payne, Jr.*, by the Payne Limner, oil on canvas, *c.* 1791, Virginia, 41¾" x 35⅝". A southern gentleman of means frequently had his favorite hunting dog included in his portrait. Perhaps this was an attempt to re-create the famous fox hunts of merry England in the New World. (Mr. and Mrs. William E. Wiltshire III)

220 (below, right). *Martha Payne* by the Payne Limner, oil on canvas, *c.* 1791, Virginia, 43⅞" x 37¾". This painting and that of Archer Payne, Jr., above, are from a group of ten portraits of members of the Archer Payne family. With the exception of two of the sitters, all are shown out of doors, probably on the grounds of New Market, the Payne plantation in Goochland County, Virginia. (Mr. and Mrs. William E. Wiltshire III)

222 (above). *Miss Huysche* by Charles Bridges, oil on canvas, 1735–1740, South Carolina, 24¹³/₁₆″ x 30¹/₁₆″. Inscribed on the lower stretcher is "Miss Huysche." Research has established that the sitter resided in Charleston. (Greenfield Village and Henry Ford Museum)

223 (below). *Ralph Izard* by Jeremiah Theus (b.c. 1719–d.c. 1774), oil on canvas, South Carolina, 37¹³/₁₆″ x 30¾″. (Greenfield Village and Henry Ford Museum)

221 (above). *Edward Jaquelin, Jr.* (1716–1734), attributed to the Jaquelin Limner, oil on canvas, *c.* 1722, Virginia, 31½″ x 26″. Wealthy southern planters preferred to have their portraits painted in England rather than by native itinerant artists. Consequently there is no large body of seventeenth-century southern painting. The Jaquelin Limner was probably a semiprofessional artist working in and around Williamsburg during the first quarter of the eighteenth century. Like William Fitzhugh, a painter working in Virginia in 1698, the Jaquelin Limner most likely ordered his supplies from London. Fitzhugh, in a letter to John Cooper, requested that he forward "six three quartered Lacken book frames for pictures, well burnished, about 40 or 50 shillings worth of colours for painting wt., pencils, walnut Oyl & Linseed Oyl proportionably together with half a doz 3 quarter clothes to set up a painter."[10] (Virginia Museum of Fine Arts; lent by the Ambler Family)

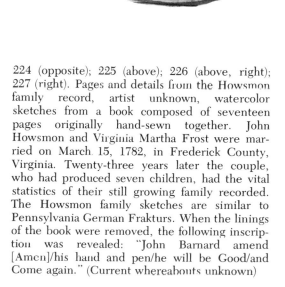

224 (opposite); 225 (above); 226 (above, right); 227 (right). Pages and details from the Howsmon family record, artist unknown, watercolor sketches from a book composed of seventeen pages originally hand-sewn together. John Howsmon and Virginia Martha Frost were married on March 15, 1782, in Frederick County, Virginia. Twenty-three years later the couple, who had produced seven children, had the vital statistics of their still growing family recorded. The Howsmon family sketches are similar to Pennsylvania German Frakturs. When the linings of the book were removed, the following inscription was revealed: "John Barnard amend [Amen]/his hand and pen/he will be Good/and Come again." (Current whereabouts unknown)

228 (right). *The Family of Mrs. John Morel,* artist unknown, oil on canvas, third quarter of the eighteenth century, Savannah, Georgia, 51½" x 41" (the painting has been cut down). It is believed that this family portrait was executed prior to the death of John Morel, husband of the woman and father of the children in the picture. The portion of the painting that included John Morel, who probably stood to the right of the two children holding the birds in the hat, was cut off after his death in 1776. The widowed Mrs. Morel married Richard Wylly of Savannah in 1801, and the painting descended through the Wylly family. Mrs. Morel's dress is nearly identical to the one worn by Mrs. Archibald Bullock, also of Savannah, in a similar conversation piece. (Telfair Academy of Arts and Sciences; gift of Miss Caroline Lamar Woodbridge)

229 (below). *Alexander Spotswood Payne and His Brother John Robert Dandridge Payne with Their Nurse,* attributed to the Payne Limner, oil on canvas, *c.* 1790, Goochland County, Virginia, 56½" x 69". Elaborate conversation pieces were far more popular in the South than in New England. (Virginia Museum of Fine Arts; gift of Miss Dorothy Payne)

154

230 (above). *The McCormick Family* by Joshua Johnston (1765–1830), oil on canvas, 1805, Maryland, 50⅞" x 69⅝". Johnston, a black man, was one of the few artists of his race to achieve significant recognition during the early Federal period. Many of the South's most prominent citizens sat for him. (Maryland Historical Society)

231 (below). *Mr. James Raglen and Wife* by Dupue, watercolor on paper, dated August 1820, Clark County, Kentucky, 12" x 14½". England's cultural ties to the South were strong, and Dupue relied upon the British convention of placing the subjects close to the viewer and allowing their impressive ancestral estate to fill the background. The Raglens sit in painted country chairs. (Private collection)

of New Orleans. In 1803 the Louisiana Territory was purchased by the United States. Because of the constant change of political authority, there was no consistent development of artistic activity in the area. Certainly very little folk painting, other than religious works, remains from the early French and Spanish days.

As settlements sprang up along the entire length of the Mississippi during the nineteenth century, New Orleans became a melting pot of humanity. The folk artist flourished.

In the portions of the South settled by English colonists, lifestyles also tended to be conducive to the arts —both academic and folk. While there were some cities— such as Jamestown and Williamsburg, Virginia; Charleston, South Carolina; Louisville, Kentucky; and Annapolis, Maryland—most southern Colonials lived on large plantations and concerned themselves with agrarian pursuits. In 1686 Durand de Dauphine recorded in a description of Virginia how the successful plantation

155

owners lived: "they barter with tobacco as though it were specie. With it they buy land, they rent it, they buy cattle, & as they can get anything they need in exchange for this commodity, they become so lazy that *they send to England* for clothes, linen, hats, women's dresses, shoes, iron tools, nails, & even wooden furniture, although their own wood is very fine."[102]

Rich and powerful plantation families like the Carters, the Shirleys, and the Pages set a precedent by pyramiding their holdings and squeezing the independent small farmer into a position of tenant laborer. Their wealth and power enabled them to build mammoth, stylish plantation manors. Obviously the folk artist had little place in this society, for it was certainly more fashionable to have one's portrait painted in London while there on a business trip trading tobacco than to sit for itinerant painters who trekked through the hinterlands in search of commissions.

In opposition to this lavish lifestyle, Thomas Jefferson described the homes of the tenant farmers, who barely managed to eke out a living: "The private buildings are very rarely constructed of stone or brick, much the greatest portion being of scantling and boards, plastered with lime. It is impossible to devise things more ugly, uncomfortable, and happily more perishable. There are two or three plans, on one of which, according to its size, most of the houses in this state are built."[103]

For the more successful tenant farmer and for the modest plantation owner, the work of the traveling portraitist sufficed.

Baltimore received its name from the family of the Barons Baltimore, who established Maryland in the early seventeenth century. This "tobacco port" was chartered in 1729. Within the next twenty years local landowners switched to the cultivation of wheat, which they milled for export.

By the beginning of the American Revolution Baltimore had developed into a bustling port with a population of around seven thousand. The imagination of the folk artist was fired by the sparks that flew from the conflict. Wartime heroes such as George Washington became household gods for the newly independent American.

The Baltimore painter Frederick Kemmelmeyer (active 1788–1803) is best known for his Washington-related paintings, which include *Washington Reviewing the Western Army at Fort Cumberland, Maryland.* Kemmelmeyer announced in a 1788 issue of the *Maryland Gazette* that he had "opened a Drawing-School for young Gentlemen." He also advertised that he executed "Miniatures and other Sizes in Oil and Water-Colour." In 1800 he again advertised as a portrait painter in miniature and watercolor and announced the establishment of "An Evening Drawing-School for the instruction of young gentlemen who may have a desire of learning that polite art."[104]

By the time the American Revolution had ended, several black artists had earned a reputation for their skillful portraits.

Joshua Johnston, the best documented of all eighteenth-century black artists, was listed in the Baltimore directory as a portrait painter or limner between 1796 and 1824. A "free householder of color," it appears that he was probably a slave or house servant who obtained his freedom.

Johnston's work strongly recalls the paintings of Charles Peale Polk, who had been very active in Baltimore during the 1790s. His exceptional talent earned for him a considerable number of commissions from prominent Baltimore families. In all of his portraits the poses are similar, and like many folk painters, the artist appears to have had great difficulty with hands. Decorative accessories were used and reused and quite possibly were props. It is thought that Johnston might well have been a servant to the Moale family, for whom he executed numerous portraits, including one of Colonel John Moale. At one time the artist was listed as residing on the same street as the Moales. It is possible that he even maintained a studio adjacent to Colonel Moale's house.

Johnston had black competitors in Baltimore, for G. W. Hobbs, a Methodist minister, is believed to have

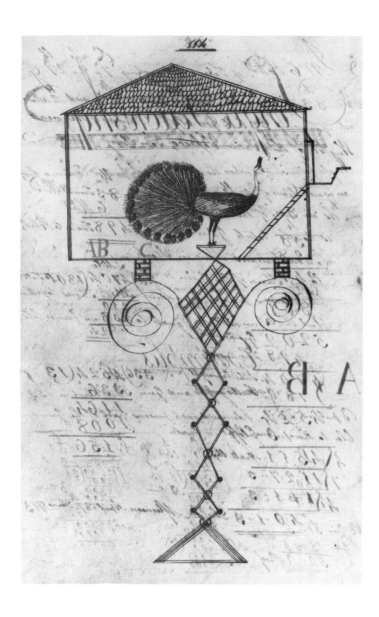

executed, in 1784, a pastel portrait of Richard Allen, the first bishop of the African Methodist Church. Hobbs too was successful and established himself as the official portrait painter of the Methodist Episcopal church in the area.

During the eighteenth century black artists enjoyed considerable success in other American cities. The following advertisement appeared in a Boston newspaper: "Negro artist. At McLean's Watch-Maker, near Town-Hall, is a Negro man whose extraordinary Genius has been assisted by one of the best Masters in London; he takes faces at the lowest Rates. Specimens of his performance may be seen at said Place." [105]

Even Gilbert Stuart obtained some of his rudimentary training from a black artist, for Peterson's *History of Rhode Island* states that he "derived his first impression of drawing from witnessing Neptune Thurston, a slave who was employed in his master's cooper shop, sketch likenesses on the heads of casks." [106]

Portraits painted by "colored mechanics" named Vidal and Wilson were displayed in Philadelphia in 1852, and Joe, a runaway slave who fled to Milwaukee,

Wisconsin, in the mid-nineteenth century, executed a creditable portrait of a grocer's son and daughter (fig. 322) after his escape.

A partial list from the 1856 census of free colored people in Charleston, South Carolina, indicates the variety of trades practiced by blacks. Listed by profession, they included 50 tailors, 2 coopers, 11 shoemakers, 4 dressmakers, 2 cabinetmakers, and 6 painters.

Blacks often reverted to their pre-American heritage and attempted to adapt it to the lifestyle they encountered in the New World:

The transition from Africa to America must have been extremely difficult. The Africans were, literally, torn "between two cultures," and struggled to adjust themselves to a new way of life while at the same time trying to retain what little they could of their African heritage. This was made especially difficult because there was a need to adjust not only to the European culture in which they found themselves, but also to the Africans of other tribes with whom they were thrown. [107] On the large southern plantations there were some factors that helped the slave to bridge the gap between the two cultures, European and African, in spite of their many differences. For one thing, although there were some cities of note in West Africa, most of the slaves came from an agricultural society rather than an urban one. The cultivation of such crops as cotton, rice, or indigo was familiar to them. The work in the fields, the opportunity to hunt and fish occasionally, to plant a small "patch" of one's own, to spend some spare time at handcrafts such as woodcarving, basketry, or net-making, was not dissimilar to life in an African village—at least on a superficial level.

The African had come from a society in which the individual identified his welfare with the welfare of the group. Stringent behavioral patterns were set by that society, and punishment of infractions was harsh and swift. The individual was expected to share with others and in turn expected others to share with him. Land was not owned by individuals, but by the community or family. Gold did not belong to the commonality, but to the king. Suffering, even death, were sometimes required of the individual for the benefit of king or community. But if the king's demands seemed at times cruel and arbitrary (like the master's in America) the African

nevertheless had the assurance of his patriarchal guidance and protection. All these aspects were more or less true of the plantation community.[108]

In the slave society of the South, therefore, it is not surprising that traditional African ideas should permeate plantation paintings. *The Old Plantation* (fig. 234), by an unknown artist, depicts a slave wedding and includes several Africanisms. The dancing figures quite probably are executing a traditional African dance. The custom of using scarves and canes as an integral part of dance movement was and continues to be widespread in Africa. The stringed instrument has been identified as a molo and the drum as a gudu-gudu. Many of the participants in the festivities wear textile headdresses of Yoruba cloth. In the distant background of this striking picture stands the master's imposing plantation house.

The Old Plantation was probably executed by a black artist, for the portraits of the men and women are highly individualized. There is a complete lack of the stereotyping that is so often encountered in the early pictures in which whites depicted blacks. This painting was originally found in South Carolina, an area where black slaves were received directly from Africa and where the survival of African traditions tended to be especially strong.

Savannah, like Charleston, was an English settlement and boasted a fine seaport located at the mouth of the Savannah River. The site was laid out by James Oglethorpe according to plans drawn in England. The original settlement was established in 1733 and by the mid-eighteenth century had become the center of a vast export and import business, with many of the ships clearing port headed directly for England. Throughout the entire Revolution, the city remained for the most part sympathetic to the Loyalist forces.

Northern settlers who fought in Georgia during the Revolution were attracted by the temperate climate and remained when hostilities had ceased. Georgia granted land to over nine thousand veterans after the war. Of those, only two thousand were native Georgians. One North Carolinian who settled in the new state in 1782 wrote home, "Georgia must in a few years be one of the Richest States in the Union, and Where I've no doubt you may live happy and secure a lasting and Valuable Estate for your self & family." [109] James Jackson wrote a friend in 1797, "Some thousands of people are now moving into this State. They will rush like a torrent in search of subsistence." [110]

Cotton, lumber, rice, tar, and turpentine were among the early exports. Upon the development of the cotton gin by Eli Whitney in 1793, cotton became the primary economic basis for a burgeoning plantation system. The importance of the port increased and transportation to the interior was developed, making it easier for the folk portraitist to travel to the back country.

234 (opposite). *The Old Plantation*, artist unknown, watercolor on paper, *c.* 1800, South Carolina, 11¾″ x 17⅞″. During the eighteenth century, black slaves from the Hausa and Yoruba tribes of northern and southwestern Nigeria and British West Africa were brought directly to Charleston. The blacks represented in this picture were probably engaged in a secular dance that was a frequent part of festivals or other nonreligious celebrations. The cane held by the man might indicate that this scene was a slave wedding, for an important part of the marriage ceremony was jumping over a stick. The stringed instrument resembles an African *molo*. The drum of Yoruba origin is called a *gudugudu*. The plantation house in the background of the painting is believed to have stood between Orangeburg and Charleston, South Carolina. (Abby Aldrich Rockefeller Folk Art Center)

235 (above, left); 236 (above). Pair of pinprick portraits signed "Miss M. Brook," watercolor on paper, *c.* 1800, New Orleans, 8¼″ x 6¼″. The textured surface on these pictures was created by pricking the paper repeatedly with a pin. This technique was utilized primarily during the eighteenth and nineteenth centuries. (America Hurrah Antiques, N.Y.C.)

237 (left). Birth and baptismal certificate for Elias Hamman by Barbara Becker, watercolor on paper, 1806, Shenandoah County, Virginia, 15″ x 12½″. (Mr. and Mrs. William E. Wiltshire III)

When John Vinton was sent to Georgia on a mission in 1827 by President Adams, he recorded that he found himself "amidst a rude homely people, full of pride & high-toned republicanism." [111]

The vitality of the lifestyle on the Georgia frontier inspired many folk painters to record the rough and tumble life of a westward-moving nation.

Contrasting with that lifestyle is the portrait of Robert Ransome Billups (fig. 243) from Georgia, which illustrates the favorite English and southern pastime: riding to the hounds. Billups was killed by Creek Indians at the Battle of Shepard's Plantation in Stuart County on June 9, 1836. He and his wife, Elizabeth Ware Fullwood Billups, had three children. The paintings of the Billupses are attributed to Edwin B. Smith, portraitist and historical painter, who is known to have worked in Cincinnati, Ohio, in 1815; at Troy, Ohio, in 1832; and in New Orleans in 1841.

Though Louisville, Kentucky, was visited by the French in the last half of the seventeenth century and by French and British traders during the mid-eighteenth century, no real effort was made to chart the wilderness area until Captain Thomas Bullitt received a commission from William and Mary College in Virginia to survey the land in 1773.

In 1780 the Virginia legislature incorporated a growing settlement under the name of Louisville, in recognition of the assistance given by the French King Louis XVI to the Colonial effort during the Revolutionary War.

During the next thirty-one years the infant town became a frontier and flatboat trading center that grew significantly as a result of the introduction of steam navigation.

In 1811 when Nicholas Roosevelt docked the *New Orleans*, the first steamboat on the western waters, at Louisville, he inaugurated a new era. With it came unprecedented prosperity for the developing community. Successful Louisville merchants provided a likely clientele for the folk portraitist, and in the second and third quarters of the nineteenth century Louisville became a frequent stop on the itinerary of the wandering folk painter.

Nearly 100,000 acres in the central Carolina piedmont was acquired by the Moravian church during the mid-eighteenth century. The colonists who began to build a large town on the Wachovia tract in North Carolina in 1766 already had well-established folk traditions that had been developed over nearly three centuries. The Moravians had attempted to colonize elsewhere in America previously. Under the leadership of Count Zinzendorf of Saxony the Moravians first came to America. The count acquired land in Georgia in 1734, and in 1735 an establishment party was sent to colonize the New World.

The Georgia settlement was abandoned in 1740 because of hostilities between the English and the Spanish in Florida; the colonists left Savannah and moved north to Pennsylvania. In the northern state they instituted numerous towns, including Bethlehem and Nazareth.

Because of their great skill in utilizing natural resources, the Moravians were encouraged by the lord proprietors of the North Carolina colony in 1752 to explore the possibility of building a new Moravian settlement in that area.

By 1753 colonists traveled from Pennsylvania and founded Bethabara. In 1759 new settlers developed Bethania, and in the following years several other farm settlements were built on the Wachovia tract, which had been named in honor of the ancestral Zinzendorf estate. Salem, the place of peace, was from the first intended to be the large central town of the entire Moravian colony.

The Moravian church grew out of the beliefs of a small band of followers of the Bohemian John Huss, who had been burned at the stake in 1415 by the Roman Catholic church for his heretical ideas. Prior to their arrival in America, the Moravians suffered persecution at the hands of various other religious groups.

The Moravian way of life followed concepts popular in the primitive Christian church and the belief that good deeds were more important than dogma. In the communal society each person contributed what he could and shared according to his need. Communities were divided according to age, sex, and marital status into groups called *choirs*. Land was owned by the church. Prices for goods produced were determined by ruling elders. In fact, every aspect of daily life was administered by one of three ruling boards, which had to give approval even for marriages.

Folk arts in the Moravian settlements were extensive, and painting flourished in the conservative settlements, where tradition tended to be the ruling doctrine.

In Salem there was a lively interest in music that in part came out of the chorales sponsored by the church. Musical instruction, including vocal training, instrumental technique, and theoretical study, was an integral part of the school curriculum.

A watercolor birthday greeting for Jacob Van Vleck, a minister and musician of Bethlehem, Pennsylvania, is dated 1795. This fascinating document shows Brother Van Vleck accompanying Moravian sisters or possibly young girls in a Bethlehem boarding school for which he was the local inspector. The watercolor might well have been executed by a student of John Valentine Haidt (1700–1780), a portrait and religious painter who had been born in Danzig and came to America in 1754, settling in the Moravian community in Bethlehem, Pennsylvania. Haidt, who had some academic training prior to coming to America, painted numerous portraits and several religious pictures that were used to decorate local Moravian churches.

A Moravian artist who achieved recognition beyond the religious community was Christian Daniel Welfare (Wohlfahrt) (1796–1841) from Salem. Welfare's portrait of Wilhelm Ludwig Benzien (1797–1832), who was business manager and music instructor of Salem, is a sound indication of the community's concern for music, for Benzien is shown with a violin in his hand. The view through the window is of Salem.

During the first quarter of the nineteenth century conservative church elders maintained a tight rein upon the community. In the second quarter of the century better transportation and increased communication with the outside world caused the individual member of the Moravian church to reject the communal way of life. The free enterprise system emerged. This dissolution of inherited cultural traditions, brought about by inroads of Victorianism resulting from increasing American industrialization, was a phenomenon that occurred wherever isolated cultural groups had established themselves during the eighteenth century.

John Toole (1815–1860) was born in Dublin, Ireland, and taken to Charlottesville, Virginia, as a young boy. Many documents relating to him and his art survive. From them it is possible to reconstruct both his private and his professional life and to see how a primitive painter could blossom into a highly competent artist.

Toole began painting at the age of seventeen, and soon after his marriage in 1836 he began to rely entirely on commissions to support his growing family.

Little is known about Toole's general education, but it is certain that in either 1832 or 1833 he journeyed to Harper's Ferry, where he achieved a fair measure of success. A letter from a gentleman in Harper's Ferry to Toole reveals, "Mr. Hoffman tells me that you are 'John Toole pinx' and I suppose that he told you that I had got to be a 'dubber that could but make resemblance faint'—True, true—I'm glad of your success and congratulate you—but I do it not without some Idea of the 'row you have had to hoe' for to be a painter is to be bandied about from pillar to post and never satisfying others and never satisfied with yourself." [112]

Toole undoubtedly relied upon drawing books for part of his self-training, for he owned two: *The Key to the Art of Drawing the Human Figures Commencing With the Features and Progressing to Heads, Limbs and Trunks, with their Principles of Proportion, and their Application to Attitude, Comprised in Twenty Four Lithographic Plates, Each Plate Accompanied with Letterpress Instruction Showing How to Proceed on Simple and Correct Principles Well Calculated for a Self-Instructor, an Amateur's Companion, or a Teacher's Assistant. The Whole Designed and Executed by John Rubens Smith, Teacher of Drawing, Painting, and Perspective. Published by Samuel M. Stewart, No. 122 Chester Street, Philadelphia. C. Alexander, Printer, 1831;* and *Heads, Representing the Various Passions of the Soul, as They Are Expressed in the Human Countenance: Drawn by*

238 (below). View of the west front of Mount Vernon, showing a family group on the bowling green, artist unknown, oil on canvas, c. 1794, southern, 21½" x 28¾". This picture was carried from the area of Old Point Comfort, Virginia, to New England soon after the Civil War. It was bequeathed to the Mount Vernon Ladies' Association by a descendant of a Union soldier. (Mount Vernon Ladies' Association of the Union)

that Great Master Monsr. Le Brun, and Finely Engraved on Twenty Folio Copper Plates: Near the Size of Life (London 1794).

Toole was a Mason and found his association with the secret order valuable beyond its social implications. Some eight years after he began painting, he recorded his success in obtaining commissions for portraits and his use of the Masonic Order to seek out the financial reliability of prospective sitters:

> I have engaged a good many faces to do in this place, and many of the neighboring farmers talk of having their portraits painted. I have 5 portraits on hand at twelve dols. apiece, they are most finished. I have done 2 miniatures at 10 dols. and one crayon likeness at 3 dols. My reason for being so particular is to show you that I am doing something more than clearing expenses. I pay 5 dols. a week for myself and horse, and the use of a room to work in, and I think it is enough. I will have to credit some of the work: but I first find out whether a man is responsible or not before I engage work from him on those terms. But you wish to know how I a stranger can ascertain this. I will tell you; I have found 5 good brother Masons here and if a man talks of having work done I go to one of them and inquire whether or not he is good pay, and he tells me all about him. It is true any other man could do so, but perhaps he would then go and tell such a man that I was doubtful about him, and by so doing render me unpopular. My brother will do nothing to injure me.[113]

Being an itinerant painter had its disadvantages. Toole recorded at one time in his career that he was engaged to paint six portraits, and evidently they were all for members of the family of an ancient gentleman. He wrote to a friend his fear that the old man might be taken sick and perhaps not recover, and though it would keep him on the road for an extended period of time, he felt the necessity for postponing his return home to avoid the possibility of losing the old man before he finished the commission and received payment.

In addition to full-sized portraits, Toole painted numerous miniatures, a branch of portraiture that he found difficult since the small work obviously bothered his eyes: "but owing to my working on a very small miniature for Mr. Hill (which Sarah saw) my eyes got to be very sore, and then being very busy here since, they were so bad on Saturday that I had to use something to ease them. But O! such care! On Sunday I had to sit in a dark room, and could not even look at the light therefore I could not write . . . My eyes are greatly better although still quite sore."[114]

Like many folk painters, Toole developed formulas that enabled him to execute portraits in a remarkably quick period of time. Under satisfactory conditions he could finish five portraits a week: "I have commenced five portraits, one of which is complete. I shall finish all during this coming week, if my health continues good,

239 (opposite). *Wilhelm Ludwig Benzien* (1797–1832) by Daniel Welfare (1796–1841), oil on linen, c. 1830, North Carolina, 21½" x 17½". Benzien was business manager and music instructor for the Moravian settlement in Salem, which is visible through the window. (Old Salem, Inc.)

240 (above). *A View of Salem in North Carolina* by Ludwig Gottfried von Hedeken, watercolor, dated 1787, dimensions unavailable. (Current whereabouts unknown)

241 (below). *Salem Square* by Elias Vogler, watercolor, c. 1845, southern, dimensions unavailable. (Current whereabouts unknown)

242 (bottom). *Bethabara Church and Parsonage, Salem, North Carolina*, by Julius Mickey (1832–1916), pencil drawing, 1846, North Carolina, 11½" x 16". Bethabara Church was built in 1788; the artist was a tinsmith at Salem. (Old Salem, Inc.)

243 (above). *Robert Ransome Billups*, attributed to Edwin B. Smith, oil on canvas, *c.* 1827, Clarke County, Georgia, 33½″ x 34¾″. Edwin B. Smith must have traveled extensively in search of commissions, for he is known to have worked in Cincinnati, Ohio, in 1815; to have been located in Troy, Ohio, in 1832; and to have moved on to New Orleans, the Crescent City, in 1841. Billups married Elizabeth Ware Fullwood in Clarke County, Georgia, in 1818. He was killed by Creek Indians in the Battle of Shepard's Plantation in Stuart County in 1836. This portrait and the accompanying portrait of Mrs. Billups, opposite, hung in Eagle Tavern at Watkinsville, Georgia, until 1945. The tavern was built in 1789 as Fort Edwards, a precaution against Indian attack. In 1801 it was converted to a stagecoach stop and remained in continuous use as a hotel through 1930. Southern gentlemen, in the traditional English manner, frequently had a hunting scene included in the background of their portraits. (William and Florence Griffin)

244 (left). *Elizabeth Ware Fullwood Billups* by Edwin B. Smith, oil on canvas, *c.* 1827, Clarke County, Georgia, 33¾″ x 26¾″. The portrait of Mrs. Billups is inscribed on the reverse of the canvas: "Painted and presented by Edwin B. Smith, Junr. to Mrs. Elizabeth W. Billups, March 1, 1827." (William and Florence Griffin)

245 (below). *Hunting Scene* by Mary Catherine Noel, watercolor on velvet, first half of the nineteenth century, North Carolina, dimensions unavailable. The artist and her three sisters attended the Salem Female Academy, a school founded by the Moravians in 1772 at Winston-Salem, North Carolina. It is believed that this piece was painted while the young woman was at the academy in either 1833 or 1834. Although countless theorems were executed on velvet, realistic scenes such as the one depicted here are far more rare. (Salem Academy and College)

246 (left). *Charleston Square* by Charles J. Hamilton, oil on canvas, 1872, South Carolina, 36⅝" x 38⅝". The artist is well known for his carved wooden tobacconist figures and studies for them executed in watercolor and ink on paper. He was born in Philadelphia and at the age of twenty-three (in 1855) was listed in the local directory as a carver. In 1859 he moved to Washington, where he entered into partnership with Elias W. Hadden, another carver. He resided in Charleston from 1872 to 1873 and was listed in the local directory as a painter. The central building in this painting is the Old Market in Charleston, which was completed in 1841. The structure still stands and now serves as a Confederate Museum; the arcaded space at the street level continues to be used as a marketplace. (Abby Aldrich Rockefeller Folk Art Center)

247 (above). *The Plantation*, artist unknown, oil on wood, c. 1825, southern, 19⅛" x 29½". Nearly every aspect of southern plantation life is evident in this striking and famous painting. The manor house at the top of the hill was obviously maintained by the residents living in the auxiliary buildings. A mill powered by a waterwheel is in the lower right-hand corner of the painting. Imported goods were delivered by ship to the waterfront warehouse. (The Metropolitan Museum of Art; gift of Edgar William and Bernice Chrysler Garbisch)

248 (below). *View of Savannah, 1837,* by Joseph Louis Firmin Cerveau (1812–1896), tempera, dated 1837, Savannah, Georgia, 27½″ x 49½″. This painting was given to the Georgia Historical Society in 1879 by G. B. Carhart of Brooklyn, New York. Carhart had been a Savannah merchant and is believed to have acquired the painting in a raffle. Buildings from many different periods are evident in this panoramic view of one of the South's most beautiful cities. (Georgia Historical Society)

249 (above). Room end from the Alexander Shaw House, Wagram, North Carolina, signed and dated "I. Scott August 17, 1836." The interior of the room was entirely wood-sheathed. The frieze was composed of a decorative border of swags and tassels. The painting over the mantel and between the two windows is titled "Vue of New York." (Abby Aldrich Rockefeller Folk Art Center)

250 (opposite, top). Catawba dining room from a house owned by the Perkins family, who settled in Catawba County, western North Carolina, in the latter part of the eighteenth century. The painted woodwork is inscribed "M. J. Cocker," and the date 1811 was found on the back of a cornice. This painted interior shows the influence of the Classical movement in England, where urns and draped festoons were especially popular during the late eighteenth and early nineteenth centuries. (Museum of Early Southern Decorative Arts)

251 (opposite, middle); 252 (opposite, bottom). Painted walls from the Winemiller House, Helvetia, West Virginia, artist unknown, c. 1880. Country people often attempted to embellish their modest homes with painted decoration and scenes as well. Several vignettes of rural life are included on these sheathed walls. The lower quarter of the wall is marbleized. (Photograph courtesy J. Roderick Moore)

which it has been since I came down. My appetite is ravenous owing to the increased quantity of quinine which I have been taking while here." [115]

While visiting Richmond in 1847, the artist first mentioned the intrusion of the daguerreotype into his life. He noted numerous painters' signs, and referring to the artists, he recorded, "It really appears that they, (and myself in the crowd) have laid regular siege to this place. There are now no less than seven of the male order, (including your humble servant) and one lady, who offer their professional services in Portrait and miniature to the citizens of this Metropolis. Now multiply this number by two or three, it does not matter which, and you can ascertain within a dozen or so, the number of Daguerreotype factories. I was astounded when I discovered so many here, and I give you my word, if it were not for the pictures which I had been engaged to paint here, I would as soon think of setting up as a *Lawyer* or *Dr.* in *Charlottesville*, as a face maker here." [116] Like Erastus Salisbury Field, John Toole used the daguerreotype to assist him with his art: "I am now engaged copying a daguerreotype, and will next paint a child's portrait." [117]

Upon his death in 1860 Toole left behind a large body of work, which in recent years has been catalogued and studied. Though this artist frequently is criticized for the sameness of his characterizations, his pictures reveal the lifestyle, the working methods, the trials, and the tribulations of the journeying painter in the South and his never-ending quest for commissions.

The miniature portrait that was so popular in the North also enjoyed great popularity in the South. Henry Tuckerman, writing in *The Book of the Artists* in 1867, noted the devastating effect that photography had exerted on portraiture in general and miniature painting specifically: "Photography has done and is doing much to banish mediocrity in portraiture and it has in a great measure superseded miniature painting . . . but mechanical ingenuity and scientific success can never take the place of art; for the latter is a product of the soul." [118]

Many of the best miniature portraits were cut from colored paper and pasted onto painted backgrounds. William Henry Brown (1808–1883) carried this technique to a fully realized art form when he created his now famous "black pasties" (fig. 258). The backgrounds have been skillfully rendered in watercolor.

Many black artists suffer a sense of alienation to the white-oriented world they live in. As Cedric Dover so knowingly observed, "The art of American Negroes has always been a minority art in the main stream of American culture. It is a continuity without birthdays. It began when the American Negroes emerged as a group and it will continue as long as they think of themselves as a group, which they will do for generations after they are full partners in their native democracy." [119]

Contemporary southern black artists like Sister

253 (right). *The American Star* by Frederick Kemmelmeyer (active 1788–1803), oil on paper, late eighteenth century or early nineteenth century, southern, 17¾" x 22". Military and political heroes such as George Washington were favorite subjects for the folk artist. (The Metropolitan Museum of Art; gift of Colonel Edgar William and Bernice Chrysler Garbisch)

254 (below). *Howard's Grove Hospital, Richmond, Virginia,* unidentified Confederate soldier, oil on canvas, 1862–1864, southern, 21" x 30⅛". The soldier who painted this picture is believed to have been cared for at the hospital during the Civil War. (Chicago Historical Society)

255 (opposite). *Civil War Military Encampment,* artist unknown, oil on canvas, 1860s, southern, 14¼" x 17⅝". Several of the boats included in the painting are steam operated. Note that the three-masted ship is fitted to run both by sail and by steam. (Private collection)

Gertrude Morgan, Clementine Hunter, Mose Tolliver, Jimmie Suddouth, and Bruce Brice deserve a detailed study, for the painting of black naïve artists in America is decidedly different from that of white artists.

During the twentieth century the black artist continues to reach back to his African heritage. Paintings such as those executed by Thomas Jefferson Flanagan (born 1896) provide a link with a cultural past that the artist can only subconsciously relate with.

Clementine Hunter of Melrose Plantation, Natchitoches Parish, Louisiana, is perhaps the most celebrated of all southern contemporary painters. Hunter knows well the black life that she so touchingly portrays, for as an illiterate black servant she spent over sixty-five years in the fields and as kitchen help at Melrose. It was not until her late sixties that Clementine Hunter began to paint her radiant naïve pictures that depict life and death in a rural southern setting.

Clementine Hunter is a memory painter in that she looks back in time to her childhood on the Little Eva Plantation, where she was born, just up the road from Melrose. She first began painting during the late 1940s, when, serving as a cook, she discovered that a visiting artist from New Orleans had left his paints. She borrowed the pigments and found that she could "mark a painting." Through the years this gifted artist has earned a reputation that causes her admirers to speak of Grandma Moses as the "North's Clementine Hunter." Of her work, she explains, "Cotton's right in front of you; you just have to pick it from the bush. You have to study your head to paint." [120]

Sister Gertrude Morgan, a former gospel singer and street preacher, was born around 1900 and now lives in New Orleans. In 1956 a commandment from the Lord inspired her to become the "bride of the Father and the Christ." [121] Since that time she has opened the Everlasting Gospel Mission, where her efforts to rebuke the devil often bring solace and comfort to supplicants.

Sister Gertrude's mission consists of a room fitted with seats for visitors. Her dress is of fine white linen

256 (right). *Little Eva and Uncle Tom*, artist unknown, oil on canvas, *c.* 1880, southern, 16½″ x 14¾″. Soon after Harriet Beecher Stowe's novel *Uncle Tom's Cabin* was published in 1852, enthusiasm for the emancipation of slaves swept the northern states. Moralistic paintings depicting the voluntary education of blacks were especially popular in the South. (Museum of American Folk Art; gift of Cyril I. Nelson)

257 (below). Immortelle—"A Mon Épouse," artist unknown, enamel on glass and zinc, nineteenth century, France or southern, Diam. 5¼″. Immortelles were reverse paintings on glass that were attached to tombstones to serve as commemorative plaques. Although most immortelles were imported from France, it is believed that some were executed in French-American cities such as New Orleans. (The Historic New Orleans Collection)

258 (below). *Hauling the Whole Week's Picking* by William H. Brown, watercolor and paper collage, *c.* 1842, southern, four panels totaling 108³/₁₆″ x 19⅜″. Silhouette cutters sometimes made "pasties," which were usually pictures cut out of trade magazines and glued onto painted landscapes. In this instance, Brown himself executed the parts to be glued down. These pasties were executed for the young children of Mr. and Mrs. William Henry Vick of Nitta Yuma Plantation, north of Vicksburg, Mississippi. Brown was born in Charleston, South Carolina, in 1808 and died there in 1883. A well-known silhouette artist in later life, he traveled throughout the South as well as New England. (The Historic New Orleans Collection)

259 (above). *Child in a Georgia Interior*, artist unknown, oil on canvas, second half of the nineteenth century, southern, 14⅝″ x 11⅛″. The artist who executed this picture recorded several Victorian conventions. Of special interest are the fireplace and its fire tools and the clay pipe and the glass on the table. (Museum of American Folk Art; gift of Cyril I. Nelson)

260a and 260b (above). *Martha Morris Suddarth* and *Richard Pleasants Suddarth* by John Toole, oil on canvas, first half of the nineteenth century, southern, dimensions unavailable. Mr. and Mrs. Suddarth commissioned the artist to paint their portraits during the early years of their marriage. Stylistically the portraits are similar to any number of likenesses taken during the same period. They are, however, especially interesting when compared to the illustrations opposite, which are daguerreotypes of the same two people at a much later date. Photographs courtesy The New York Public Library. (Current whereabouts unknown)

and the entire mission interior is painted white; even the seats have covers made from sheeting. A sign on the wall reads, "Christ is the head of this house, the unseen host at every meal, the silent listener at every conversation. Missionary Morgan, prophetess." [122] Of her talent, she explains, "When I was a little girl I was always trying to draw something. I used to draw on the ground with a stick. Then sometimes I had a pencil or a crayon and some paper. One day I drew a mountain and a train, and I was in the train waving, and my momma said, 'That girl is goin' to go far away from here'—and she was right." [123]

Sister Gertrude believes her painterly technique is a consequence of divine inspiration. Referring to God, she notes, "He moves my hand. Do you think I would ever know how to do a picture like this by myself?" [124]

Most of Sister Gertrude's paintings include calligraphic inscriptions, and writing becomes an intimate part of the overall design. Her intense religious fervor permeates each of her pictures, and like her art, she is filled with His spirit.

Mose Tolliver of Alabama, one of the most recent discoveries, paints a world that is only his own. Single, quasi-representational figures, hauntingly abstracted, are placed in a reality that is the private domain of the

artist, accessible only through his art. With lyric beauty and iron-fisted surety, this self-taught naïve conjures images that invite comparison with Pablo Picasso and Karel Appel, both names unknown in the Tolliver world.

Jimmie Suddouth, also an Alabama artist, has developed his own technique to produce raw, vital pictures of compelling beauty. Suddouth paints with mud and grows plants in a nearby garden to expand his natural palette. When asked about the source of colors for his forceful pictures, he exclaimed, "Watch this." Striding to the garden, he broke off an amber-hued plant and meticulously began to rub the mud picture on which he was working. "I grows my own," he noted with pride and with dancing eyes, his timeworn hands skillfully dabbing at the unfinished picture, staining it the right color in just the right place. Finished, he stood back from his work of art and grinning broadly, exclaimed, "And that's how I does it. It's one of my best." Each new picture is "one of my best." [125]

Bruce Brice grew up in the French Quarter of New Orleans, where he now resides. Much of his brightly colored festive art centers on the urban world that surrounds him. Brice began painting in his late teens and exhibited with numerous other folk artists on the famed New Orleans landmark, Jackson Square. By 1973 he had been invited to exhibit with two other southern black artists, Sister Gertrude Morgan and Clementine Hunter, at The Museum of American Folk Art in New York City, where their works brought new attention to the contemporary black artist working in America.

Brice, whose first exposure to painting came while he was working as a framer at a New Orleans art gallery, thoroughly enjoys the life of an artist. As he explained, "Painting is what I want to do for the rest of my life." [126]

Philo Levi Willey was born in Canaan, Connecticut, in 1886 and left home at the age of twelve with a five-dollar bill in his pocket and a desire to travel to the big city: New Haven. There he obtained a job as a helper in a furniture warehouse and later worked for a wholesale grocer. Throughout his colorful life he has held jobs as a fireman, a deckhand on a steamboat, a coal hauler, a teamster for the Barnum & Bailey Circus, a lumberman, a farmer, and a cowboy on the Buffalo Bill Ranch in Wyoming. In 1932 he began a job for the Sewerage and Water Board in the City of New Orleans. In time promotions led him to the top position in the organization. He headed the police force and was fondly called "The Chief" by his employees. The Chief began painting in 1970 with watercolor pencils at the encouragement of his artist wife. His more recent works

are executed in acrylic. When asked about his painting *Hilltown*, he wrote,

> The story is about a country boy who worked with his father to hold together and cultivate a part of his ten acres of fertile land for growing cotton. Each year it produced a better crop than the previous year. Using good judgment, he invested the earnings in stock which developed into millions of dollars. This town is named after the sponsor.

> At the age of 32 years, young and healthy, the son built a town on his farm and retired. He first cleared all the unnecessary hills, trees and bushes so that the animals and birds could roam without fear of a hunter. He then built some houses for those people he employed to work on the upkeep of the town. His next project was to build a railroad which ran from other small towns to bring the children to his high school, it also carries mail and freight, he also built a church and a home for a retired preacher. The depot was handled by a retired railroad employee who also had a home over the depot, along the side of the railroad track. He had a park for recreation of the schoolchildren, also there was a river which ran through the land, where fishing was good and boats traveled to large cities, on the

261a and 261b (below). *Martha Morris Suddarth* and *Richard Pleasants Suddarth*, photographs, nineteenth century, dimensions unavailable. In several instances, early painted portraits and photographic portraits of the same sitters exist. Mr. and Mrs. Suddarth sat for the photographer during the later years of their lives. Photographs courtesy The New York Public Library. (Current whereabouts unknown)

262 (left). *Jackson Square, New Orleans,* by Mrs. A. A. Flotte, colored pastels on marbledust paper, third quarter of the nineteenth century, Louisiana, 20¹⁵/₁₆″ x 27⅜″. Around 1850 Jackson Square was updated by the Baroness Pontalba, who erected buildings on two sides of the park. St. Louis Cathedral, the focal point of the square, was redesigned and rebuilt, and the Jackson monument was placed in the center of the square. The ironwork around Jackson Square serves as an outdoor art gallery where contemporary folk artists like "The Chief" (Philo T. Willey) currently exhibit on a regular basis. (The Historic New Orleans Collection)

263 (below). *New Orleans Mansion* by Peter Minchell, watercolor on paper, late 1960s, Florida, 20″ x 24″. Minchell was born in Trier, Germany, in 1889 and came to America in 1906. (Private collection)

Peter Minchell

A LITTLE TOWN WHERE SOME HAD MUCH AND GAVE TO THEM WHO HAD LITTLE AND AMONG THEM ALL THERE WERE NONE WHO WERE IN WANT, THERE WERE JUST ANOUGH

265 (above). *Evergreen Plantation* by James Pritchard, pastel or marbledust paper, last half of the nineteenth century, southern, 8¹¹/₁₆″ x 11¼″. (The Historic New Orleans Collection)

264 (above). *There Were Just Enough* by the Reverend Howard Finster, enamel on plexiglass, 1970s, Georgia, 20″ x 26″. Finster first began to paint biblical scenes as decorative accompaniments to his fantastic outdoor sculpture garden. The artist executes his pictures on found material and will move abandoned refrigerators, stoves, and even bicycle fenders into his sculpture garden and decorate them with scenic views. (Jay Johnson: America's Folk Heritage Gallery)

266 (below). *Fantastic Building* by Jimmie Lee Suddouth, clay fixed to plywood, 1970s, Alabama, 27″ x 37½″. Suddouth paints with clay that he digs from the ground and "fixes" with sugar. He colors his paintings by rubbing plants from his garden over the rough clay surfaces. (Private collection)

267 (right). *The U.S.S. Texas* by William O. Golding (1874–1943), crayon and watercolor on paper, late nineteenth or early twentieth century, Georgia, 9″ x 12″. Golding, a black seaman, recorded many of the ports he had visited. He once wrote: "I have been all over the World, from North, South, East and West and plenty of ports in the Seven (7) Seas, from England to China, Japan, India, Australia, Africa, West Indies, Central America and South America around Cape Horn 23 times Cape of Good Hope 25 or 30 times. . . . Can't get along like I use to do on the ship, so I have to give up going to Sea now only go to Sea now in my sleep."[11] (Hirschl & Adler Galleries)

268 (below). *Cotton Time in Columbus* by Thomas Jefferson Flanagan, oil on canvas, 1959, Georgia, 16″ x 50¼″. The Reverend Thomas Jefferson Flanagan was born in 1896 and grew up near Columbus, Georgia. He taught science and English in the public school system for nine years and became a Methodist minister. His most prolific period as an artist was during the 1950s and 1960s. (Columbus Museum of Arts and Crafts)

269 (opposite). *The Last Judgment* by Robert Hemp (b. 1916), oil on canvas, 1975–1976, Virginia, 48″ x 68″. Hemp was a black house painter who ultimately worked for the State of Virginia and painted the interiors of the public buildings. Religious scenes and depictions from the Bible continue to be popular subjects for the contemporary folk painter. (Private collection)

270a, 270b, 270c (above). *The Family* by Mose Tolliver, house paint on cardboard, *c.* 1976, Alabama, 8½" x 14". Tolliver was injured while working for a furniture store and has been unable to work since. He began painting early in the 1970s, and his imaginative style has brought considerable attention to his work. These three paintings are inscribed on the backs, "Polo Marco," "Parker Dorothy," and "Shakespeare." (Private collection)

other side of the river. He built for himself a nine hole golf course between the river and the state highway which offered a place to ride horses and motorcycles, also to walk, on the other side of the road were two homes for the help, who cared for the cotton patch and raised chickens and pigs, a cow to furnish the milk, a long warehouse to store cotton and a cart to haul the cotton into the warehouse. The women enjoyed doing their washing.

You will notice that as the train approaches the town the station master, the blonde school teacher who has an apartment above the school and the preacher are all out to welcome the children on the first trip to the high school after the vacation. All this was done by a man who loved children, his country, and pleasure for retired people, to help the people to live in a world which "GOD" meant for them to live in peace.

You will notice that there are no police in this town, as all who live there are law abiding and love one another. I suppose you wonder why the large white bird is in the picture. It has been trained to make a lot of noise if he sees a stranger in the town at night. He also has an assistant in the cotton field location, they are sort of watch dogs.[127]

Peter Minchell was born on October 11, 1889, in Treves, Germany, where between 1895 and 1903 he attended a trade school for two-and-a-half years. In 1906 he set sail for New Orleans, Louisiana, and in 1911 moved to Florida, where he worked in the building trade.

By 1960 the artist began to create extraordinary watercolors based upon flora. In 1972 he began to paint his Geological Phenomena series, which brought him to the attention of museum curators across the country.

Minchell's vision is highly personal and derives its strength from his deeply introspective nature.

John William Dey (born *c.* 1915), better known as "Uncle Jack," is a retired policeman who now lives in Richmond, Virginia, where he paints his brittle, enamellike pictures with Tester's airplane paint. Uncle Jack enjoys painting and is extremely demanding of himself: "When I've finished with a painting, I put a bright light on it, and I go over the whole thing with a magnifying glass to see if anything's wrong. Sometimes a picture just doesn't look like it's level, and then I have to put something on to anchor it—something like a cow or a rabbit."[128]

Much of Uncle Jack's art recalls his career at a Maine lumber camp in 1933. The woods, the cabins, the animals, and the birds reappear again and again in his brilliantly colored pictures. He spends much of his time scouting the neighborhood for old frames and then takes immense pleasure in painting the picture to suit the frame.

The Reverend Howard Finster, who lives in a small Georgia town, has only recently turned to painting. Much of his life has been devoted to the construction

271 (above). *Portrait of "Artist, Bone"* (Jimmie Lee Suddouth) by Rance Maddov, Jr., oil on cardboard, mid-1970s, Alabama, 14″ x 20″. Rance Maddov maintained that he was Jimmie Lee Suddouth's grandson. The older artist had taught the young boy to paint; however, he indicated that they were not related. This portrait of a black field hand has great power. (Private collection)

of a "Paradise Garden," which was originally conceived as a plant farm museum. Herbert Hemphill, writing in *Missing Pieces: Georgia Folk Art,* recorded, "There, sparkling in the sunlight is what at first appears to be a giant jeweled ossuary. This remarkable vision, which is actually made of white painted concrete, inset with mirror fragments and all manner of materials, is the incredible shop and 'paradise garden' of the Reverend Howard Finster, a preacher and repair man who has spent years constructing this paean to his God and the Bible. The result is Paradise, a promise of salvation, and a threat of damnation to the sinner." [129]

Anna Wadsworth also noted,

Reverend Finster has slowly installed an assortment of memorabilia contributed by local people. "One little boy came and brought his tonsils. The doctor had put 'em up in alcohol and he wanted them molded in. . . ." The garden walls are concrete, reinforced with hubcaps; and photographs encased in plastic are inset in the walls. Some of the photographs are cut from magazines, and others picture local people.

In 1976, paintings began to appear on boards mounted under television-screen glass and nailed into the wall of Finster's lawn mower repair shop. "Back in the winter I got shut in by cold weather and so these pictures come on my mind and I began to paint 'em while the cold weather was on and I just painted a sluice of them. I have to use car lacquer to paint these pictures so they'll stand the weather."

The light walls of the garden and the mirror fragments everywhere make the sunlight shining on Reverend Finster's flowers and vegetables seem overwhelmingly intense in the heat of the day. But as the day ends, the garden changes. "By nighttime here, there's a couple of pole lights. I have a little chandelier that turns by the breeze . . . the evening breeze . . . and it has mirrors hanging down on it. And every once in a while, you'll look and you'll see shadows going across the trails. . . . And the pumphouse made out of cokecola bottles, you can turn the red lights on in the pumphouse. It's nice to walk of a night in the Garden when everybody's gone, in the cool of the evening. Just you and the Lord. And you can talk and He can tell you things to do. And when He does, there's just something about it that makes us understand real well." [130]

Artistic activity in the South has changed dramatically from the day when Frances Trollope described the quilting techniques and other artistic accomplishments and intellectual achievements of southern women in a very derogatory way: "There is an idleness, a sauntering listlessness, that gives what we call a 'creole manner' to the fine ladies of Baltimore and Washington, which, though not quite what would be most admired, is yet infinitely more a drawing-room manner than any thing to be seen in Ohio; but I did not find that the leisure obtained by the possession of slaves was in many cases employed in the improvement of the mind. The finest ladies I saw either worked muslin or did nothing. The very trifling attempts at music are rarely continued after marriage. The drawings I saw were always most ludicrously bad, though perhaps as good as the masters', and the stock of what is called general information less than I believe any one would believe possible who had not witnessed it." [131]

Were Mrs. Trollope alive today, she would be forced to reevaluate her appraisal after viewing the extraordinary folk paintings of the Georgia artist Mattie Lou O'Kelley. When asked to write a brief autobiographical account of her life, Miss O'Kelley wrote a brief poem that reveals much about her life. A few stanzas are quoted below.

I made no friends, I had no beaus,
I stayed at home.
I piddled at this and that,
I did not roam.

I read and read, each moment lovely
A twilight's purple down.
Invisible stars filled my silent head,
They would not let me down.

But unknowingly we breathe time's grip,
We ride a legless horse,
We go each to our very own,
Happiness or remorse.

A public job I acquired and never liked,
Ten public jobs I got,
Ten jobs I never did like,
The boss never forgot.

Now my one room house has only me,
I never roam,
No lessons have I, but I paint
And paint
And stay at home.

This brilliant artist does indeed paint and paint and stay at home. Through her pictures she has earned a well-deserved place in the history of American folk art.

Miss O'Kelley's poem poignantly illustrates the life-style of many of America's rural artists, who often work in cultural isolation even today.

272 (opposite, above). *The Lighthouse* by Earl Cunningham, oil on board, *c.* 1960, Florida, 18″ x 24″. (Jay Johnson: America's Folk Heritage Gallery)

273 (opposite, below). *Self-Portrait* by Bruce Brice, acrylic on canvas, 1971, Louisiana, 24″ x 30″. (Artist's collection)

274 (above). *Gathering Gourds* by Clementine Hunter, house paint on cardboard, second half of the twentieth century, Mississippi, W. 96″. This painting is said to have been part of a wall on a field hand's house at Melrose Plantation, Mississippi. Clementine Hunter, a black artist, is one of the South's most famous contemporary naïve artists. (Private collection)

Plate 51 (left). *Alabama Gentleman*, artist unknown, oil on canvas, 1866, Huntsville, Alabama, 36″ x 30″. The document that the gentleman holds is inscribed with two names: J. K. Collins and P. M. Rose. Perhaps these are the names of the sitter and the artist. (America Hurrah Antiques, N.Y.C.)

Plate 52 (below). *McMeens's Surgeons Call at Camp Taylor, Huntsville, Ala.*, artist unknown, watercolor on paper, late nineteenth century, 8½″ x 11½″. Dr. McMeens was a regimental surgeon of the Ohio Volunteers. He was highly praised for his work in the Battle of Perryville, Kentucky, October 8, 1862. Suffering from exposure and overwork in connection with that battle, McMeens died on October 30, 1862. (America Hurrah Antiques, N.Y.C.)

Mc Meens's Surgeon's Call at Camp Taylor, Huntsville Ala.

Plate 53 (above). *Mrs. Keyser*, artist unknown, watercolor on paper, dated December 1, 1834, Baltimore, Maryland, 23″ x 18″. Inscribed on the back of the picture is the address "20 N. Eutaw Street." The original framer's label indicates that it was made by "M. Barret & Bros. Carvers & Gilders No. 82 Howard Street, corner Saratoga, Baltimore; Looking glasses, portrait and picture frames and gilt work in all its variety, also plain and fancy wood frames and importers of French and German looking glass plates, fine engravings." This extraordinary watercolor is a prime example of the best in American folk painting. (Burton and Kathleen Purmell)

Plate 54 (opposite, **above**). *Modern Inventions* by Sister Gertrude Morgan, oil on cardboard, *c.* 1970, Louisiana, 14″ x 18″. Sister Gertrude, a black New Orleans artist, uses the Bible as a source of inspiration for her paintings, which she frequently inscribes. She has written on this picture "Modern inventions fulfilling Prophecy. Many shall Run to and fro and knowledge shall Be in creased. Dan. 12:4." (Private collection)

Plate 55 (below). *Portrait of Miles B. Carpenter* by Uncle Jack Dey, airplane model paint on board, *c.* 1973, Virginia, 20″ x 24″. Uncle Jack has depicted Miles B. Carpenter, the well-known contemporary folk sculptor, in a complex rural setting that is characteristic of Dey's paintings. (Private collection)

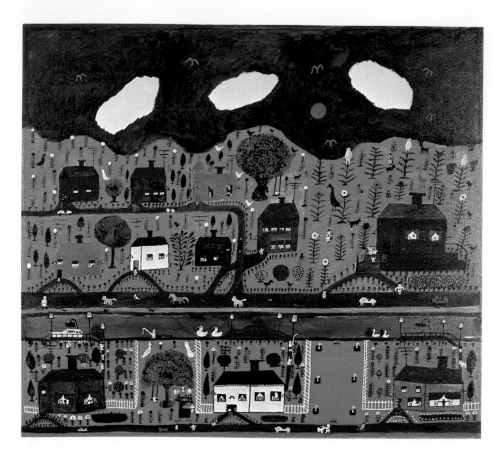

Plate 56 (left). *Suburb of Hill Town* by "The Chief" (Philo T. Willey), oil on canvas, 1976, New Orleans, 40″ x 40″. The artist's wife is a professional portraitist who has exhibited in several different galleries in New Orleans. Her husband, a self-taught primitive, began painting late in life and first showed his work on "the fence" that surrounds historic Jackson Square in New Orleans. (Private collection)

Plate 57 (below). *Picking Blackberries on the Fourth of July* by Mattie Lou O'Kelley, oil on board, 1974, Georgia, 24″ x 36″. Miss O'Kelley's paintings abound with detail revealing much about the rural southern life in and around her hometown, Maysville, Georgia. With an unfailing sense of design, she depicts a way of life fast disappearing. (Jay Johnson: America's Folk Heritage Gallery)

THE WESTERN RESERVE, FIRELANDS, VIRGINIA MILITARY LANDS, THE OLD NORTHWEST TERRITORY, AND THE NORTHWEST

275 (preceding page). *Brigham Young and His Wife and Six Children* by William Warner Major, oil on canvas, *c.* 1847, Utah, 28″ x 36″. Major, who was born in England, joined the Church of the Latter-Day Saints there in 1842 and immigrated to America in 1844. He accompanied the Mormon trek from Illinois to Utah in 1846–1848. This idealized portrait of the Brigham Young family was completed around 1847. © LDS. (Church of Jesus Christ of Latter-Day Saints)

276 (right). *Mr. John Jackson* by Sheldon Peck, oil on wood panel, *c.* 1820, Vermont, 21½″ x 16¼″. John Jackson (1765–1830) was born in Massachusetts and lived there until 1794, when he moved to Milton, Vermont. *Mr. John Jackson* is one of a pair of paintings that is the second earliest known work by the artist, who worked first in New England, eventually moved to western New York, migrated west, and finally settled in Illinois. This painting is included in this section because it shows the stylistic difference between the artist's New England pictures and those executed in the Midwest, as seen below. (Private collection)

THE WESTERN RESERVE, FIRELANDS, VIRGINIA MILITARY LANDS, THE OLD NORTHWEST TERRITORY, AND THE NORTHWEST

Throughout the entire nineteenth century Americans continued to trek westward. This movement of the population in part became possible because France ceded all of her American lands as far west as the Rocky Mountains to the United States in the Louisiana Purchase of 1803. By 1848, at the close of the Mexican-American War, the territories of Texas, New Mexico, and California also became part of the United States.

During the early decades of the nineteenth century keen interest in western exploration was expressed in Washington, the new political capital, and in Philadelphia, the young nation's intellectual center. Exploratory expeditions were sent forth to record the lands that previously had been the domain of the native American.

The original charters granted to the seaboard Colonies gave them the right to all territories in their latitude from the Atlantic to the great sea in the west. The area of Pennsylvania, north of the Ohio River, and east of the Mississippi River came to be referred to as the Old Northwest Territory. Following the Revolution, the western claims of the seaboard states were surrendered to the new national government. There were exceptions. The Virginia Military Lands in the southern part of Ohio were reserved by the State of Virginia and were used to compensate soldiers for their part in the Revolution. The Western Reserve, made up of a strip of land some 120 miles long, starting at the western edge of the Pennsylvania border and running along the forty-first parallel straight west 120 miles and north to Lake Erie, was held by the State of Connecticut. The Western Reserve of Connecticut was settled almost exclusively by people from New England and represents the single largest homogeneous migration ever to take place in this nation. This would explain the reappearance later in the Western Reserve of techniques used by folk artists in Connecticut.

At the western edge of the Western Reserve two counties were set aside for people living along the Connecticut shore whose homes had been burned during the Revolutionary War. Folk paintings from this area, known as Firelands, also show strong similarities to Connecticut examples.

In 1803 Ohio became the first section of the Old Northwest Territory to be admitted as a state. By 1825 the national road had extended across Ohio and into Indiana. In the same year the Erie Canal was completed

277 (opposite, below). *Mr. and Mrs. David Crane* by Sheldon Peck, oil on canvas, *c.* 1845, Illinois, 35¾" x 43¾". Peck's earliest pictures from his New England period, as seen above, are usually waist-length portraits painted on panels. During his New York period, he painted both half-length and three-quarter-length portraits on panels, and during his Illinois period, he executed several portraits featuring the subjects in dramatic settings. Many of his later paintings are on canvas, and often the frames for them are also painted directly on the canvas, as in this example. (Mr. and Mrs. William E. Wiltshire III)

278 (above). *Mrs. Isaac Augustus Wetherby* by Isaac Augustus Wetherby, oil on canvas, *c.* 1845, 32½" x 25". Wetherby, like Peck, began his artistic career in the East and ultimately traveled west to seek his fortune. (The New-York Historical Society)

279 (above). *Indians on the Detroit River*, signed F. E. Cohen, oil on canvas, *c.* 1840, Michigan, 43″ x 27″. (Mr. and Mrs. James O. Keene)

280 (below). *Scene on the Detroit River* by F. E. Cohen, oil on canvas, *c.* 1840, Michigan, 43″ x 27″. Cohen, an English Jew, came to the Detroit area from Upper Canada during the Canadian Rebellion of 1837. In 1855 he moved from Detroit to Oberlin, Ohio. His romantic depictions of the Old Northwest Territory are striking documents. (Mr. and Mrs. James O. Keene)

to Buffalo. Canals never extended very far into the Northwest Territory, however, for the railroad eclipsed their purpose. The railroad provided better transportation and brought the banker with his money. Prior to this time the Old Northwest Territory had been relatively poor and without the means to transport goods economically. With the railroad came numerous local industries, which in time mushroomed into major manufacturing concerns that encouraged the building of large cities.

Though landscape painting became more common along the East Coast in the first half of the nineteenth century, portraiture was still paramount. In the Old Northwest Territory the situation was the same. Folk art represented a strong artistic undercurrent, and professional and semiprofessional itinerant artists in rural communities traveled from town to town and farmhouse to farmhouse taking likenesses. Folk portraits added a dash of color to otherwise modest homes.

Charles Dickens recorded in his *American Notes*, written during a visit to America in 1842, one of the first critical estimates of primitive painters in the Midwest. While describing a visit at an inn in the village of Lebanon, Ohio (probably The Golden Lamb, which has a room named in his honor), he recalled, "In the best room were two oil portraits of the kit-cat size, representing the landlord and his infant son, both looking as bold as lions and staring out of the canvas with an intensity that would have been cheap at any price. They were painted, I think, by the artist who had touched up the Belleville doors with red and gold; for I seemed to recognize his style immediately." [132]

These pictures could have been from the brush of any of the more than one hundred itinerant portraitists known to have been working in this general area during the 1820s, 1830s, and 1840s. Many New England artists journeyed west to the frontier to paint for a brief time and then returned to the East. Others made the long trek and, finding conditions to their taste, stayed. Erastus Salisbury Field is believed to have journeyed to the Old Northwest Territory, for a newspaper article written thirteen years after his death stated, "When he and his daughter went to Michigan . . . he devoted his time to portrait painting." [133]

Ammi Phillips's father and mother journeyed to Colebrook, Ohio, where his father died in 1842 and his mother in 1861. It is possible that the artist visited them on one of his painting expeditions.

One of the first fully documented folk artists to work

281 (above). *King Strang and His Harem on Beaver Island,* attributed to F. E. Cohen, oil on canvas, c. 1850, Michigan, 28⁵/₁₆" x 41⁹/₁₆". King Strang was the self-proclaimed king of Beaver Island. He led a faction of Mormon followers to the island, which served as their refuge. (Greenfield Village and Henry Ford Museum)

282 (above). *Unknown Man with a Book* by Gildersleeve Hurd, oil on canvas, 1830–1840, Detroit, Michigan, 28⅛″ x 23¼″. (Greenfield Village and Henry Ford Museum)

on the western frontier was Isaac Augustus Wetherby (1819–1904). His account books remain virtually intact. He was born at Providence, Rhode Island, and for several years as a youth was placed in various New England academies for young men. He first learned to draw while at Norway, Maine, when "A miserable Botch of a Painter came to Norway Village & Painted Ol Es. Whitman & others & my father had me go to learn to Paint Portraits with him. His name was Rice. I had not been with him long before I could Paint Better Portraits than he could." [134]

Beyond this, Wetherby probably was entirely self-taught. He headed toward the frontier during the 1840s, and the Louisville *Dime* of 1844 carried the following notice: "Mr. Wetherby is an artist of no ordinary merit, and we hope your friends will evince their appreciation of his talents by liberally patronizing him and thus secure his permanent location here. He is every inch a gentleman, and a visit to his rooms he will render both pleasant and agreeable." [135]

Wetherby returned to New England later the same year. In 1846 he married and decided to travel west again with his bride. An account book entry records their travels to Louisville, Kentucky, "over the mountains via Cum-berland Road by State Coach &c. to Wheeling, Va., and down the Ohio River by Steamboat." [136]

The painting business evidently was slow, and a few months later the newlyweds returned to Boston, where Wetherby painted numerous portraits. In 1849 commissions were so few that the artist was forced to earn a living by making oil copies of Gilbert Stuart's portrait of George Washington, both bust and full-length, which he sold for $10 to $15. Wetherby, like William Matthew Prior, must have found this segment of the painting business profitable, for he is known to have turned out at least thirty pictures of American heroes.

As early as 1841 Wetherby had purchased a daguerreotype outfit for $25, money earned from painting portraits. His success in the new field was relatively modest until he ultimately moved to Tama County, Iowa, where he secured a land grant and opened a photography parlor. Traveling in Illinois in 1852, he created a series of political caricatures of the Democratic Party that he lithographed and sold for seven cents each. In 1856 he executed campaign banners at Rockford and in nearby Davenport, Iowa. A local paper notified the readers that the artist was willing to execute banners for either of the rival political parties. One might expect such activities to cause unhappiness and resentment in an artist who had enjoyed success and acclaim in the East. This appears not to have been the case. Wetherby's account books indicate that he continued to execute oil portraits of adults and children. He even painted likenesses for bereaved families, often working beside the coffin and on occasion snapping a daguerreotype that served as the model. His last two known portraits were executed in Iowa City, Iowa, in 1862, when he was forty-three. Nearly forty-two years later Isaac Augustus Wetherby died, leaving an immense body of work and a wealth of information about the nineteenth-century itinerant folk artist.

Sheldon Peck (1797–1868), like Isaac Wetherby, undoubtedly was self-taught. Peck's painting activities have recently been carefully researched and documented, and an exhibition of his work, entitled "Sheldon Peck," was shown at the Whitney Museum of American Art in New York City in 1975. Peck's life, while perhaps not as colorful as Wetherby's, is more interesting to study, for his artistic contribution is certainly more significant. Peck, like William Matthew Prior, was born into a New Eng-

284 (above). *Miss Helen Sophia Harris* by H. A. Pease, oil on canvas, 1842, Ohio, 27⅜" x 24". The back of this canvas is inscribed: "Miss Helen Sophia Harris/Aged 7 years/Amherstville Lorain County/Ohio/A.D. Dec 28th 1842/By H. A. Pease of Oberlin, Ohio." Pease later went by the name Alanzo H. The seascape behind Miss Harris has been identified as Lake Erie and the Vermillion River Light. (Private collection)

285 (below). *Lumber Mill at Plymouth, Michigan,* by Celestia Young, oil on paper, 1856, Michigan, 11½" x 16⅞". The Adams Mill was located some four miles southeast of Plymouth, Michigan. The midwestern landscape was dotted with similar lumberyards. (Greenfield Village and Henry Ford Museum)

286 (top). *The Red Mill near Yellow Springs, Ohio,* artist unknown, oil on board, *c.* 1850, 27″ x 15″. Over six mills stood in Yellow Springs when this painting was executed. The painting's strong visual impact comes from its stark simplicity. (Greenfield Village and Henry Ford Museum)

287 (above). *Locomotive* by E. West, watercolor on paper, 1862, Ohio, dimensions unavailable. The inscription on this painting gives the artist's name and indicates that it was executed while he attended the Young American House located in Cleveland, Ohio. (Private collection)

land family that could trace its ancestral lineage to the earliest American settlers. The Peck clan had been among the founders of the New Haven Colony in 1635. Jacob Peck, his father, had fought in the Revolution and was one of the first settlers of Cornwall, Vermont. Quite possibly Peck learned about the rudiments of painting from art manuals contained in the library of the Cornwall Young Gentleman's Society, which had been founded in 1804.

Sheldon Peck's work can be divided into three distinctive phases. His earliest paintings were executed in Vermont, a second group were painted in New York State, and a third group record the sturdy settlers who were his neighbors and friends during his final years in Illinois.

Peck married Harriet Corey (1806–1887) of Bridport, Vermont, in 1824. His portraits executed at this time appear to be the result of a formula worked out by an artist attempting to catch a likeness in a brief period of time. Marianne E. Balazs, organizer of the Whitney show, writing of Peck's art of this period, indicates that there is "a decorative motif that reappears throughout the artist's work in one form or another—a long stroke flanked by two shorter ones, like the print of a rabbit's foot. The frequent recurrence of the motif on clothes and furniture indicates that Peck may have thought of it as a sort of trade mark. In portraits done about this time Peck elaborated on his sitters' coiffures and costumes by painting in curls, lace-trimmed collars and bonnets, and gold buttons." [137]

In 1827, when their second child, Charles, was born, Sheldon and Harriet Peck were in Burlington, Vermont. From Vermont the Pecks quite possibly traveled down

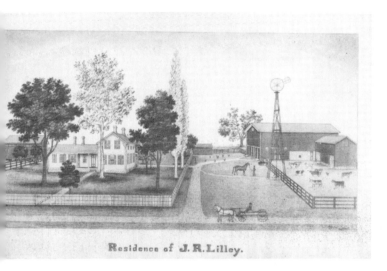

Residence of J. R. Lilley.

288 (left, above). *House on the River*, artist unknown, oil on canvas, *c.* 1875, Washington, 20⅛″ x 27¼″. This painting from the far Northwest is framed in a rustic extravaganza made from stripped fir branches and pine cones. (Greenfield Village and Henry Ford Museum)

289 (left, below). *Residence of J. R. Lilley* by William Stanley, pencil on paper, *c.* 1880, midwestern, 17⅝″ x 25¹¹/₁₆″. Ohio and Michigan abound with Late Classical Revival farmhouses such as the one shown in this picture. (Greenfield Village and Henry Ford Museum)

290 (below). *Mackinac Island*, artist unknown, watercolor on velvet, 1830–1840, Michigan, 12½″ x 19″. This painting is one of the truly great midwestern pictures. Unhappily, it is very difficult to photograph well; no one has yet captured the incredible quality of this picture. (Mackinac Island State Park Commission)

291 (above). *Star of Bethlehem*, artist unknown, pencil and watercolor, *c.* 1840, Ohio, 16½″ x 15¾″. German Separatists settled in a communal colony at Zoar, Ohio, in 1817. They brought with them knowledge of traditional German design and decorative motifs, which appear on this stylish piece. (Joan and Robert Doty)

Lake Champlain, the Hudson River, and finally west along the Mohawk River and the Erie Canal. By 1828 they had established residence at Jordan, Onondaga County, New York, a bustling canal town. During the New York period Peck executed half- and three-quarter-length portraits on wood panels as he had done in Vermont. In general his palette was brighter and the pictures are more detailed in their execution. Likenesses of this period are occasionally embellished with draperies, painted furniture, and other accessories. The rabbit's foot motif continues to be much in evidence. Peck was obviously successful, for by 1835 he had purchased a fifty-acre parcel of land just outside the village of Jordan. A brief announcement published by Hezekiah Gunn in the November 9, 1836, issue of the *Onondaga Standard* indicates that the Pecks must have departed rather abruptly: "Be it known to all people, that one Sheldon Peck, and Harriet his wife, not having the fear of God before their eyes, being instigated by the devil, have with malice aforethought most wickedly and maliciously hired, flattered, bribed or persuaded my wife Emeline, to leave me without just cause or provocation. It is supposed that said Peck has carried her to some part of the state of

Illinois. This is therefore to forbid all persons harboring or trusting my wife Emeline, for I will pay no debts of her contracting." [138]

It is speculated that the Pecks were Mormons and that Mrs. Gunn left her husband to practice polygamy. This conjecture, however, lacks substantiation, for Emeline Gunn is nowhere listed in the Illinois census with the Pecks. Apparently she did not join their household.

The Pecks traveled to Chicago, where they are thought to have purchased property near Washington and State streets. While there, Peck seems to have returned to his simple Vermont style so that in an era of financial depression he might reduce his prices, thereby attracting additional customers.

Portraits from this period are painted on canvas. Perhaps by now it was more accessible. The preparation of the wood panels that he used during the Vermont and New York period must have taken a considerable amount of time.

Family tradition indicates that Peck traded his Chicago holdings for an impressive team of horses, which he used to move his family and their belongings to Babcock's Grove. This hamlet, now known as Lombard, was

292 (left). Confirmation certificate by John George Nuechterlein, watercolor and pinprick on paper, 1869, Frankenmuth, Michigan, 12″ x 18″. This certificate is actually known as a *Patenspreich,* or a godchild's thank-you prayer for his godparents at his confirmation. Germans settled in Frankenmuth, Michigan, during the nineteenth century and have been steadfast in their preservation of cultural traditions. (Frankenmuth Historical Society and St. Lorenz Church)

293 (below). *The American War Horse* by J. W. Zook, watercolor on paper, *c.* 1880, Oak Grove, Illinois, 18½″ x 22¼″. Two versions of this delicate painting are known. The artist paid particular attention to such American symbols as the American flag and the American eagle with flags and shield. (Greenfield Village and Henry Ford Museum)

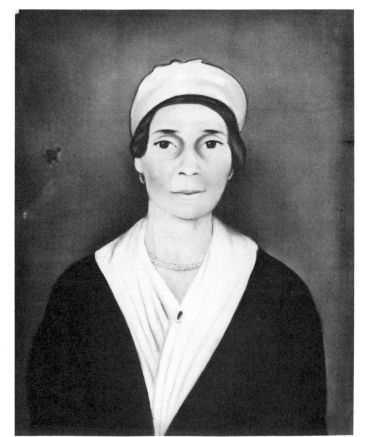

294 (opposite, above). *The Ruggles Family from Vermillion, Ohio*, artist unknown, oil on canvas, *c.* 1860, Ohio, 35½" x 51¼". (Ohio Historical Society)

295a, 295b (below, left and right). *Sully and Susanna Watson*, artist unknown, pastel on paper, second half of the nineteenth century, Ohio, 24" x 19¼". The Watsons were members of a small black community in Milwaukee. They first lived in Virginia and moved to Ohio sometime in 1828 and once again moved westward to Milwaukee in 1850. (Mr. and Mrs. William E. Wiltshire III)

296 (below). Detail of a panorama by John Stevens, oil on canvas, midwestern, overall length approx. 220'. The thirty-six-scene panorama created by the artist, *c.* 1870, dealt with the attack of the local Indians on New Ulm in 1862. Other scenes in the panorama include landscapes, townscapes, Indian massacres, and portraits of many of the people lost in the attack. (Minnesota Historical Society)

297 (above). *The Family*, artist unknown, watercolor on paper, *c.* 1875, midwestern, 11¼″ x 17¼″. The Victorian parlor is furnished with a Renaissance Revival secretary-bookcase and a wall bracket for magazines that might have been manufactured in Grand Rapids, Michigan. Attractive wallpaper and a red, green, and black carpet soften this interior. (Greenfield Village and Henry Ford Museum)

298 (right). *Portrait of a Young Woman*, artist unknown, oil on canvas, *c.* 1842, Illinois, 31″ x 27½″. Though this young woman lived on what could have been considered the frontier, she was thoroughly familiar with eastern styles. Her dress and coiffure are in the latest New York mode. This might have been made possible by a subscription to the style-setting magazine *Godey's Lady's Book*, which began publication in 1830. (George E. Schoellkopf Gallery)

299 (left). *Andrew Sailer's Farm* by Ernst Damitz (1805–1883), watercolor on paper, midwestern, 12½" x 17⅞". Ernst Damitz was born in Germany and came to America in the late 1840s. He moved to Chicago and finally settled in Greenbush Township, Warren County, Illinois, where in 1847 he paid $574 for a farm. Andrew Sailer was also born in Germany and after immigrating to America married the artist's daughter, Paulena. This painting is the least European of all Damitz's landscapes. (Helen R. Sailer) Photograph courtesy The Art Institute of Chicago)

300 (below). *Residence of Mr. Gottfried Walder* by Paul Seifert, watercolor on paper, *c.* 1880, Wisconsin, 22⅛" x 27⅞". Seifert's simple, bold renditions of northwestern farms are beautiful examples of American folk painting. (Greenfield Village and Henry Ford Museum)

Residence of Mr Gottfried Walder.

301 (above, left). Detail of the operating mechanism for Thomas Clarkson Gordon's panorama. (Greenfield Village and Henry Ford Museum)

302 (above, right); 303 (below). Paintbox and detail from panorama titled *Battle Scenes of the Rebellion* by Thomas Clarkson Gordon, oil on canvas, 1884–1886, Indiana; each of the fifteen paintings in the panorama measures approximately 84″ x 98″. (Greenfield Village and Henry Ford Museum)

304 (above). *Civil War Battle Scene,* artist unknown, oil on canvas, *c.* 1870, Michigan, 14″ x 28″. The Union Army is shown crossing a river. The Rebels appear to be massing for an attack on the hilltop. Because the detail is so realistic in this picture, it is likely that it was executed by a soldier who survived the engagement. (W. D. Ray)

305 (left). *Civil War Banner,* artist unknown, fabric and paper appliqués, *c.* 1861, Bern, Ohio, 47″ x 47″. Stenciled within a floral wreath on the opposite side of the banner are the words: "Union is Strength. Presented by the ladies of the young democracy of their town. Be true to your cause. Harmony is victory." (America Hurrah Antiques, N.Y.C.)

306 (above). *Masonic Painting*, artist unknown, oil on canvas, *c.* 1860, Holt, Michigan, 53″ x 43″. Masonic fraternities were popular in the Midwest during the period of settlement. They provided a sense of comradeship for their members. Photograph courtesy Thos. K. Woodard: American Antiques & Quilts. (Private collection)

307 (below). *The House of the Charles Hawkins Family Located West of Onsted, Michigan,* artist unknown, oil on canvas, c. 1880, 18″ x 24″. Chairs of the "kitchen" and "firehouse" variety dot the front yard. The stove under the spreading tree was probably used for summer cooking. (Current whereabouts unknown)

308 (left, above and below). *Portraits of an Unidentified Man and Woman* by M. Wilson, oil on board, 1830–1840, Kalamazoo, Michigan, 24″ x 30″. The competent artist who executed these pictures probably moved west with the settlers. Stylistically, the paintings are very similar to the works of numerous folk painters working in New England at the same time. (Mr. and Mrs. James Fostey)

AND A LITTLE CHILD SHALL LEAD THEM

309 (left). *The Peaceable Kingdom* by Olof Krans, oil on canvas, second half of the nineteenth century, Illinois, 18″ x 24″. Compare this version of the theme to the Edward Hicks version, plate 32. (Mr. and Mrs. Edwin Braman)

situated approximately twenty miles west of Chicago. The Pecks lived in a covered wagon for some two years while Sheldon built the home, which still remains in the family today.

In time Peck became a respected farmer and community leader, a landscape painter, a successful photographer, and a founding member of the august Chicago Academy of Design. The 1840 census indicates that he was employed in agriculture, and the 1850 census lists him as a professional portrait painter. Farming during the summer, Peck probably traveled during the winter months. Portraits from this period are often full-length and on occasion include several likenesses in a single canvas. His palette grew brighter, and many pictures feature bright reds and yellows. He sometimes avoided the necessity of additional expenditure for framing by painting a trompe l'oeil grained frame directly on the canvas. Peck developed a style designed to compete with the inexpensive daguerreotype currently offered by competitors. His handsome, stylish pictures must have made even the finest daguerreotype seem insignificant.

Between 1854 and 1855 Sheldon Peck maintained a studio at 71 Lake Street in Chicago and frequently advertised himself as a decorative painter. His son Charles was also an artist and photographer and in 1860 and 1866 was listed in St. Louis, Missouri, directories.

While many itinerant painters continually attempted to refine their technique and increase their income by executing increasingly realistic likenesses, Sheldon Peck seems to have deliberately taken the opposite course: "he appears to have consciously chosen to paint in a simple style that would appeal to relatively unworldly patrons. Facial features are treated as simple planes rendered by flat areas of color. Unlike most artists, who flocked to the cities to compete for the patronage of wealthier merchants and manufacturers, Peck chose his style and went to the frontier where he would find people to appreciate it." [139]

While some settlers journeyed westward in pursuit of new lands, others hoped to find religious tolerance. Joseph Smith, founder of the Mormon Church, was born in Vermont in 1805. In the spring of 1820 he had a vision in which two shining figures appeared and told him of their divine origin. Some years later an angel named Moroni and his father, Mormon, appeared before Smith and related facts that had been disclosed to no living man. Moroni told him of a book with thin gold pages inscribed in new Egyptian buried in a nearby mountain. In 1827 the angel Moroni appeared again and guided Smith to the spot where the fabulous book lay hidden. Smith saw on the ground a pair of spectacles with large lenses, and by looking through the spectacles, he was able to translate the inscriptions. He took the book to Harmony, Pennsylvania, where his father-in-law lived, and translated it, making the Book of Mormon. Smith returned to his Palmyra, New York, home, where he printed the Book of Mormon.

In 1830 the Church of Jesus Christ of Latter-Day Saints was officially established at Fayette, Seneca

310 (opposite, below). *The Days of Harvest* by Olof Krans, oil on canvas, second half of the nineteenth century, Illinois, 29½" x 47". The Swedish settlers who founded the communal society at Bishop Hill, Illinois, looked upon the settlement in the New World as utopia. One member said, "God visited the old nation that he might send choice grain over into this wilderness. The men cut the wheat and the women gathered and bound it as the great fields of gold grain fell before the scythe and cradles in the hands of men who moved in unison in the torrid heat of the summer sun. Behind them their womenfolk tied the grain in bundles to be pounded with flails, the earliest method of threshing." [12] (Illinois Division of Historic Sites)

311 (above). Mechanical calendar by a Zoar craftsman, painted pine wood, 1836, Zoar, Ohio, 36" x 18". The German peasant origin of the Zoarites is evident in their use of German names and their decorative themes, including castles and flowers. There are movable dials on the reverse of this calendar. (Index of American Design)

312 (right). *St. Paul* by S. Holmes Andrews, oil on canvas, 1855, midwestern, 15″ x 26″. This view of the city is from the west side of the river and shows many of its most prominent buildings, including the state capital. Steamboats travel the river; one is docked at the foot of the palisades. (Minnesota Historical Society)

313 (right, middle). *Barn Bluff, Red Wing, Minnesota,* artist unknown, oil on canvas, c. 1860, midwestern, 23⅞″ x 32″. Red Wing was an important riverboat stop on the Mississippi. A sawmill, warehouses, and the Metropolitan Hotel, which opened in 1857 and "was built against a bank so steep that the third floor is about level with the back yard," are illustrated. (New York State Historical Association)

314 (below). *Indiana Yearly Meeting of Friends, 1844,* by Marcus Mote, oil on canvas, drawn by Mote in 1844, repainted and enlarged in 1885, Indiana, 17″ x 27″. Mote gave this painting to Earlham College in 1885. The site depicted is part of the present Earlham College campus, although the buildings no longer exist. (Earlham College)

315 (opposite). *The Burning of Harper's Opera House* by Nicholas Wirig (1860–1896), oil on canvas, dated 1887, midwestern, 47¾″ x 71⅞″. Harper's Opera House was built in 1881 at Rock Island, Illinois, and burned on New Year's Eve in 1887 during a performance of *Uncle Tom's Cabin.* An inscription in the lower right corner of the painting reads "Presented by B. Brahm and N. Wirig/The ABE Awake/H[ose] H[ook] and L[adder] Co. No. 2/ Dec. 31, 1887." In the two upper corners, the artist added the slogans of the fire company: "The Eye That Never Winks" and "The Wing That Never Tires." Young women who had been portraying angels in the play are shown fleeing through the streets. (Abby Aldrich Rockefeller Folk Art Center)

County, New York. The congregation numbered six. In following years Joseph Smith received other visitations, and additional religious followers joined the sect.

Mormon converts answered the call of the West and by 1836 had migrated in sufficient numbers to build a temple at Kirtland, Ohio, a short distance from Cleveland. Local hostility was so fervent that the Saints were forced to move westward once again, to Missouri. They settled briefly at Nauvoo, Illinois, on the Mississippi River. At Nauvoo Joseph Smith's enemies whipped up a violent mob that attacked the jail, in which he was imprisoned. He had been indicted for treason. On July 27, 1844, Smith was killed by the mob.

The Mormons then elected Brigham Young as their new leader, and in 1846 they marched to Council Bluffs, Iowa, where they spent the winter while they sent an exploratory expedition farther west. Under Brigham Young they traveled to Great Salt Lake, where they established a large community and enjoyed the much-sought freedom from religious persecution.

The history pictures from a large panorama by Carl Christian Anton Christensen record the religious persecution and difficult migration of the Mormons. Christensen immigrated to the United States from Denmark in 1857. The young man, who had been born in Copenhagen in 1831, met two Mormon missionaries in 1850 and was converted to the Mormon faith. He too became a missionary, and upon his arrival with his Norwegian wife he made his way to the Mormon colony in Iowa City. They completed the trek westward and arrived at the Mormon Zion, Salt Lake City, in 1857. Christensen had had artistic instruction in his native land and carried with him his paints and brushes.

In 1869 Christensen began to record the significant incidents that dealt with the formation of the Mormon church. By 1890 "C.C.A.," as he was fondly called by fellow Mormons, had completed twenty-two of the eight-foot by ten-foot pictures. These he had sewn together and rolled onto a long wooden pole. He used the paintings as illustrations for a lecture on Mormon history in the local Utah country. The rolls of paintings were hung over loops of rope suspended by portable tripods. The individual scenes were rolled forward as he spoke. The Mormon artist died in 1912, and the paintings then became the property of the Brigham Young University at Provo, Utah.

The bright, crisp vitality and the well-conceived composition give these Mormon history pictures a unique place in the annals of American folk art.

Religious persecution was responsible for the organization of several other colonies of people hoping to worship as they chose. A group of German Separatists from

Württemberg settled on the east bank of the Tuscarawas River in the state of Ohio in 1817. They named the settlement Zoars, suggesting a sanctuary, and established a communal society as a means of guaranteeing economic stability and maintaining a social and religious entity. The members were predominantly farmers, but there were artisans and professional men as well.

The Zoarites had left behind Biedermeier furniture and oftentimes attempted to approximate that style in the pieces they created for their homes in the new settlement. More frequently, however, peasant designs and decoration appeared on the furniture, which was constructed from several different types of native wood. Painted chairs, wardrobes, and even a mechanical calendar clock suggest the origins of the communal group. Although the communal experiment of the Separatists came to an end in 1898, examples of their craftsmanship still remain.

In Wisconsin, where heavier concentrations of Scandinavian immigrants settled, painted and decorated furniture also flourished. The retardataire pieces have a vigor and boldness greatly admired by collectors today.

The Swedish religious dissenters who founded Bishop Hill, Illinois, in 1846 never knew that their efforts would best be known through the work of Olof Krans (1838–1916), a self-taught painter. Early in the nineteenth century Eric Janson and his followers found the doctrines of the established church of Sweden unbearable and migrated to Illinois. In the years that followed other Swedes joined the colony at Bishop Hill, which at one time boasted nearly eleven hundred members. This Chris-

tian communistic organization began with only sixty acres and by 1860 could boast a "balance stock on hand" of $770,630.94. Agriculture was the primary source of income, and every member of the community, from the oldest man to the youngest child, was expected to contribute. Paintings executed by Olof Krans, preserved in the colony church at Bishop Hill, indicate the strengths and weaknesses of the system.

Olof Krans was born Olof Olson at Silja, Nora Parish, Vestmanland, Sweden. Krans as a youth early demonstrated his ability as an artist: "Before he was twelve years old, his father, having decided to emigrate to America, visited a shipwright in Gefle to ascertain the value of a boat and skiff which constituted part of the property he had to sell. Each member of the colony was required to sell his possessions and to contribute the proceeds to the common fund. The shipwright wanted to see what the property looked like, so the father made some sketches. Olof, who had accompanied his father, glanced at the drawings, remarked that they were not correct, and proceeded to draw the boat and skiff with the comment, 'This is the way they look.' The shipwright scanned the picture, looked intently at the little boy, then turned to the father, and said: 'Let me have him, and I shall give him an education and he will make his mark in the world.' But the father would not think of giving him up."[140]

As a mature man Olof worked in the paint and blacksmith shops at Bishop Hill. When he joined the 57th Regiment Illinois Volunteer Infantry in 1861, he took the

316 (opposite). *Sun River, Montana*, artist unknown, wash on paper board, *c.* 1885, Montana, 6″ x 9½″. Frontier towns all across America must have looked similar to Sun River. The wagon trains passing through the town are an interesting touch. (Herbert W. Hemphill, Jr.)

317 (left, top). *View of Fort Snelling* (near Minneapolis, Minnesota) by Edward K. Thomas, oil on canvas, second half of the nineteenth century, midwestern, 27″ x 34″. In the foreground are what appear to be several stone buildings with stepped caps, a European style of architecture. Since much of the Midwest was settled by immigrants from the Old World, this is not surprising. (The Minneapolis Institute of Arts)

318 (left, middle). *View of Cincinnati* by John C. Wild (1804–1846), gouache, *c.* 1835, midwestern, 21¹³/₁₆″ x 31⅜″. Because of its location on the Ohio River, a major waterway, Cincinnati grew rapidly and its population was larger than that of many other frontier cities during the first half of the nineteenth century. Several of the giant sidewheel, steam-propelled boats that plied the river are docked on the city's edge. (Museum of Fine Arts, Boston; M. and M. Karolik Collection)

319 (left, bottom). *Homer, Minnesota*, by John Sperry, watercolor on paper, 1869, midwestern, 14¼″ x 17″. This is a crude yet fascinating painting. Note the strange perspective and the log raft on the river. (New York State Historical Association)

320 (above). *Great Bluff* by Dave Gier, oil on board, 1965, Michigan, 16″ x 20″. The artist, like many contemporary naïves, has painted in several styles and has ultimately settled on an impressionistic rendering of nature. (Private collection)

321 (above). *Child from the Merriman Family Dressed in a Scots Outfit*, artist unknown, oil on canvas, *c.* 1860, Jackson, Michigan, 49″ x 37″. The convention of using pets in a painting prevailed throughout the entire nineteenth century. (Ella Sharp Museum)

name Olof Krans and retained it for the rest of his life. After returning to Bishop Hill in 1862 because of a disability, he clerked in a general store and at one point maintained a photographic gallery on wheels.

In time Krans moved to Galesburg, where he married Christiana Aspequist, and in 1867 they moved to Galva, Illinois, where they raised three sons and a daughter. At this time of his life Krans worked as a house painter and handyman and frequently grained woodwork in the High Victorian style. He also contributed theatre curtains and scenery for special performances at the Galva Opera House.

Krans had no formal training. His scenes of the Bishop Hill colony were executed from memory and done long after the society experiment had been dissolved. Most appear to date between 1896 and 1911. Many of his portraits were copied from photographs.

Panoramas mounted on giant turntables appeared frequently in the late eighteenth and early nineteenth centuries. One of the first recorded instances of a truly successful panorama was that produced by Robert Barker, a portrait painter of Edinburgh, Scotland, who during the 1780s created several successful panoramic views that depicted landscapes, architecture, and historical events. By 1790 New Yorkers were treated to a panoramic view of Jerusalem. As the nineteenth century progressed, the popularity of panorama paintings grew. Travel and military subjects were among the most favored.

The Civil War made a deep impression upon the folk artist and inspired numerous panoramas that attracted great national interest. In 1860 the Indiana artist Aurelius Smith created a thirty-seven-scene panorama devoted to John Brown and his attempt to spark the southern slaves to rebellion. In 1862 Louisville, Kentucky, hosted a showing of *Views of the Battle for the Union*, and again in 1863 Goodwin and Wilder showed their thirty-eight views of the *Gigantic Polyorama of the War* in the same city. Polyoramas were occasionally presented in specially constructed circular buildings with conical roofs. The spectator stood in the center of the room with the painting surrounding him.

Sometime during the 1820s or early 1830s the canvases were mounted on huge rollers and wound from one to another. The panorama could be large because the size was limited only to the amount of canvas able to be wound from roller to roller.

Thomas Clarkson Gordon, an Indiana folk artist born in 1841 on a rural farm near Spiceland, Henry County, Indiana, served in the Civil War in Company A, 36th Infantry and recorded, "I was always at the front, on the move, or in action. I took part in the battles of Shiloh, Stone River, Chickamauga, Lookout Mountain, Missionary Ridge, Tunnel Hill, Rocky Face, Dalton, Resoca, Kenesaw Mountain, and Atlanta."[141]

Years after the cessation of hostilities, Gordon married and settled again at Spiceland, where he and his wife, Mary Ellen, raised five daughters. He worked as a house painter and during leisure hours constantly at-

322 (opposite, below). *Children of John Rooney* by Joe, oil on canvas, *c.* 1850, Milwaukee, Wisconsin, 38″ x 41″. This painting is the earliest known work of art by a Milwaukee black. John Rooney, a local merchant and abolitionist, hired a fugitive slave, known only as Joe, to work in his store. The children in this painting are Rooney's daughter and son. The doll held by the girl was made for her by the former slave, as well as the clothing worn by both children. The dress and suit, along with the painting, are on exhibit at the Milwaukee County Historical Society. (Milwaukee County Historical Society)

323 (right). Photograph of Parrish C. Allen, the young boy depicted in the memorial picture below. (Susan Taylor Martens)

324 (below). *Memorial Picture for Parrish C. Allen* (1876–1896) by Almira Nickols, oil on fabric, *c.* 1896, Dover, Illinois, 17″ x 21″. Almira Nickols was a teacher of instrumental music, drawing, and painting at the Dover, Illinois, Academy of Higher Learning. This charming memorial picture is a tribute to her nephew Parrish Allen, who died following the heroic rescue of his cousin from an Illinois river. (Susan Taylor Martens)

tempted to teach himself the art of painting: "He was always drawing pencil or pen pictures to satisfy himself; or making cartoons, for the appreciation and amusement of his many friends; or giving chalk-talks to the children in his Sunday School classes. A few more permanent scene paintings and portraits, in crayon or oil, were made and later preserved by his family. His early works were mostly of local interest and only preparatory for his later large panoramic paintings that had wider public appeal."[142]

Sometime in the early 1880s Thomas Gordon decided to record his experiences as a member of the Union forces, and many of his scenes were ultimately worked into a large panoramic painting. He sought depictions of places or battles that he was not personally involved with, and these too he incorporated into his gigantic effort, which he attempted to make as factual as possible. Nearly everyone agreed "his artistic ability found its fullest expression in the painting of a large collection of war scenes."[143]

In 1884 and 1885 he continued to work at his war panorama, which he had set up in John S. Stiggleman's furniture factory at Spiceland. He used unbleached sheeting, sized to make it waterproof, and oil paints that he skillfully mixed to achieve the various hues he desired. His scheme was to lay the canvas out in broad areas with two-thirds of the height for geographical detail and military activities and one-third left for the sky. He attempted to make each view important in itself and yet an integral part of the entire picture narrative. In fact, the panorama was painted on separate canvases 7 feet high and 14 feet wide and then joined into one continuous canvas 105 feet long by 14 feet wide. Gordon developed a mechanism that allowed him to move the canvas vertically: "As the canvas was unwound from the front roller, it passed up to and over the top one, seven feet above, thus giving sufficient surface exposure for showing the full painted scenes in succession. Then the canvas was carried down to the back roller where it was wound up again. Before another showing, the canvas was wound back onto the front roller to start all over again with the first scene. The framework, when set up, measured sixteen feet across and eleven feet high, the lower rollers being attached to the frame about four feet above the floor. For purposes of storage or shipment, the exhibition frames were taken down, part by part, by removing bolts and screws and the panorama roll carefully wrapped for its protection."[144]

In 1886 Gordon first showed his completed panorama, *Battle Scenes of the Rebellion*, at Hoover's Hall in Spiceland. A few weeks later he began a tour of the rural towns in eastern Indiana, where playbills were distributed and the fantastic wonder was advertised in the local press. Success was apparent and local newspaper critics enthusiastically noted "that every town and village in Eastern Indiana will give Mr. Gordon a welcome, and honor themselves by honoring his genius with full and paying houses."[145]

In Gordon's later years he purchased a small dwelling near his home to store his treasure. People continued

325 (above). *Pier Fishing Scene with Self-unloading Lake Freighter Entering Grand River* by William Perry (1882–1967), oil on canvas, *c.* 1960, Ohio, 17″ x 26½″. Perry, a Finnish immigrant who settled in the Midwest, recorded many of the old streets, buildings, and harbor scenes around Fairport Harbor, Ohio. (Gene and Linda Kangas)

326 (below). *The Steamer "Dove"* by H. Cluczs, oil on canvas, 1876, Detroit, Michigan, 20″ x 32″. (Dossin Great Lakes Museum)

327 (opposite, above). *Upper Reaches of Wind River* by Steve Harley, oil on canvas, 1927–1928, found in Scottsville, Michigan, 35″ x 20″. Though this scene was found in Michigan, it is believed to represent a location in Washington State. Harley painted with a magnifying glass to help him refine his brush strokes. Though only three of his paintings are known, he is considered by many to be one of the great twentieth-century naïve artists. (Abby Aldrich Rockefeller Folk Art Center)

328 (opposite, below). *Dance on the Sequoia Stump* by F. R. Bennett, oil on canvas, *c.* 1875, western United States, 20″ x 28″. It seems likely that this scene represents either northern California or southern Oregon. A passageway has been cut through the sequoia tree to the right of the stump. (New York State Historical Association)

to clamor to see his great Civil War panorama, and he set it up in the house and installed kerosene footlights and reflectors and for a number of years held showings for visitors. Gordon lived to be eighty-one years of age, and his Civil War panorama certainly was his greatest artistic achievement.

The watercolor artist Paul Seifert was born at Dresden, Germany, in 1840. His elegant farm portraits of Wisconsin scenes span the period between the late 1870s and 1915. One of his granddaughters has recorded,

> In later life, he set up a shop near Gotham, where he practiced his art of painting and taxidermy. Besides the watercolor work he did oil painting on glass. These were castle scenes, as he remembered them in his native land. He died in 1921.
>
> . . . You asked if he painted at home or traveled to do his farm scenes. Sometimes he left home for days, walking from one farm to the other with his sketch book. Some sketches were brought home and painted, others, as I understand, were done at the farms. Along with his paintings, he set out groves of shade trees at farms he visited, and started small fruit gardens for the farm folk, supplying the plants from his own garden.
>
> The farm scenes were all painted in watercolors. As money was very scarce in those days, not more than $2.50 was paid for the paintings. He did not have a shop until later. These were done at home or on the farms.
>
> His first shop was set up at Gotham, then later moved one and one half miles west of Gotham on this farm where I now live. The little shop, about 20 x 20, was painted a gay red with a white sign adorning the front, bearing the name of *Paul A. Seifert, Taxidermist* in black letters. Here my grandfather practiced many arts. It had two rooms and in one corner of the large room was a window and a table where he did his painting.
>
> In the shop he did the glass painting. The sketches were made on drawing board, then the glass 16 x 20 inches was laid over the board and scenes of lofty castles with gold and silver foil windows were painted with oil on the glass. Later on, he painted winter scenes of churches and country churchyards. These sold for $5.00, a small fee considering his work and the making of the frames, but the country people were his customers and could not afford higher prices.[146]

Paul Seifert possessed a clarity of vision that is unusual in the history of American landscape painting. His color sense and his attention to detail are as pleasing today as they must have been to the farm folk who purchased his paintings when they were freshly painted.

Steve Harley has captured the essence of the primeval Northwest with greater strength than perhaps any other naïve painter. The artist was born in Scottsville, Michigan, in 1863. He lost the family farm that he had inherited and sometime early in the 1920s moved westward, traveling to Washington, Oregon, California, and finally Alaska. When his attempts at photography failed to capture the breathtaking wooded landscapes that were so much a part of his life, he turned to painting. His concern with detail was so intense that he laid his tiny brushstrokes on the painting with the aid of a magnifying glass.

Sometime in the early 1930s Steve Harley returned to Scottsville and lived in a shack with his paintings. Though he left behind a limited body of work, he is deeply respected for his three masterpieces.

Tella Denehue Kitchen of Adelphi, Ohio, is a contemporary memory painter. Her pictures reach back to scenes and situations from her childhood, which she records with sure strokes.

Mrs. Kitchen was born in 1902 on a small farm in the hills of Vinton County, Ohio, near the tiny village of Londonderry. Her father's family migrated from County Cork, Ireland, and her mother's from Pennsylvania. While still young, Tella Denehue moved with her parents to a small farm near Independence, Indiana. In 1920 she married Noland Kitchen and returned to Ohio.

The Kitchens raised four children, and today Tella boasts seven grandchildren and thirteen great-grandchildren.

In 1963 Mrs. Kitchen was left a widow. She recalls,

> My husband was mayor of our small village when he passed away and I, too, served as mayor for two years after my husband's death—the first woman to be so honored in the history of our county.
>
> I have had a busy, good life. I have been a member of the Order of Eastern Star for fifty years and have had the pleasure of seeing my family follow their father and me through the Chairs of Masonry and the Order of the Eastern Star.
>
> After I was left alone and trying to keep busy, my youngest son, knowing my love for art, gave me a set of paints and said, "Now, get busy!" So when I read in the paper where an art teacher was offering free art lessons to Senior Citizens, I decided to go, which I did. But the first lesson was enough for me. I was too old to paint new-fangled things and I just began to paint the simple things I remembered and loved.[147]

Tella Kitchen's paintings bustle with the daily activities of small-town and country life. Her brilliantly colored pictures provide a detailed view of rural America in the early twentieth century.

Michigan artist David Gier considers himself a folk artist even though his paintings are oftentimes impressionistic. He is primarily self-taught and has arrived at his highly individual style through experiments that continue incessantly, each canvas representing a new challenge. Most of his pictures are painted in acrylic, and when asked about his art, he indicated that his work "tends to be decorative—viewers get a lift from my paintings." [148]

The youthful Katherine Jakobsen paints Michigan landscapes and genre pictures in both watercolor and oil. When asked about her past, Katherine wrote,

When I came along my active and adventurous brothers, age two and four, had already defeated my parents in their attempts at training. I soon joined them and we did as we pleased. (My official title was "The Queen of the Jungle.")

Our parents were generous. Though we lived near a city, our yard was a wooded acre and our sandpile had two truckloads of sand. The neighbors kept chickens and a horse, which I rode. We all had dogs and cats. We spent our allowances on all kinds of books. At one time we had over one thousand comic books.

Our family was not rich in money, but we traveled frequently, especially in the Northern Peninsula where my mother was raised and where her 87-year-old mother still lives.

When I was very young I decided that when I grew up I was going to be a boy, an artist, or a horse trainer. Well, I stayed a tomboy for as long as I could and eventually traded my horses for boyfriends.

I lived in Antigua for a while and sailed through the British West Indies (and the Bermuda Triangle) on my brother's 1908 53-foot Herreshoff sloop.

Katherine Jakobsen's art is based upon her keen interest in calligraphy, and her modern-day illuminations and Frakturs are without precedent in the contemporary naïve art world.

Emily Lunde reveals through her paintings much about the early twentieth-century immigrants living in northern Minnesota, where she spent most of her childhood with Swedish grandparents. She frequently depicts scenes from the isolated northern woodlands, where telephones and radios were nonexistent and peddlers and tramps or traveling evangelists were the only contacts with the outside world.

When referring to the way of life still experienced by the friends and neighbors she grew up with, she observes,

Fortunately they are slowly getting modern but traces of the old culture hang on with the older folk.

I was deprived of a decent education, having only finished eighth grade. I have not had any painting lessons.

My husband was a mechanic and construction worker all his life. We are now on Social Security. I guess that fairly sums it up. [149]

Emily Lunde now lives in North Dakota, where her keen artist's eyes never fail to see a picture in the neighboring farmyards and towns. Her Polish neighbors, the nearby Indians, and the burly millworkers all provide inspiration for this talented artist.

Because the Midwest was settled by people with such diverse ethnic backgrounds, many of the naïve artists find inspiration for their art in different cultural sources. There are so few parallels that generalizations about the midwestern and northwestern folk painter are meaningless.

329 (above). *Farm Scene with Fanning Mill Factory* by Nettie Cortrite, oil on board, 1887, Detroit, Michigan, 18" x 24". (Dr. and Mrs. Henry Raskin)

330 (below). *Interior Scene* by Miss Anna C. Freeland, oil on board, late nineteenth century, Three Oaks, Michigan, 9½" x 12½". (The Museum, Michigan State University)

331 (above). *Popeye and Dancing Girls Mural* (detail) by Clarence Hewes, painted wall, *c.* 1940, Lansing, Michigan, dimensions unavailable. Clarence Hewes (1894–1970) began working for the Lansing Board of Water and Light when he was thirty. To relieve the boredom of his long hours on duty underground, he created a personal world of paintings, murals, and sculpture in the tunnels of the Cedar Street Pumping Station. (Lansing Board of Water and Light)

Plate 58 (opposite). Detail from a panorama of twenty-two pictures illustrating Mormon life by Carl Christian Anton Christensen, oil on canvas, nineteenth century. The 175-foot scenic roll was designed to illustrate Christensen's lectures on the principal events that mark the first decades of the Church of Jesus Christ of Latter-Day Saints. The artist recorded in his dramatic work the persecutions, the wanderings, the hardships, and the ultimate peace and prosperity of the Mormon experience. When Joseph Smith and other hostages were released from jail in Liberty, Missouri, in April 1839, the governor's order made it imperative that the Mormons move on. Smith and his people loaded their possessions into wagons and began their trek again, following the Mississippi northward into the sparsely settled town of Commerce, Illinois. They established a settlement and named it Nauvoo, which in Hebrew signifies a beautiful place. This painting depicts their flight from Missouri. Christensen began to paint his history of the Mormon church in 1869, and by 1890 he had completed all twenty-two of his pictures. In 1878 he first began to sew the initial group of eight paintings together and rolled them on a long wooden pole. He used these pictures as illustrations for a lecture on Mormon history and drove a wagon through Utah advertising his lectures. By 1888 nineteen paintings were assembled and exhibited in Sanpete County, Utah. While he was lecturing, the roll of paintings was hung over loops of rope that were suspended from portable tripods. The individual scenes were revealed as he spoke. In 1912 the artist died at Ephraim, Utah. (Brigham Young University Art Gallery)

Plate 59 (opposite, above). *The Steamboat Washington*, artist unknown, oil on canvas, *c.* 1820, Ohio, 19¾" x 28½". (Mr. and Mrs. Samuel Schwartz)

Plate 60 (opposite, below). *Farm of H. Windle* by Henry Dousa, oil on canvas, 1875, Indiana, 34" x 48½". The artist is believed to have been born in Lafayette, Indiana, around 1820. Between 1879 and 1885, he worked at Newcastle, Indiana, and then returned to Lafayette, where he died. Dousa is best known as a painter of farm scenes and prizewinning livestock. He later turned to portraiture, and five examples of his work in this genre are known. Dousa's livestock pictures are all similar in concept and show the animals in profile against a green background much like the bull and background in this painting. The bull was named William Allen and evidently was the homeowner's prize possession. Its large proportion compared to the other elements of the painting and its specific identification ("WilliamAllen/property of H. Windle/age Five Years/Weight 2500") indicate its importance. The inscription was probably added to the painting by the owner and not placed there by the artist. Photograph courtesy George E. Schoellkopf Gallery. (Mr. and Mrs. William E. Wiltshire III)

Plate 61 (below). *The Burning of the Buck Stable* by Tella Kitchen, oil on canvas, 1974, Ohio, 30" x 36". The horses running from the burning stable are as varied in shape as the horse weathervanes that once stood atop rural barns across the country. © Tella Kitchen. Photograph courtesy Jay Johnson: America's Folk Heritage Gallery. (Private collection)

Plate 62 (left). *Cottage Meeting* by Emily Lunde, oil on board, 1976, North Dakota, 20″ x 24″. Emily Lunde, a memory painter, nearly always depicts scenes from her childhood. (Private collection)

Plate 63 (below). *House on Barnum Street, Ishpeming, Michigan* by Kathy Jakobsen, oil on canvas, 1978, 22″ x 28″. Colorful and lovingly detailed, this delightful Victorian house is the creation of one of the most talented folk painters working today. Photograph courtesy Jay Johnson: America's Folk Heritage Gallery. (Private collection)

THE SOUTHWEST

332 (preceding page). *San Acacio* by José Aragón, tempera and gesso on pine panel, *c.* 1830, New Mexico, 17½″ x 14½″. José Aragón was probably Spanish-born; he came to New Mexico during the early nineteenth century. He appears to have traveled extensively, for several panels similar to this example are signed and inscribed with the location of execution. It is generally believed that Aragón maintained a studio or workshop and actually had an assistant who helped him with some of the painting. (Charles D. Carroll Bequest, Museum of International Folk Art, a division of the Museum of New Mexico)

333 (above). *Crucifixion* by the "Calligraphic" artist, tempera and gesso on pine panel, 1880–1825, northern New Mexico, 23½″ x 14½″. (Taylor Museum of the Colorado Springs Fine Arts Center)

THE SOUTHWEST

The Spanish were the first Europeans actively to occupy North America, and by the mid-sixteenth century, they had secured possession of most of South America, Mexico, and the Caribbean Islands. Forts and missions were established in what is now Florida by the 1560s, in New Mexico by the opening of the seventeenth century, in Texas by the close of the seventeenth century, and in Arizona and California during the eighteenth century.

Spanish interest in America grew out of a legend that centered on the belief that a bishop of Lisbon, fleeing the Moorish invasion in the eighth century, took to the sea. He and his followers finally landed and settled in the New World to the west, where they constructed seven cities made of gold. This legend was revived sometime in the early sixteenth century and inspired fortune hunters such as Álvar Nuñez Cabeza de Vaca to attempt to locate these fabulous cities.

When De Vaca reached Mexico in 1536, local Indians told him of the white men who had risen out of seven caves to the north. He returned to Spain with the tale, which spurred the formation of numerous expeditions to search for the mythical cities.

One of the search expeditions was led by Fray Marcos de Niza, who personally viewed a terraced Zuñi Indian pueblo, which he believed represented one of the bishop's seven cities. Upon his return to Spain news of the discovery spread like wildfire, and the influential Franciscan Order supported the idea of colonization, hoping to build missions to convert the heathens.

Francisco Vásquez de Coronado led an expedition in 1539 and in 1581 another Franciscan, Fray Agustin Rodriguez, followed Coronado's trail up the Rio Grande valley. In 1582 Antonio de Espejo thrust deeper into northern territory, and finally during the last years of the sixteenth century the Spanish began to refer to what is now the southwestern United States as New Mexico.

Despite the astounding success of the Catholic church, which by 1617 had brought some fourteen hundred Pueblo Indians into the Christian fold, the Indians seldom fully accepted the Christian faith and tenaciously clung to ancient rites.

334 (above). Reredo, artist unknown, tempera on cottonwood, eighteenth century, dimensions unavailable. This piece was found in a chapel located on the original plaza of Chimayó, New Mexico. (New Mexico Department of Development)

335 (right). Retablo, or small altarpiece used in a home, artist unknown, tempera on panel, eighteenth century, New Mexico, dimensions unavailable. The large center panel depicts the Holy Family. (New Mexico State Tourist Bureau)

219

Warfare between the Spaniards and the Indians frequently flared. In 1680 the Santa Fe uprising brought about the death of nearly all of the some four hundred Spanish settlers. Those that could escape fled to El Paso for refuge. As a result of the uprising, nearly all traces of the Spanish civilization disappeared. The churches and the homes were destroyed and the acceptance of the Christian religion dissipated.

In 1692 Don Diego de Vargas retook Santa Fe and with an army of one hundred soldiers, eight hundred colonists, and seventeen Franciscans reestablished Spanish dominance in the territory. Soon after, the first outpost was established at the Mission of Saint Xavier del Bac in what is now Arizona.

The Spanish often failed to build permanent colonies; thus, their hold upon the New World was never secure. The Spanish ambassador Zuñiga informed Philip III of the first English settlement in Virginia and expressed the hope "that you will give orders to have these insolvent people quickly annihilated." [150] Though the

336 (above). *Nuestra Señora de Refugio de Pecadores* (*Our Lady of Refuge*), artist unknown, tempera on board, *c.* 1840, northern New Mexico, 25″ x 14″. (Charles D. Carroll Bequest, Museum of International Folk Art, a division of the Museum of New Mexico)

337 (right). *Nuestra Señora de los Dolores* (*Our Lady of Sorrows*) by Molleno (working *c.* 1804–1845), tempera on panel, first quarter of the nineteenth century, New Mexico, dimensions unavailable. Molleno is often referred to as the "chili" painter because many of his paintings contained red chili-pepper-like designs. They may represent naïve simplifications of acanthus leaves that the artist saw on eighteenth-century prints from Mexico. (Museum of International Folk Art, a division of the Museum of New Mexico)

338 (opposite). *God the Father* by José Rafael Aragón (*c.* 1797–1862), tempera and gesso on pine panel, 1825–1860, northern New Mexico, 25″ x 14¼″. This retablo is an extremely rare concept of the deity, where He is surmounted by the dove, a symbol of the Holy Ghost. (Taylor Museum of the Colorado Springs Fine Arts Center)

221

339 (left). *St. Francis of Assisi*, artist unknown, tempera on cottonwood, second half of the nineteenth century, Las Vegas, New Mexico, 11¾″ x 16″. (Mr. and Mrs. James O. Keene)

340 (below). *Taos Pueblo* by Juanita Lucero, oil on board, 1889, Southwest, dimensions unavailable. (Mr. and Mrs. James O. Keene)

341 (above). Detail from a painted box, artist unknown, first half of the nineteenth century, New Mexico, pine, dimensions unavailable. (Index of American Design)

342 (above). *St. Anthony of Padua*, artist unknown, print, second half of the eighteenth or first half of the nineteenth century, Mexico, dimensions unavailable. This print probably served as the source of inspiration for the santero who executed the retablo at the right. (Museum of International Folk Art, a division of the Museum of New Mexico)

343 (right). *San Antonio de Padua*, anonymous santero, tempera on cottonwood, nineteenth century, New Mexico, 18″ x 11″. This painting is attributed to the still unidentified santero, A. J., and is believed to date from 1822. (Museum of International Folk Art, a division of the Museum of New Mexico)

West Side Main Plaza SanAntonio Texas 1849 WGMSamuel

Virginia experiment failed, within fifty years the English established numerous other colonies and Spanish influence on the East Coast faded rapidly. In the Southwest, however, the Spanish military, in search of gold and converts for the Catholic church, continued to push northward and spread the influence of the Spanish crown.

The final thrust of the Spanish empire in the New World was in the form of a string of Franciscan missions that secured the California coast. The first was established in 1769. When Mexico broke with Spain in 1821, this mission system dissolved. During the same year American settlers poured into Texas and Florida, and during the spring of the following year wagon trains carried them west from Missouri over the Santa Fe Trail. Only ten years after the Spanish domination of the Southwest ceased, a large number of eastern settlers permanently established themselves in what is now California, and by the mid-nineteenth century all of the Spanish territorial lands had become part of the United States.

Spanish colonial art in America, from its beginning, was inspired by religion. The three-dimensional repre-

344 (opposite, above). *West Side of the Main Plaza, San Antonio, Texas,* by W. M. G. Samuel, oil on canvas, 1849, Texas, 20¾″ x 35¾″. Samuel was born in Missouri and went to Texas shortly after the fall of the Alamo. A well-known Indian fighter, he participated in the Mexican War. During the Civil War, he served as a captain of artillery and was connected with the Quartermaster's Department of the Confederate States of America. Although Samuel's paintings are crude, they document well the flavor of life in early Texas. (San Antonio Museum Association)

345 (opposite, below). *View of Austin* by William Sandusky, watercolor on paper, *c.* 1840, Texas, dimensions unavailable. Sandusky hailed from Columbus, Ohio, and worked as a draftsman and surveyor after moving west to Austin, Texas, in 1838. The artist ultimately was appointed secretary to President Mirabeau Lamar after serving the state as registrar of the General Land Office. By 1844 he had retired from his position in the president's office and announced in the *Galveston Press* that he could "Execute all kinds of maps, charts, landscapes, plans of cities and towns, also instruments of writing of every description in the neatest style and on the most liberal terms."[13] (Photograph courtesy Austin-Travis County Collection, Austin Public Library)

346 (below). *The Funeral of an Angel* by Theodore Gentilz, oil on canvas, 1840s, Texas, 9″ x 12¼″. (Daughters of the Republic of Texas Library)

347 (above). *St. Joseph* by the "Franciscan B" painter, possibly Fray Carlos Delgado, oil on hide, eighteenth century, New Mexico, dimensions unavailable. (Fred Harvey Foundation Collection)

sentations of Christ, the saints, and other religious figures were fashioned not only for the churches but for personal shrines, which nearly every family maintained in their home. Painting, when it occurred, almost always centered on religious themes as well. Woodcuts from the title pages of Bibles and other religious books served as a guide to native-born craftsmen-artists. Pictures were painted on soft pine panels and on tanned animal hides frequently referred to as *anta blanca*. Portraiture or landscape art was rarely attempted in Spanish America.

There are distinct features about Spanish colonial pictures in America. There is a decided absence of a light source and a failure on the part of the artist to model the figures or to give them individuality.

Because of the great distance from centers of culture, the settlers had to fashion many of their own religious decorations. At first the Franciscans painted the ornaments for the churches and the domestic shrines. When it became apparent that it was impossible to satisfy the demand for such pictures, they taught the colonists and the Indian converts to execute similar ornaments.

In time santeros, or santo makers, developed enough skill to earn their living exclusively by painting religious pictures and carving three-dimensional, freestanding representations of religious figures. Some, like the itinerant limners of New England, traveled from house to house and settlement to settlement, where they made and sold their inspirational pieces.

Altar decorations, or reredos, were also painted by the santero. Most of the early reredos were replaced through the years and very few have survived. The late E. Boyd, Curator Emeritus of Spanish Colonial Art at The Museum of New Mexico, wrote of the santero or image-maker, "At the end of the past century the itinerant santero was still in demand in rural areas that were far from town stores. While part of the santero's time was spent in the repair and renovation of old santos, there were enough families who wanted new statues of their preferred patron saints to keep several men busy in three widely separated districts of northern New Mexico. Rural villages loved their familiar forms of santos long after townspeople had discarded them in favor of zinc or plaster statuary, chromos, and mission cards. Town parishes had contributed the funds to buy the zinc figures, but as their prices ran as high as one hundred dollars, according to size, the country folk could more easily afford those made by the santero who lived with a family while he did his work, and was was paid in goods or livestock."[151]

The santo maker began to suffer a loss of patronage when Currier & Ives and their contemporaries began to produce bright, colorful, inexpensive religious prints. Few were willing to pay the price for a hand-painted picture when a print could be had for a fraction of the cost. By 1850 painted retablos began to disappear and by the nineteenth century had all but ceased to be made.

Much religious art in the Southwest was based upon graphic arts imported from Spain and Flanders. The first prints in what is now known as the United States were

348 (opposite, middle). *Stations of the Cross: Jesus Falls for the First Time*, Indian neophytes working under a mission padre at the Mission San Gabriel, California, painting on sailcloth, *c.* 1779, approx. 30″ x 50″. This painting and the one below are from a series of fourteen paintings that are located in the Mission at San Gabriel, California. (Index of American Design)

349 (opposite, bottom). *Stations of the Cross: Jesus Is Stripped of His Garments*, Indian neophytes working under a mission padre at the Mission San Gabriel, California, painting on sailcloth, *c.* 1779, approx. 30″ x 50″. (Index of American Design)

350 (above). *Juan N. Seguin* by Thomas Jefferson Wright, oil on canvas, 1838, Texas, 26½″ x 24¼″. Seguin, a colonel in the Texas Army, was honorably discharged to take a seat in the State Senate. Wright painted him in his army uniform. (Texas State Archives)

unquestionably brought by Franciscan priests, who came to New Spain by way of Mexico. The Spanish were completely familiar with the development of printing in Germany and Italy. Spanish printing began at Valencia in about 1474, and within three years printers in Seville began to produce books using movable type and decorative woodcuts. German printers from the Holy Roman Empire migrated to Seville from Switzerland, Poland, and Flanders before 1500. With them came their tools and their skills. Jacome Cromberger was among these immigrants. In 1519 *Suma de geografía,* written by Martin Fernández de Enciso, was printed in Mexico on a Cromberger press.

Juan Palos, an Italian member of the Cromberger clan, arrived in Mexico with fonts and a printing press in 1539. In the next fifteen years he produced strong and vital images that did much to serve the cause of Catholicism in the New World. Partially because of his work the desire for portraiture did not develop in Spanish settlements of the southwestern United States.

It is generally believed that the artists working in the Southwest who used oil pigments either brought them with them or imported them from Mexico. For the most part tempera paints made from the earth or from vegetables were used to create the flat religious pictures called *retablos.*

Fray Andrés García, born at La Puebla de los Angeles, Mexico, was a member of the Franciscan Order and was stationed in New Mexican missions at Santa Fe, Santa Cruz, and Albuquerque between 1747 and 1779. His activities were as diverse as those of the New England jack-of-all-trades. He designed and constructed buildings; he carved pulpits, altar rails, and screens; he produced religious figures or santos in the round; and he decorated shrines and painted religious pictures.

Until recently it was generally assumed that the Franciscans were responsible for most of the eighteenth-century painted and carved religious decorations used in missions. E. Boyd, in her monumental work, *Popular Arts of Spanish New Mexico,* has amply demonstrated that laymen could also paint effective religious pictures.

Captain Bernardo de Miera y Pacheco was born at Gergos, Spain. He came to the New World as a professional soldier and resided twelve years in El Paso before moving his family to Santa Fe in 1754. His firsthand experience as a traveler in the New World gave him accurate information that he incorporated into maps. Pacheco was employed as a cartographer by Governor de Anza to chart an overland route to California. His efforts as a farmer were productive, and one can only wonder where he found the time to carve and paint religious decorations. His style was distinctive:

351 (opposite). *Whaling Off the Coast of California* by Coleman, black, white, and colored chalks on prepared board, nineteenth century, California, 18⅜″ x 28″. On the back of the frame is inscribed "Ship 'Joseph Grinell' (built in Fairhaven, Mass., 1858) Captain William W. Thomas. This picture was crayoned on board the ship by mate named Coleman." (Museum of Fine Arts, Boston; M. and M. Karolik Collection)

352 (above). *Lydia Ann Mason* by Thomas Jefferson Wright, oil on canvas, prior to 1846, Texas, 27½″ x 22″. Mrs. Mason was Wright's niece. (Mrs. Bruce L. Stout)

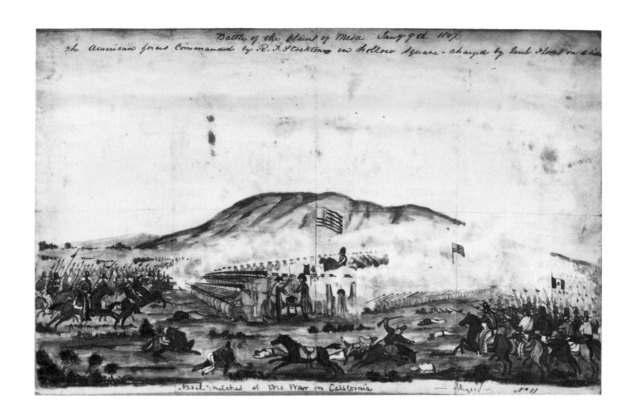

353 (above). *Battle of the Plains of Mesa Jany 9th 1847* by William H. Meyers, watercolor on paper, 1846–1847, California, 10¼″ x 16″. Meyers, a gunner aboard the U.S. sloop-of-war *Dale,* painted this watercolor along with many others during naval operations along the coast of California between 1846 and 1847. His sketchbook constitutes the only eyewitness pictorial record of the war in California. President Franklin D. Roosevelt purchased the sketchbook in 1930, and in 1939 twenty-eight of the original drawings were reproduced in a book titled *Naval Sketches of the War in California* for which President Roosevelt wrote the introduction. (Franklin D. Roosevelt Library)

354 (below). *The Presidio of San Francisco* by Louis Choris, drawing, 1816, California, dimensions unavailable. The men and horses did not appear in Choris's original drawing, but were added later when the picture was used in a book of his travels. (Current whereabouts unknown)

355 (above). *Telegraph Hill, San Francisco*, artist unknown, oil on canvas, 1849–1850, California, 22½" x 34". Telegraph Hill acquired its name because flag signals were given from the tower on the top of the hill when ships arrived in Golden Gate harbor. When gold was discovered in California, so many new settlers rushed to the area that housing was an acute problem. In the painting, Telegraph Hill is covered with tents, which were set up to alleviate the situation. (Wells Fargo Bank History Room)

356 (below). *Taking of Monterey, October 20th, 1842, by the Frigate, United States,* by William H. Meyers, watercolor on paper, 1842, California, 9¼" x 14¾". (Bancroft Library)

357 (above). *Teatro Aleigra* by William H. Meyers, watercolor on paper, c. 1841, probably California, 8¼" x 13½". Meyers painted his watercolor views of Spanish theatricals during stops along the California coast. (Bancroft Library)

Paintings attributed to the captain have several features in common, including oddly lettered inscriptions, usually muddy coloring, and robust subjects. One which he must have done soon after he came to Santa Fe is the large picture of St. Michael which now hangs on the altar screen in the chapel of San Miguel in Santa Fe. It is remarkable in that it is painted in oils on good quality linen canvas instead of on a wooden panel or on the loosely woven burlap of *ixtle* (maguey fibre cloth), on which many of the mission supply canvases from Mexico were painted. The archangel stands, with one brawny leg foreshortened, upon a sinister though amorphous-looking dragon, flourishing a sword and bearing an oval shield, this time lettered "QVIEN COMO DIOS"— a somewhat colloquial Spanish form of the Latin motto. The angel wears a well-drawn cuirass, jeweled tunic, cloak and plumed cap. The wings are impractically small to waft such a stalwart figure aloft, but are painted with the structure of live bird wings and plumage. Amateurish as the painting is, it is easily traced to its Mexican prototype, a picture of St. Michael by Cristobal Millalpando (1648–1714).[152]

Pacheco is also credited with the paintings at Halona, where Fray Francisco Atenacio Dominguez described the high altar:

It has a small new altar screen, as seemly as this poor land has to offer, which was paid for by Father Velez [de Escalante] and the Indians of the pueblo. It consists of two sections, as follows: in the center of the whole thing, almost from top to bottom, there is a framework lined with coarse brown linen and very well painted, in which a large oil painting on canvas with an old frame, newly half gilded, of Our Lady of Guadalupe, which the King had given before, hangs. Below this painting is a very old lacquer Child Jesus vested as a priest, the clothing [is] also old.

The lower niches contain St. Michael on the right and St. Gabriel at the left, new middle-sized images in the round. In the two in the second section above those [mentioned] are—St. Dominic and St. Francis —painted half life size. Above at the top a bust of the Eternal Father in half relief.[153]

Because many of the Franciscans had been stationed in Mexico over an extended period of time, they were familiar with the paintings that remained in the ancient churches in that country. The iconographic details that they incorporated in their New Mexican pictures reveal a reliance upon the conventions of European Renaissance and Baroque painting. "In many respects a more conservative order than some others of the Roman church, the Franciscans were merely continuing a tradition of fresco painting which had been in practice in the 13th century during the lifetime of their founder, Francis of Assisi. The extent of their efforts in New Mexico in painting church walls is little realized now because they used water soluble pigments on mud and plaster. Unlike true fresco these are easily damaged by water, cracking, or abrasion; they are as ephemeral as paper flowers, and have nearly all been lost to view." [154]

The Spanish colonists in America tended to be conservative and frequently repeated architectural design, construction techniques, and decorative elements of their former homeland.

Most early Spanish colonists slept on the floors in their adobe houses, which were made from unburned bricks of clay or soil and straw. Beds of hides, pelts, or wool sacks were picked up and hung from the ceiling during the day. Simple, functional design dominated domestic architecture, and ornamentation was at first reserved for religious structures. Religion was the heart of colonial Spanish life and private oratories were a feature in many houses. These were necessary when one considers the long distances and frequent absences of a priest from the rural churches that dotted the Spanish settlements.

The family chapel built for Sebastian Martín Serrano on a large land grant north of Santa Fe, New Mexico, was described in 1776:

This little chapel is adobe and resembles a small *bodega*. It faces west and is 14 to 16 varas long, five wide and six high. There is no choir loft. There is a poor window on the Epistle side facing south, and the door is squared with one leaf and a key. The roof is of wrought beams; there is a small belfry with its brass bell, and a little cemetery.

The altar screen is nothing more than a middle-sized niche like a cupboard in the wall and in this there is a middle-sized image in the round whose title is Our Lady of Solitude, although her dress is a mother-of-pearl tunic and blue mantle, all of smooth ribbed silk, silver radiance, and linen apron. On the whole wall where the high altar is there are some large paintings of saints on buffalo skins in the local style. The altar table is adobe, with its altar stone, cross, candlesticks and a little bell. It has old vestments of flowered cloth with all accessories, including linen. Chalice, paten and spoon, all of silver, and glass cruets on a Puebla plate, and an old missal. The only functions here are two novenas and a Mass annually.[155]

The number of artists creating religious pictures on hide in the early eighteenth century is rather small; however, distinctive techniques and the repeated use of decorative borders indicate that many of the remaining examples were created by a single man.

One group of pictures is signed with an impressed block letter *F*. It is conceivable that this body of work was executed by Fray Francisco Farfán, who arrived in Santa Fe in 1694. Four years later he traveled to Acoma, where his successful attempts at pacifying the dwellers

358 (left). Ceiling from the Church of Santo Tomás, Village of Las Trampas, New Mexico. Legend has it that wood from decorated chests was used in the construction of this ceiling some two centuries ago. Many of the designs are similar in character to those used by early Dutch and German settlers. (New Mexico State Tourist Bureau)

359 (left). *El Cibolero*, artist unknown, oil on pine, eighteenth to nineteenth centuries, probably New Mexico, dimensions unavailable. (Spanish Colonial Arts Society, Inc., collection in the Museum of International Folk Art)

360 (above). *San Rafael Arcángel* by Bernardo Miera y Pacheco, oil on canvas, dated 1780, New Mexico, 49¼″ x 24″. Pacheco is known to have executed at least two other images of San Rafael. The artist left many descendants who were prominent throughout the Mexican Republican period; however, by the third generation, they had dropped the y Pacheco name, thus confusing researchers. The artist's work is far more three-dimensional than that of most of his contemporaries. (Spanish Colonial Arts Society, Inc., collection in the Museum of International Folk Art)

of the mesa there earned for him a special place in Spanish colonial history. For the next thirteen years he remained in New Mexico and served at Galisteo, San Ildefonso, Pecos, Tesuque, and Santa Ana.

Some believe that it was not Fray Francisco Farfán who executed these striking pictures, but that they should be credited to Fray Lucas de Arébalo, for handsome lettering and script executed by the friar in a book of baptisms that he made in Galisteo in 1711 are similar to the design of the *F* on the pictures.

Fray Carlos Joseph Delgado, who began service in New Mexico in 1710, also decorated church record books with freehand, ornamental designs and letters that are similar to the impressed block letter *F* found on the pictures. Fray Delgado is believed to have played a major part in the repainting of the Pecos mission, which was much heralded for its ornamentation.

Tanned hides were also used as protective shields or dust guards for altars; an inventory begun in 1712 for the Santa Ana mission records, "Two painted skins that serve as *el cielo* [the sky] for the altar." [156] Some twenty years later these were again mentioned as "two old hides that serve as *guardo-polva* [dust-guard] for the main altar." [157] The practice of mounting these canopies in adobe churches, where dust and dirt constantly fell from the roof, continued well into the mid-nineteenth century; an inventory of 1840 at the San Jose mission in Laguna includes "a canopy of bison, well painted and very nicely attached to the ceiling." [158] Their use is recorded as late as 1895 through photographs of the interiors of the mission that show the canopy, altar screen, and frontal and wall paintings still intact.

Not everyone viewed the native animal hides as a proper support for religious pictures. Don Juan Bautista Ladrón del Niño de Guevara, visiting New Mexico during 1817–1820, insisted upon the removal of religious images painted on skins. At Santa Fe he dictated that "the painting of Santa Barbara on elkskin must be removed and done away with completely as it is improper as an object of veneration and devotion of the altars." [159] At Santa Cruz he required that six paintings on hide be removed from the local church. He was silent about the use of hides in a domestic context.

Hides were hung at doorways and substituted for doors. Fray Dominguez also recorded painted hides being used at San Ildefonso as floor coverings: "the carpet is a painted buffalo skin, now old but large and serviceable." [160]

In California, Spanish culture prospered in a significant way. Artistic developments differed from those in New Mexico·

The California missions were elaborate complexes situated strategically not only for the conversion of the Indians but to protect the coast from British and Russian encroachment. They included grain fields and orchards, water supply systems, quarters for Indians and soldiers, and shops where the natives were taught to produce weaving, pottery, tanned hides, soap, and other commodities. Despite the efforts of the *padres* to make them self-sustaining however, the Indians were not ready for independence when the process of secularization began with the Mexican Revolution. Neither had the period of development been long enough for distinctive new art forms to ripen. What we see in California is a mixture of imported Mexican art, local workmanship based upon Mexican and European design, and some remarkable combinations of Spanish and Indian elements—e.g., the delightful mural paintings or the Stations of the Cross at *San Gabriel Arcangel*—that indicate the beginnings of a genuine regional style and offer a hint as to what might have happened if there had been more time. [161]

One of the most beautifully preserved altar screens in all of Spanish colonial America is in the mission of San José at the Laguna pueblo (plate 64). The sophistication of the paintings is in direct contrast to the mural decoration included in several California missions where neophyte Indian artists, working under the supervision of Spanish priests, frequently used stencils to create decorative wall murals and patterns, vases of flowers, animals, and hunt scenes. A painted niche from the sanctuary of San Antonio de Paolo is rich in Indian murals. Natural pigments derived from local roots and plants were used in the creation of this decorative mural.

During the entire Spanish colonial period furniture forms mirrored Old World designs. Pine, spruce, and oak were the most popular woods. Chests, cupboards, benches, tables, and chairs were decorated with flat carvings that frequently were gaily painted with colors derived from natural sources. During the late eighteenth and early nineteenth centuries the familiar rampant lions and pomegranates gave way to a more stylized geometric decoration. Much Spanish colonial furniture was intended to be painted. Numerous pieces reveal successive layers of paint, which indicate that when a decorated surface began to fade, it was brightened by the addition of a fresh coat of paint.

A number of brilliantly decorated small chests that had long been thought to have been brought north from Chihuahua have recently been positively identified as originating in the upper Rio Grande valley. Floral borders surround detailed scenes, which include people in boats, helmeted dragoons, and fanciful turreted architecture. It is believed that these pieces were painted by an immigrant from Mexico who brought oil pigments with him. The decorative example (fig. 341) illustrates a successful fishing party; the joyous sportsmen appear to be catching large red snappers, indicating that the artist was familiar with the West Coast or the Gulf of California region. The floral motifs on this piece are similar to those found on lacquered boxes from Olinala, a town in the state of Guerrero. The color schemes used on the Olinala boxes and chests are believed to have been derived from contacts with China that resulted from the China trade during the nineteenth century.

Folk painting in Texas was not unlike that found

elsewhere in the United States and included work by unknown primitive and naïve painters who earned their living as explorers, soldiers, surveyors, or limners. After the first waves of settlement, limners, genre painters, landscape painters, and historical painters appeared in increasing numbers during the period of transition from outpost settlements to built-up towns.

Jerry Bywaters, in his introduction to *Painting in Texas* by Pauline A. Pinckney, observed that Texas

> was like the hub of a giant gambling wheel, radiating its magnetic attraction into the Old South, into the states of Virginia, Tennessee, and Kentucky, deep into Mexico, and across the ocean to England, Germany, and France. With each turning year fortunes and lives were staked, and great areas of land changed hands through the gambling instincts of a few men who chanced their way into history.

> In this center of activity, the southwestern push of American settlers and armies met the Plains Indians and the soldiers of Spain and Mexico. It was a time and place of challenges, nationalistic and ethnic, of stirring events taking place against a landscape which itself was an extreme of forests and treeless prairies, of mountains and deserts.[162]

During the 1830s painters such as George Catlin, who came to record the Indians and the cowboys, realized that the wild West, even at such an early date, was fast disappearing. Catlin, upon a visit to northwest Texas in 1834, recorded his concern about the native American: "Art may mourn when these peoples are swept from the earth, and the artists of future ages may look in vain for another race so picturesque in their costumes, their weapons, their colours, their manly games and their chase." [163]

In 1836 Texas cast aside its allegiance to Mexico and an infant republic emerged. One of the first and most successful folk painters to work in the new republic was Thomas Jefferson Wright (1798–1846), who came to the frontier from Mount Sterling, Kentucky, and announced in a Houston paper his hope of receiving portrait commissions from the prominent citizens. Wright, a "gentleman of the brush," frequently included objects in the background of his pictures that indicated the special interest or profession of the sitter. He attracted great attention, and in 1837 a Houston paper reported, "We have recently visited a small gallery of paintings in this city from the palette of Mr. Wright and we are highly pleased with their appearance. The portraits of this gentleman bear evidence of much genius and application. We recommend him to the notice of the amateurs of the Fine Arts." [164]

Wright, like his contemporaries in New England, was not above other activities that would augment his income. He occasionally journeyed to Cincinnati, where he joined his two brothers and sometimes worked as a cabinetmaker. While in Houston, he advertised fancy lettering as one of his secondary accomplishments.

It seems reasonable to believe that Wright might have had the benefit of some instruction from his friend Matthew H. Jouett, a portrait painter of Fayetteville, Kentucky. Jouett wrote a letter of introduction for Wright to his former teacher, Thomas Sully, that revealed a great deal about the esteem in which the well-established Philadelphia artist was held by lesser artists of the day:

> Dear Friend The kindness with which you have heretofore honored my letters and commissions of every sort leaves but little ground to distrust the entire success of this application in favor of my young friend Jefferson Wright to whose acquaintance I hereby entreat you to be introduced. You will find Mr. W. amiable, modest and entirely upon the reserve. He visits Phila. with the view to avail himself of the helps of the academy and the artists in portrait painting. Of his abilities I cannot speak decisively—they are reputed promising in this country and I believe them to be so. By his enthusiasm and industry he has become enabled to visit your city and with prospects of a tolerably longer stay—Altho entirely devoid of the graces of early learning —you will find him by no means destitute of those lights characteristic of a good mind attentive to the object of its pursuit. He earnestly solicited to be made acquainted [with] you. Indeed all the young gentlemen of the brush in this country look upon you as the Elijah in the arts, and push forward with hopes of immortality if they can but touch the hem of your cloak—and so you see if you are annoyed by we poor provincial children of the brush, you must attribute it mainly to that good report that accompanies your name. Be assured of one thing, the amiable subject of this letter will never obtrude upon one busy moment of your time whilst in the city—; you will only have to say to him go and he goeth; do and he doeth. "Your advice will be law and your council, will be as strength unto Weakness."

> For an introductory I think I have said enough. You will please let me hear from you, often. If I cannot see you I love to hear what you are engaged about. Your sincere friend Matt H. Jouett" [165]

Among the very first artists to work in the Texas area were those who created pictorial records that related to cartography or plans for settlement. This specific interest in geographical places continued to fascinate the Texas artist and men like William H. Sandusky (1813–1849), who first executed watercolor views that he later copied for engravings. Sandusky, a resident of Austin, came to the Texas territory from Ohio in 1838. He served the state as a surveyor and registrar of the General Land Office and in 1840 was appointed secretary to President Lamar. Sandusky's bird's-eye views of local scenes parallel the numerous town and city views that were so popular on the East Coast.

361 (above). *The Day the Bosque Froze Over* by Clara McDonald Williamson, oil on composition board, 1953, Dallas, Texas, 20″ x 28″. In the section of Texas where the artist grew up, it was rare that the weather was sufficiently cold to freeze the rivers. This painting is a memory picture and recalls the only time that the river was frozen solidly enough for a team of horses to be driven across it. (The Museum of Modern Art, New York; gift of Albert Dorne)

362 (right). *Women Picking Maize* by Lady Dorothy Brett, tempera on tin, first quarter of the twentieth century, Taos, New Mexico, 24″ x 20″. During the nineteenth century, metal cans and drums that had been shipped to the Southwest filled with processed food and other supplies were saved by thrifty natives and converted into frames for mirrors and paintings. (Mr. and Mrs. James O. Keene)

363 (left). *Paeter Verse* by Bertha Staffel, watercolor on paper, 1885, Texas, 18″ x 14″. The Staffels were Germans, and several members of their family painted. This watercolor is composed of a variety of flowers and foliage, which surround a verse in German. It was painted in San Antonio after the artist's family moved there in the third quarter of the nineteenth century. (Mrs. Clara Mae Staffel Michel)

364 (below). *My Dream* by Nounoufar Boghosian, mixed media, 1967, Pasadena, California, 42″ x 68″. Mrs. Boghosian was born in Istanbul, Turkey, to Armenian parents. She came to America in 1913 and moved to California in 1949. Like those of many eighteenth- and nineteenth-century artists, her paintings are centered on inherited cultural traditions from her native land. She focuses upon her recollection of the Armenian world of her childhood. (Photograph courtesy The American Federation of Arts)

Folk painting in Texas was rich and varied. At its best it records in bright strokes the vitality of the early settlers and the zest for frontier life.

William M. G. Samuel (1815–1902), who probably arrived in San Antonio, Texas, in the late 1830s or 1840s, was an immigrant soldier from Missouri. In time he became a law officer for the town of San Antonio and recorded various scenes viewed through the courthouse windows (fig. 344). His crude, vital depictions of frontier town life teem with activity and provide documentary evidence of the social integration of town dweller, cowboy, and Indian.

Jean Louis Theodore Gentilz (1819–1906) created a rich pictorial account of Texas in his genre pictures. Gentilz, the son of a Parisian manufacturer of fine coaches, arrived in Texas in 1843. A smattering of European training enabled him to create paintings that were more sophisticated than those executed by many of his contemporaries, such as Thomas Jefferson Wright and William M. G. Samuel. Gentilz was especially fascinated by the Spanish Americans and time and again recorded them in their celebration of traditional religious ceremonies and pursuit of pleasurable pastimes. In time Gentilz became a very proficient artist, and as in the case of John Singleton Copley, his early naïve paintings appear to have been only one step in a series of experiments that finally evolved into his own personal style.

During the second half of the nineteenth century several important naïve painters were born in the great Southwest.

Velox Ward (born 1901), a Texas artist, grew up near Hopewell, where as a youth he enjoyed the security and warmth of a happy family life. His father died while Velox was still in the seventh grade. The youth left school and went to work, first as a fur hunter and then as a farmer. A restless man, he once said, "I have been painting for ten years. That is the longest time I have ever spent in any vocation." [166] He has held a variety of jobs, including that of a car painter, a shop foreman, a sales manager of a car shop, a shoe shop owner, a furniture restorer, a wrestler, and a minister. Ward frequently looks back to the early days of his childhood and depicts western life in the early twentieth century.

Clara McDonald Williamson is also best known for her memory pictures. This creative artist was born in 1875 in Texas, where her father and mother had settled after traveling west on a wagon train. Her pictures recall the frontier life of her home town, Iredell, which she viewed as "my world; that was all I knew, that little town, and of course that's all I have to remember and put on canvas, and I think a painter ought to paint what he knows like an author ought to write what *he* knows." [167]

Eddie Arning, another Texas artist, was born near Kenney in 1898. After his release from a mental institution at the age of sixty-seven, he began drawing. His first efforts were memory pictures executed with wax crayons. Later he turned to "inspiration pictures," which derived their design from four-color advertisements in magazines and books. His highly creative mind could take a very commonplace advertisement and turn it into a masterpiece of design and color. Arning's best pictures are full of strength and vitality.

The California artist P. M. Wentworth is best known for his pictures executed during the late 1930s and early 1940s, when he used pencil, crayon, and wash on heavy paper. The paintings are dotted with fanciful stone castles and bizarre free-form buildings and are peopled by mystical figures in floor-length capes. Their surrealistic quality provides a striking contrast to the works of Peter Mason Bond (1882–1971).

Bond, who was born in Australia, immigrated in 1905 to San Francisco, where he resided until his death. This religious eccentric, who signed his works with the acronym "PEMABO," created an extraordinary peace garden, which was filled with painted signs that spoke out for peace and a love of God. Bond also painted on canvas symbolic pictures that were permeated with his spiritual beliefs.

Probably Martin Ramirez (c. 1880–1960) is the most significant twentieth-century southwestern folk artist. He became mute when he was in his mid-thirties and began painting as he neared the age of sixty. Ramirez died in the DeWitt State Hospital in California. His highly patterned, sensitively executed pictures on paper depict not only the cowboys of his youth but the hustle-bustle of the modern-day California city as well. Ramirez's extraordinary sense of design has brought many new devotees to the field of contemporary folk painting. As with all great folk painters, his pictures have a quality that transcends the barriers of time and place.

365 (above). *Kingdom of Heaven* by P. M. Wentworth, pencil, crayon, gouache, and erasure on heavy paper, c. 1940, California, 29½" x 25¾". (Courtesy James Nutt)

366 (above). *"Holiday,"* A *Scene on* STOW LAKE *in famed* GOLDEN GATE PARK, *San Francisco,* by Peter Mason Bond, oil on canvas, *c.* 1950, California, 48″ x 60″. (Sydney E. Bond)

367 (below). *The Tree of Life* by Velox Ward, oil on canvas, 1961, Longview, Texas, 16″ x 20″. The artist indicated that this painting was inspired by a double-exposure photograph. He recently stated: "I will be striving the rest of my days to attain what I want on canvas." [14] (Donald Vogel)

Plate 64 (above). The altar screen at the San José de la Laguna Mission, Laguna, New Mexico, artist unknown, late eighteenth century, dimensions unavailable. As the execution of the painting of this screen and a corresponding screen in Acoma, New Mexico, are relatively sophisticated, it is believed that the unknown artist who painted them had extensive working experience and probably decorated screens in Mexico before he received the commissions in New Mexico. This screen is inscribed on the reverse "Se pintó este coral y se yso a costa del alcalde mallor Dⁿ José Manuel Aragon este año de 780 [sic]. [This screen was painted and made at the expense of the chief magistrate Don José Manuel Aragon, this year of 780.] (Church of San José de la Laguna Mission)

Plate 65 (right). *El Santo Niño de Atocha* by Rafael Aragon, tempera and gesso on pine panel, *c.* 1840, New Mexico, 15″ x 10″. Rafael Aragon frequently made use of the profile, and his three-quarter view pictures were executed with ease and conviction. He worked until around 1865 in a style that combined innocence and refinement. (Museum of International Folk Art, a division of the Museum of New Mexico)

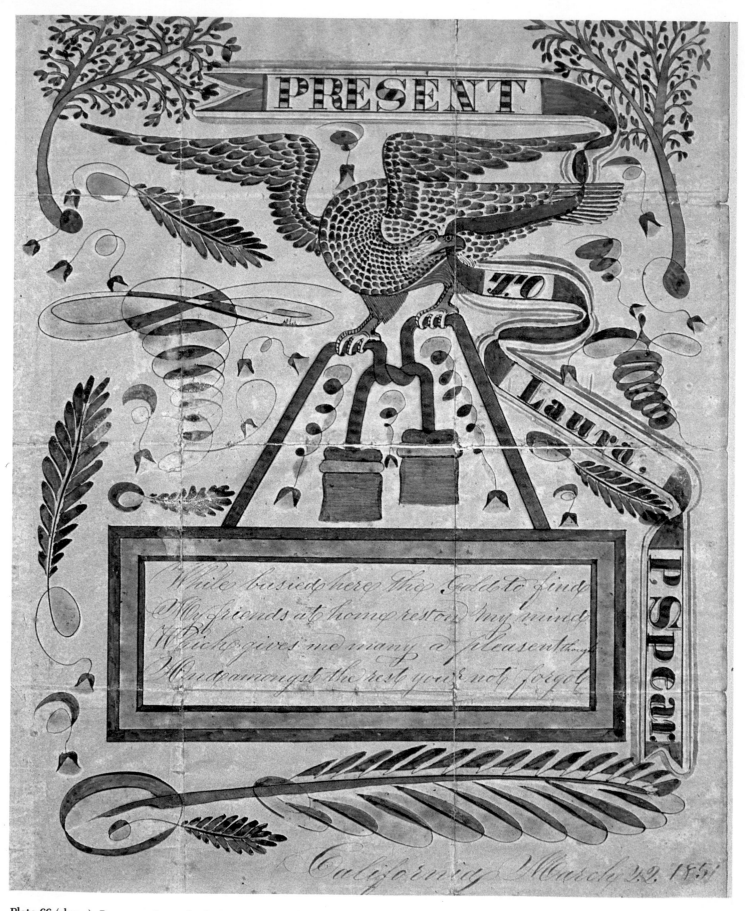

Plate 66 (above). *Present to Laura* by P. Spear, watercolor on paper, March 22, 1851, California, 9¾″ x 7¾″. This piece is inscribed: "While busied here the Gold to find/ My friends at home rest on my mind/ Which gives me many a pleasant thought/ And amongst the rest youre not forgot." (Howard and Catherine Feldman)

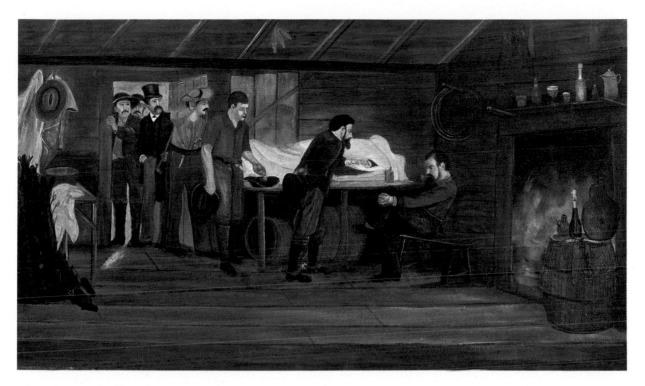

Plate 67 (above). *The Luck of Roaring Camp* (after the story by Bret Harte) by A. Levill, Jr., oil on canvas. *c.* 1885, Western States, 28″ x 42½″. (America Hurrah Antiques, N.Y.C.)

Plate 68 (above). *Indian Attack on a Covered Wagon,* artist unknown, oil on academy board, 1880–1910, Western States, 23″ x 45½″. (America Hurrah Antiques, N.Y.C.)

Plate 69 (left). *Egyptian Scroll* by Martin Ramirez, crayon on paper, *c.* 1960, California, 100½″ x 24½″. Ramirez was an illiterate and mute Mexican laborer, who during the last thirty or forty years of his life was incarcerated in a state mental hospital in California. Photograph courtesy Phyllis Kind Gallery.

Plate 70 (below). *The Dinner* by Eddie Arning, crayon and pastel on paper, *c.* 1970, Texas, 24″ x 28″. Arning began to "make pictures" at the age of sixty-seven after his release from a mental institution, where he had been a patient for several years. The artist very frequently "borrowed" his designs from illustrations in popular magazines. He developed a highly personal style, which evolved from a complex, singular vision. (Jay Johnson: America's Folk Heritage Gallery)

NOTES

NOTES

PREFACE

1. Jean Lipman and Alice Winchester, *The Flowering of American Folk Art, 1776–1876* (New York: The Viking Press in cooperation with the Whitney Museum of American Art, 1974), p. 8.

2. Stuart P. Feld, *American Paintings for Public and Private Collections* (New York: Hirschl & Adler, 1967), Foreword.

3. William Dunlap, *History of the Rise and Progress of the Arts of Design in the United States,* 1834. Reprint. (New York: Dover Publications, Inc., 1969), vol. 1, p. 3.

4. S. G. W. Benjamin, *Art in America* (New York: Harper & Brothers, 1880), Preface.

5. Clarence Cook, *Art and Artists of Our Time* (New York: Selmar Hess, 1888), vol. 3, pp. 16–17.

6. Jean Lipman and Alice Winchester, *Primitive Painters in America 1750–1790* (New York: Dodd Mead & Company, 1950), p. 8.

7. *American Folk Art, The Art of the Common Man in America, 1750–1900* (New York: The Museum of Modern Art, 1932), p. 27.

8. *American Primitives, An Exhibit of the Paintings of Nineteenth Century Folk Artists* (Newark, N.J.: The Newark Museum, 1930), pp. 7, 9.

9. Clara Endicott Sears, *Some American Primitives: A Study of New England Faces and Folk Portraits* (Boston: Houghton Mifflin Company, 1941), p. v.

10. Lipman and Winchester, *The Flowering of American Folk Art,* p. 7.

11. Carl W. Drepperd, *American Pioneer Arts and Artists* (Springfield, Mass.: Pond-Ekberg Company, 1942), pp. 6–7.

12. Lipman and Winchester, *The Flowering of American Folk Art,* p. 8.

INTRODUCTION

13. Marshall Davidson, *The American Heritage History of American Antiques from the Revolution to the Civil War* (New York: American Heritage Publishing Co., Inc., 1968), p. 72.

14. Albert Ten Eyck Gardner and Stuart P. Feld, *American Paintings* (New York: The Metropolitan Museum of Art, 1965), p. 1.

15. *Ibid.*

16. *The Knickerbocker,* vol. 14, 1839.

17. *New York Observer,* March 1839.

NEW ENGLAND

18. *Historical Collections of the Essex Institute,* 1883, vol. 20, p. 9.

19. Harriette M. Forbes, *Gravestones of Early New England* (Boston: Houghton Mifflin, 1927), p. 2.

20. *Collections of the Massachusetts Historical Society,* 1878, Fifth Series, vol. 5, p. 470.

21. Alice Ford, *Pictorial Folk Art, New England to California* (New York: Studio Publications, Inc., 1949), p. 7.

22. *Collections of the Massachusetts Historical Society,* 1863, Fourth Series, vol. 6, p. 450.

23. Louisa Dresser (Ed.), *XVIIth Century Painting in New England* (Worcester, Mass.: Worcester Art Museum, 1935), p. 23.

24. *Ibid.,* p. 26.

25. Roger B. Stein, *Seascape and the American Imagination* (New York: Clarkson N. Potter, Inc., 1975), p. 9.

26. Albert Ten Eyck Gardner and Stuart P. Feld, *American Paintings, A Catalogue of the Collection of the Metropolitan Museum of Art,* vol. 1 (New York: Metropolitan Museum of Art, 1965), p. 1.

27. Henry Wilder Foote, "Mr. Smibert Shows His Pictures March, 1730," *New England Quarterly,* 1935, vol. 8, no. 1, pp. 14–18.

28. C. Bridenbaugh (Ed.), *Gentleman's Progress, The Itinerarium of Dr. Alexander Hamilton, 1744* (Westport, Conn.: Greenwood, 1973).

29. William Dunlap, *History of the Rise and Progress of the Arts of Design in the United States,* 1834, vol. 1. Reprint. (New York: Dover Publications, Inc., 1969), pp. 223–224.

30. Rita Susswein Gottesman, *The Arts and Crafts in New York 1777–1799* (New York: The New-York Historical Society, 1954), p. 5.

31. Nina Fletcher Little, "J. S. Blunt, New England Landscape Painter." *Antiques* Magazine, September 1948, p. 174.

32. *Portsmouth Directory,* 1827, p. 81.

33. Unpublished letter from Christopher Tahk to Dr. Dorothy Vaughan, June 2, 1974.

34. Jean Lipman and Alice Winchester, *Primitive Painters in America 1750–1950* (New York: Dodd Mead & Company, 1950), p. 82.

35. *Ibid.*

36. Nina Fletcher Little, "William M. Prior, Traveling Artist and His In-Laws, the Painting Hamblens." *Antiques* Magazine, January 1948, p. 44.

37. Grace Adams Lyman, "William M. Prior, The 'Painting Garret' Artist." *Antiques* Magazine, November 1934, p. 180.

38. *Ibid.*

39. Lipman and Winchester, *Primitive Painters,* pp. 88–89.

40. *American Folk Art, The Art of the Common Man in America* (New York: The Museum of Modern Art, 1932), p. 13.

41. Jean Lipman, *American Primitive Painting* (New York: Oxford University Press, 1942), p. 7.

42. Unpublished letter, Nina Fletcher Little to Mrs. Nathalie Coss Turner, July 19, 1974.

43. Little, "William M. Prior, Traveling Artist," *Antiques* Magazine, p. 47.

44. Gardner and Feld, *American Paintings,* p. 238.

45. *Ibid.*

46. *Ibid.*

47. Gail and Norbert H. Savage and Esther Sparks, *Three New England Watercolor Painters* (Chicago: The Art Institute of Chicago, 1974), p. 22.

48. *Ibid.*

49. *Ibid.*

50. Herbert W. Hemphill, Jr., and Julia Weissman, *Twentieth-Century American Folk Art and Artists* (New York: E. P. Dutton & Co., 1974), p. 62.

NEW YORK AND NEW JERSEY

51. Mary Black and Jean Lipman, *American Folk Painting* (New York: Clarkson N. Potter, Inc., 1966), p. 2. George C. Groce and David H. Wallace, *The New-York Historical Society's Dictionary of Artists in America 1564–1860* (New Haven, Conn.: Yale University Press, 1957), p. 200. Rita S. Gottesman, *The Arts and Crafts in New York 1726–1776* (New York: The New-York Historical Society, 1937), p. 130.

52. Louis C. Jones, "The Genre in American Folk Art." In *Papers on American Art,* John C. Milley (Ed.) (Maple Shade, N.J.: The Edinburgh Press, 1976), p. 41.

53. Edgar P. Richardson, *Painting in America, The Story of 450 Years* (New York: Thomas Y. Crowell Co., 1956), pp. 26, 27.

54. Robert G. Wheeler, "The Albany of Magdalena Douw," *Winterthur Portfolio 4* (Charlottesville, Va.: University Press of Virginia, 1968), p. 63.

55. Alexander Hamilton, *Hamilton's Itinerarium*, A. B. Hart (Ed.) (St. Louis: William K. Bixby, 1907), p. 89.

56. Wheeler. "The Albany of Magdalena Douw," *Winterthur Portfolio 4*, p. 63.

57. John Romeyn Brodhead (Comp.), *Documents Relative to the Colonial History of the State of New-York: Procured in Holland, England and France*, vol. 6, E. B. O'Callaghan (Ed.) (Albany, New York: Weed, Parsons and Co., 1855), p. 122.

58. *Hudson Valley Paintings 1700–1750 in The Albany Institute of History and Art* (New York: The Albany Institute of History and Art, 1959), p. 12.

59. *The New-York Gazette or The Weekly Post-Boy*, October 13, 1755.

60. *The New-York Mercury*, March 30, 1761.

61. Theodore Bolton and Irwin F. Cortelyou, *Ezra Ames of Albany, Portrait Painter, Craftsman, Royal Arch Mason, Banker 1768–1836* (New York: The New-York Historical Society, 1955), pp. xviii, xix.

62. Letter from John Vanderlyn to John Vanderlyn, Jr., September 9, 1825. Senate House, Kingston, New York.

63. Barbara C. and Lawrence B. Holdridge, *Ammi Phillips: Portrait Painter 1788–1865* (New York: Clarkson N. Potter, Inc., 1969), p. 14.

64. *Ibid.*, p. 18.

65. Donald Smalley (Ed.), *Domestic Manners of the Americans by Mrs. Frances Trollope* (New York: Vintage Books, 1949), pp. 394–395.

66. Herbert W. Hemphill, Jr., and Julia Weissman, *Twentieth-Century American Folk Art and Artists* (New York: E. P. Dutton & Co., Inc., 1974), p. 104.

67. Sidney Janis, *They Taught Themselves* (New York: The Dial Press, 1942), p. 18.

68. Jean Lipman and Helen M. Franc, *Bright Stars, American Painting and Sculpture since 1776* (New York: E. P. Dutton & Co., 1976), p. 123.

69. Hemphill and Weissman, *Twentieth-Century American Folk Art and Artists*, p. 220.

70. Excerpted from *New York Magazine*, October 30, 1972.

71. Hemphill and Weissman, *Twentieth-Century American Folk Art and Artists*, p. 207.

72. Elinor Lander Horwitz, *Contemporary American Folk Artists* (Philadelphia: J. B. Lippincott Company, 1975), p. 58.

73. *Ibid.*

74. *Ibid.*, p. 60.

75. Hemphill and Weissman, *Twentieth-Century American Folk Art and Artists*, p. 217.

PENNSYLVANIA

76. *Encyclopaedia Britannica*, s.v. "Philadelphia."

77. *Ibid.*

78. Marshall Davidson, *The American Heritage History of Colonial Antiques* (New York: American Heritage Publishing Co., Inc., 1967), p. 119.

79. Roger B. Stein, *Seascape and the American Imagination* (New York: Clarkson N. Potter, Inc., 1975), p. 6.

80. Frances Lichten, *Pennsylvania Dutch Folk Arts* (Philadelphia: Philadelphia Museum of Art, n.d.), p. 8.

81. Jean Lipman and Alice Winchester, *The Flowering of American Folk Art 1776–1876* (New York: The Viking Press, 1974), p. 105.

82. A. Howry Espenshade, *Pennsylvania Place Names* (Harrisburg, Pa.: The Evangelical Press, 1925), p. 43.

83. Albert Ten Eyck Gardner and Stuart P. Feld, *American Paintings* (New York: Metropolitan Museum of Art, 1965), p. 150.

84. Arthur Edwin Bye, "Edward Hicks, Painter-Preacher," *Antiques* Magazine, January 1936, p. 13.

85. Paul Svinin, "The Observations of a Russian in America," quoted in William B. O'Neal, *Primitive Into Painter* (Charlottesville, Virginia: University Press of Virginia, 1960, p. 1.

86. Jane Barton, "Theorem Painting Past and Present," unpublished manuscript, p. 4.

87. *Ibid.*, p. 9.

88. Lipman and Winchester, *The Flowering of American Folk Art*, p. 281.

89. Herbert W. Hemphill, Jr., and Julia Weissman, *Twentieth-Century American Folk Art and Artists* (New York: E. P. Dutton & Co., Inc., 1974), p. 50.

90. John Kane, *Sky Hooks*, Mary McSwigan (Ed.) (Philadelphia: J. B. Lippincott Co., 1938).

91. Holger Cahill and others, *Masters of Popular Painting* (New York: The Museum of Modern Art, 1938), p. 125.

92. Sidney Janis, *They Taught Themselves* (New York: The Dial Press, 1942), p. 55.

93. Hemphill and Weissman, *Twentieth-Century American Folk Art and Artists*, p. 176.

94. Unpublished letter, Clarence Perkins to Bishop, August 1975.

95. *Ibid.*

THE SOUTH

96. Ian Bennett, *A History of American Painting* (London: Hamlyn Publishing Group Limited, 1973), p. 6.

97. Alan Gowans, *Images of American Living* (Philadelphia: J. B. Lippincott Company, 1964), p. 36.

98. Marshall B. Davidson, *The American Heritage History of Colonial Antiques* (New York: American Heritage Publishing Co., Inc., 1967), p. 15.

99. Albert Ten Eyck Gardner and Stuart P. Feld, *American Paintings* (New York: The Metropolitan Museum of Art, 1965), p. 16.

100. *Ibid.*

101. *Ibid.*, p. 17.

102. Gowans, *Images of American Living*, p. 103.

103. *Ibid.*, pp. 99–100.

104. Gardner and Feld, *American Paintings*, p. 77.

105. Judith Wragg Chase, *Afro-American Art and Craft* (New York: Van Nostrand Reinhold Company, 1971), p. 95.

106. *Ibid.*

107. *Ibid.*, p. 50.

108. *Ibid.*, p. 51.

109. Mills Lane, *The People of Georgia* (Savannah, Georgia: The Beehive Press, 1975), pp. 89, 92.

110. *Ibid.*, p. 92.

111. *Ibid.*, p. 96.

112. Timothy A. Herrington, Harpers Ferry, Maryland, to John Toole, Charlottesville, Virginia, May 12, 1847.

113. John Toole, Orange, Virginia, to Jane Toole, North Garden, Virginia, May 10, 1840.

114. John Toole, Orange, Virginia, to Jane Toole, North Garden, Virginia, June 2, 1840.

115. John Toole, King William County, Virginia, to Jane Toole, North Garden, Virginia, September 9, 1849.

116. John Toole, Richmond, Virginia, to Jane Toole, Charlottesville, Virginia, January 17, 1847.

117. John Toole, Petersburg, Virginia, to Jane Toole, North Garden, Virginia, circa March 1857.

118. Henry Tuckerman, *The Book of the Artists* (New York: James F. Carr, 1966), p. 398.

119. Cedric Dover, *American Negro Art* (Greenwich, Conn.: New York Graphic Society, 1960), p. 44.

120. Herbert W. Hemphill, Jr., and Julia Weissman, *Twentieth-Century American Folk Art and Artists* (New York: E. P. Dutton & Co., 1974), p. 63.

121. *Ibid.*, p. 189.

122. Elinor Lander Horwitz, *Contemporary American Folk Artists* (Philadelphia: J. B. Lippincott Company, 1975), p. 26.

123. *Ibid.*

124. *Ibid.*, pp. 26–27.

125. Author's personal interview with artist.

126. Horwitz, *Contemporary American Folk Artists*, p. 70.

127. Unpublished letter, Philo Levi Willey to author, 1974.

128. Horwitz, *Contemporary American Folk Artists*, p. 31.

129. *Missing Pieces: Georgia Folk Art 1770–1976* (Atlanta, Ga.: Georgia Council for the Arts and Humanities, 1976), p. 12.

130. *Ibid.*, p. 106.

131. Donald Smalley (Ed.), *Domestic Manners of the Americans by Mrs. Frances Trollope* (New York: Vintage Books, 1949), p. 414.

THE WESTERN RESERVE, FIRELANDS, VIRGINIA MILITARY LANDS, THE OLD NORTHWEST TERRITORY, AND THE NORTHWEST

132. Charles Dickens, *American Notes* (New York: Cromwell & Co., n.d. [1842]).

133. *Erastus Salisbury Field 1805–1900* (n.p., n.d., unpaged).

134. Alice Ford, *Pictorial Folk Art, New England to California* (New York: Studio Publications, Inc., 1949), p. 14.

135. *Ibid.*

136. *Ibid.*

137. Marianne E. Balazs, "Sheldon Peck." *Antiques* Magazine, August 1975, p. 276.

138. *Ibid.*, p. 279.

139. *Ibid.*, pp. 282–283.

140. Jean Lipman and Alice Winchester, *Primitive Painters in America 1750–1950* (New York: Dodd Mead & Company, 1950), p. 143.

141. Joseph Earl Arrington, *Thomas Clarkson Gordon's Moving Panorama of the Civil War* (Dearborn, Mich.: Henry Ford Museum and Greenfield Village, n.d. [1959]), p. 6.

142. *Ibid.*, p. 7.

143. Agnes Fields Kirk, "The Story of the Later Life of Thomas Clarkson Gordon," undated manuscript, p. 3.

144. Arrington, *Gordon's Moving Panorama*, p. 8.

145. Unidentified clipping in Gordon papers.

146. Lipman and Winchester, *Primitive Painters in America 1750–1950*, pp. 150, 152.

147. Unpublished letter, Tella Kitchen to Bishop, 1975.

148. Author's personal interview with artist, 1976.

149. Unpublished letter, Katherine Jakobsen to Bishop, 1976.

THE SOUTHWEST

150. Alan Gowans, *Images of American Living* (Philadelphia: J. B. Lippincott Company, 1964), p. 18.

151. E. Boyd, *Popular Arts of Spanish New Mexico* (Santa Fe, N.M.: Museum of New Mexico Press, 1974), p. 407.

152. "Art in Colonial Mexico," John Herron Art Institute, 1951, No. 21.

153. Boyd, *Popular Arts of Spanish New Mexico*, p. 115.

154. *Ibid.*, p. 50.

155. *Ibid.*, p. 33.

156. *Ibid.*, p. 122.

157. Archives of the Archdiocese of Santa Fe, LD 1712, No. 1.

158. *Ibid.*, LD 1840, No. 9.

159. Boyd, *Popular Arts of Spanish New Mexico*, p. 125.

160. *Ibid.*

161. *The Art of the Spanish Southwest*, Introduction by R. L. Scholkolp (Washington, D.C.: The Index of American Design, n.d.), pp. 4–5.

162. Pauline A. Pinckney, *Painting in Texas* (Austin: University of Texas Press, 1967), p. xvii.

163. *Ibid.*, p. xviii.

164. *Telegraph and Texas Register*, Houston, May 9, 1837; June 3, 1837; October 7, 1837; December 16, 1837; February 17, 1838.

165. Matthew H. Jouett, Fayette County, Kentucky, to Thomas Sully, Philadelphia, Pennsylvania Historical Society, November 12, 1822.

166. Herbert W. Hemphill, Jr., and Julia Weissman, *Twentieth-Century American Folk Art and Artists* (New York: E. P. Dutton & Co., 1974), p. 154.

167. *Ibid.*, p. 159.

168. *Ibid.*, p. 92.

BLACK-AND-WHITE PHOTOGRAPHS

1. Nina Fletcher Little, *Paintings by New England Provincial Artists, 1775–1800* (Boston: Museum of Fine Arts, 1976), p. 74.

2. *Ibid.*, p. 154.

3. Morgan B. Brainard, *Tavern Signs* (Hartford: The Connecticut Historical Society, 1958), p. 11.

4. All quotations are from Marion Russell Deming, "George Washington Mark," The Magazine *Antiques*, July 1952, pp. 43–45.

5. *American Heritage*, December 1950, p. 58.

6. Herbert W. Hemphill, Jr., and Julia Weissman, *Twentieth-Century American Folk Art and Artists* (New York: E. P. Dutton & Co., Inc., 1974), p. 152.

7. *Six Naives* (Akron, Ohio: Akron Art Institute, 1973), n.p.

8. Hemphill and Weissman, *Twentieth-Century American Folk Art and Artists*, p. 220.

9. Printed in *The Papers of Henry Laurens*, ed. Philip M. Hamer and George C. Rogers, Jr. (Columbia, S.C., 1970), vol. 2, pp. 335–336.

10. The Magazine *Antiques*, March 1951, p. 205.

11. Letter to Miss Stiles, July 1932, quoted in *Missing Pieces: Georgia Folk Art 1770–1976* (Atlanta: Georgia Council for the Arts and Humanities, 1976), p. 47.

12. Stratford Lee Morton, "Bishop Hill: An Experiment in Communal Living," The Magazine *Antiques*, February 1943, p. 74.

13. Pauline A. Pinckney, *Painting in Texas* (Austin: University of Texas Press, 1967), pp. 149, 151.

14. Hemphill and Weissman, *Twentieth-Century American Folk Art and Artists*, p. 154.

COLOR PLATES

1. Nina Fletcher Little, *Paintings by New England Provincial Artists, 1775–1800* (Boston: Museum of Fine Arts, 1976), p. 122.

2. Alexander Hamilton, *Hamilton's Itinerarium*, ed. A. B. Hart (St. Louis: William K. Bixby, 1907), p. 89.

3. Herbert W. Hemphill, Jr., and Julia Weissman, *Twentieth-Century American Folk Art and Artists* (New York: E. P. Dutton & Co., Inc., 1974), p. 209.

BIBLIOGRAPHY

BIBLIOGRAPHY

Anderson, Marna Brill. *Selected Masterpieces of New York State Folk Painting.* New York: Museum of American Folk Art, 1977.

Andrews, Ruth, ed. *How to Know American Folk Art.* New York: Dutton Paperbacks, 1977.

Art of the Spanish Southwest, The. Introduction by R. L. Scholkolp. Washington, D.C.: Index of American Design, n.d.

Bennett, Ian. *A History of American Painting.* London: Hamlyn Publishing Group, 1973.

Black, Mary, and Lipman, Jean. *American Folk Painting.* New York: Clarkson N. Potter, 1966.

Borneman, Henry S. *Pennsylvania German Illuminated Manuscripts.* New York: Dover Publications, 1973.

Boyd, E. *The Literature of Santos.* Dallas, Tex.: Southern Methodist University Press, 1950.

———. *The New Mexico Santero.* Santa Fe, N.M.: Museum of New Mexico, 1972.

———. *New Mexico Santos: How to Name Them.* Santa Fe, N. M.: Museum of New Mexico, 1966.

———. *Popular Arts of Spanish New Mexico.* Santa Fe, N.M.: Museum of New Mexico Press, 1974.

Cahill, Holger. *American Folk Art, The Art of the Common Man in America 1750–1900.* New York: The Museum of Modern Art, 1932.

———. *American Primitives, An Exhibit of the Paintings of Nineteenth Century Folk Artists.* Newark, N.J.: The Newark Museum, 1930.

———, and others. *Masters of Popular Painting.* New York: The Museum of Modern Art, 1938.

Carlisle, Lilian Baker. *18th and 19th Century American Art at Shelburne Museum.* Shelburne, Vt.: Shelburne Museum, 1961.

Chase, Judith Wragge. *Afro-American Art and Craft.* New York: Van Nostrand Reinhold, 1971.

Christensen, Erwin O. *The Index of American Design.* Washington, D.C.: National Gallery of Art, 1950.

Dover, Cedric. *American Negro Art.* New York: New York Graphic Society, 1960.

Drepperd, Carl W. *American Pioneer Arts and Artists.* Springfield, Mass.: Pond-Ekberg Co., 1942.

Dresser, Louisa, ed. *Seventeenth Century Painting in New England.* Worcester, Mass.: Worcester Art Museum, 1935.

Dunlap, William. *A History of the Rise and Progress of the Arts of Design in the United States.* 1834. Reprint. New York: Dover Publications, 1969.

Ebert, John, and Ebert, Katherine. *American Folk Painters.* New York: Charles Scribner's Sons, 1975.

Ericson, John T., ed. *Folk Art in America. Painting and Sculpture.* New York: Mayflower Books, 1979.

Feld, Stuart P. *American Paintings for Public and Private Collections.* New York: Hirschl & Adler, 1967.

Folk Art in America: A Living Tradition. Atlanta, Ga.: The High Museum of Art, 1974.

Ford, Alice. *Edward Hicks, Painter of the Peaceable Kingdom.* Philadelphia: University of Pennsylvania Press, 1952.

———. *Pictorial Folk Art, New England to California.* New York and London: The Studio Publications, 1949.

Gowans, Alan. *Images of American Living.* Philadelphia: J. B. Lippincott, 1964.

A Group of Paintings from the American Heritage Collection of Edith Kemper Jette and Ellerton Marcel Jette. Waterville, Me.: Colby College Press, 1956.

Hemphill, Herbert W., Jr., and Weissman, Julia. *Twentieth-Century American Folk Art and Artists.* New York: E. P. Dutton, 1974.

Holdridge, Barbara C., and Holdridge, Lawrence B. *Ammi Phillips, Portrait Painter 1788–1865.* New York: Clarkson N. Potter, 1969.

Hornung, Clarence P. *Treasury of American Design,* 2 vols. New York: Harry N. Abrams, n.d.

Horwitz, Elinor Lander. *Contemporary American Folk Artists.* Philadelphia: J. B. Lippincott, 1975.

Hudson Valley Paintings 1700–1750 in the Albany Institute of History and Art. New York: Albany Institute of History and Art, 1959.

Janis, Sidney. *They Taught Themselves: American Primitive Painters of the Twentieth Century.* New York: The Dial Press, 1942.

Jones, Agnes Halsey. *Rediscovered Painters of Upstate New York, 1700–1875.* Utica, N.Y.: Munson-Williams-Proctor Institute, 1958.

———, and Jones, Louis C. *New-Found Folk Art of the Young Republic.* Cooperstown, N.Y.: New York State Historical Association, 1960.

Jones, Louis C. "The Genre in American Folk Art." *Papers on American Art.* John C. Milley, ed. Maple Shade, N.J.: The Edinburgh Press, 1976.

Kallir, Otto. *Art and Life of Grandma Moses.* New York: The Gallery of Modern Art, 1969.

———, ed. *Grandma Moses, My Life's History.* New York: Harper & Row, 1952.

Kane, John. *Sky Hooks: The Autobiography of John Kane.* Notes and postscript by Mary McSwigan. Philadelphia: J.B. Lippincott, 1938.

Lichten, Frances. *Folk Art of Rural Pennsylvania.* New York: Charles Scribner's Sons, 1946.

Lipman, Jean. *American Folk Art.* New York: Pantheon Books, 1948.

———. *American Primitive Painting.* New York: Oxford University Press, 1942. Reprint. New York: Dover Publications, 1972.

———. *Pennsylvania Dutch Folk Arts.* Philadelphia: Philadelphia Museum of Art, n.d.

———. *Provocative Parallels.* New York: Dutton Paperbacks, 1975.

———, ed. *What Is American in American Art?* New York: McGraw-Hill Book Co., 1963.

———, and Winchester, Alice, eds. *Primitive Painters in America 1970–1950.* New York: Dodd, Mead, 1950. Reprint. Freeport, N.Y.: Books for Libraries Press, 1971.

Little, Nina Fletcher. *The Abby Aldrich Rockefeller Folk Art Collection.* Williamsburg, Va.: Colonial Williamsburg, 1957. Distributed by Little, Brown & Company.

———. *American Decorative Wall Painting 1700–1851.* New York: Dutton Paperbacks, 1972.

———. *Country Art in New England, 1790–1840.* Sturbridge, Mass.: Old Sturbridge Village, 1960.

———. *Land and Seascape as Observed by the Folk Artist.* Williamsburg, Va.: Colonial Williamsburg, 1969.

———. *New England Provincial Artists, 1775–1800.* Boston: Museum of Fine Arts, 1976.

Lord, Priscilla S., and Foley, Daniel J. *The Folk Arts and Crafts of New England.* Philadelphia: Chilton Book Co., 1965.

Missing Pieces: Georgia Folk Art 1770–1976. Atlanta, Ga.: Georgia Council for the Arts and Humanities, 1976.

M. & M. Karolik Collection of American Paintings 1815–1865 for Museum of Fine Arts, Boston. Cambridge, Mass.: Harvard University Press, 1949.

M. & M. Karolik Collection of American Watercolors and Drawings 1800–1875, 2 vols. Boston: Museum of Fine Arts, 1962.

Nineteenth-Century Folk Painting: Our Spirited National Heritage (selections from the collection of Mr. and Mrs. Peter H. Tillou). Storrs, Conn.: University of Connecticut, William Benton Museum of Art, 1973.

101 American Primitive Watercolors and Pastels from the Collection of Edgar William and Bernice Chrysler Garbisch. Washington, D.C.: National Gallery of Art, n.d.

101 Masterpieces of American Primitive Painting from the Collection of Edgar William and Bernice Chrysler Garbisch. New York: The American Federation of Arts, 1961, New York: Doubleday & Co., 1962.

Pinckney, Pauline A. *Painting in Texas.* Austin, Tex.: University of Texas Press, 1967.

Richardson, Edgar P. *Painting in America. The Story of 450 Years.* New York: Thomas Y. Crowell, 1956.

Savage, Gail, Savage, Norbert H., and Sparks, Esther. *Three New England Watercolor Painters.* Chicago: The Art Institute, 1974.

Sears, Clara Endicott. *Some American Primitives: A Study of New England Faces and Folk Portraits.* Boston: Houghton Mifflin, 1941.

Shelley, Donald A. *The Fraktur-Writings or Illuminated Manuscripts of the Pennsylvania Germans.* Allentown, Pa.: Pennsylvania German Folklore Society, 1961.

Stebbins, Theodore E. *American Master Drawings and Watercolors.* New York: Harper & Row, 1976.

Stein, Roger B. *Seascape and the American Imagination.* New York: Clarkson N. Potter, 1975.

Stoudt, John Joseph. *Early Pennsylvania Arts and Crafts.* South Brunswick, N.J.: A. S. Barnes, 1964.

Tillou, Peter. *Where Liberty Dwells: 19th-Century Art by the American People. Works of Art from the Collection of Mr. and Mrs. Peter Tillou.* Privately printed, 1976.

Welsh, Peter C. *The Art and Spirit of a People: American Folk Art from the Eleanor and Mabel Van Alstyne Collection.* Washington, D.C.: Smithsonian Institution, 1965.

Wilder, Mitchell A., and Breitenbach, Edgar. *Santos, The Religious Folk Art of New Mexico.* Colorado Springs, Colo.: Taylor Museum, 1943.

INDEX

INDEX

Page references for illustrations are in **boldface** type.